Margin of Victory

Margin of Victory

How Technologists Help Politicians Win Elections

NATHANIEL G. PEARLMAN, EDITOR

New Trends and Ideas in American Politics

Raymond A. Smith and Jon Rynn, Series Editors

 PRAEGER

AN IMPRINT OF ABC-CLIO, LLC
Santa Barbara, California • Denver, Colorado • Oxford, England

Library of Congress Cataloging-in-Publication Data

Margin of victory : how technologists help politicians win elections / Nathaniel G. Pearlman, editor.

p. cm. — (New trends and ideas in American politics)

Includes bibliographical references.

ISBN 978–1–4408–0257–7 (hard copy : alk. paper) — ISBN 978–1–4408–0258–4 (ebook)—978–1–4408–2851–5 (pbk. : alk. paper)

1. Campaign management—Technological innovations—United States—History.
2. Political campaigns—Technological innovations—United States—History.
3. Internet in political campaigns—United States—History. 4. Communication in politics—Technological innovations—United States—History. I. Pearlman, Nathaniel G.
JK2281.M363   2012
324.70973—dc23   2011051416

ISBN Hardcover: 978–1–4408–0257–7
EISBN: 978–1–4408–0258–4
ISBN Paperback: 978–1–4408–2851–5

16 15 14 13 12   1 2 3 4 5

This book is also available on the World Wide Web as an eBook.
Visit www.abc-clio.com for details.

Praeger
An Imprint of ABC-CLIO, LLC

ABC-CLIO, LLC
130 Cremona Drive, P.O. Box 1911
Santa Barbara, California 93116-1911

This book is printed on acid-free paper ∞

Manufactured in the United States of America

For my wife, Connie K. N. Chang.
Still trying to prove myself worthy of you.

Contents

Series Foreword

Change is perennial within the American system of politics and government: the electoral calendar, the ebb and flow of presidential administrations, shifts along generational lines, and long-term patterns of partisan realignment—to name a few of the rhythms and cycles to be found in the political sphere. And so, one year's innovative thinking can become the next year's conventional wisdom, and then the following year's stale orthodoxy. This book series, *New Trends and Ideas in American Politics*, focuses on the most important new currents that are shaping, and are shaped by, U.S. politics and government.

The early 21st century is a particularly important time to focus on a proactive approach to the participatory processes, governmental institutions, socioeconomic forces, and global contexts that determine the conduct of politics and the creation of public policy in the United States. The long demographic dominance of the Baby Boom generation has begun to recede as the Boomers age, even as society becomes ever more open and diverse along lines of race, ethnicity, gender, and sexuality. From the waning of the worship of "the market," to the disasters of the Bush era, to the unprecedented presidential election of 2008, to The Tea Party and Occupy Wall Street, and on to the steady emergence of a more multipolar and ever-less-certain global context, Americans are faced with new challenges that demand not simply new policies and procedures but entirely new paradigms. At the same time, emerging vistas in biotechnology and information technology promise to reshape human society, the global ecological system, and even humankind itself.

New Trends and Ideas in American Politics casts a wide net, with volumes in the series unified mostly by novel, sometimes even counterintuitive, perspectives that propose new policies and approaches for Americans to govern themselves, to relate to the rest of the world, and to safeguard the future for posterity. This is no small task, yet throughout its history, the United States has proven itself capable of initiating creative, productive periods of reform and renewal. Indeed, in one of the most strikingly regular and recurrent features of American history, intense periods of political change have occurred about every 30 to 40 years, including the founding in the 1790s, the Jacksonian age of the 1830s, Reconstruction in the 1860s and 1870s, the Progressive Era of the early 20th century, the New Deal of the 1930s, and the upheavals of the 1960s.

By this reckoning, the United States is overdue for another such fertile period of political reform; indeed, all the elements of a major political realignment are already in place: the Reagan Revolution has run its course, its political coalition fragmented beyond recognition; government is proving itself unable to tackle issues from the national debt ceiling to health care to the environment, yet seems frozen in place; and citizen engagement is on the rise, as seen in such measures as exceptionally high voter turnout in 2004 and 2008; the proliferation of citizen discussion in political blogs and on social media; the Tea Party with its near-revolutionary anti-government zeal; and Occupy Wall Street raising awareness of soaring income inequality and lack of opportunity for ordinary Americans . Discerning the patterns in this welter of change will be among the chief tasks of *New Trends and Ideas in American Politics*.

This volume, *Margin of Victory: How Technologists Help Politicians Win Elections*, examines the critical and evolving role in elections and politics of a range of new technologies, including the power of new media, software tools, data, and analytics. In most coverage of technology in elections and politics, the same highlights are cited again and again: huge online fundraising totals, the mammoth size of national voter files, the complexity of micro-targeting models, or other innovations in political technology. The reality is much muddier—and more interesting. The actual use of political technology, while certainly capable of achieving comparative advantage, is still an adventure full of immature tools, imperfect data, difficulties with integration, with continual experiment, and where competition among consultants and companies produces innovation despite the constraints of time and resource.

In *Margin of* Victory, Editor Nathaniel G. Pearlman—himself one of the leading figures in this burgeoning field—brings together some of the leading practitioners in political technology to describe their current work and the state of play in their area of expertise. It puts their innovations into historical context and also asks them to make predictions about the possible future uses of technology in electoral politics. The main story line is that political technology is in an early stage: consultants, candidates, and companies are still figuring out how to leverage analytics and modeling, integrate huge amounts of data, and incorporate distributed campaigning into customary methods of fundraising, persuasion, and mobilization. And what works now is a moving target, for the world is changing and potential voters are modifying their receptivity to different forms of communication.

Raymond A. Smith and Jon Rynn
Series Editors

Foreword

If you are in the market for a standard discussion about the world of political technology suitable for a political science journal or a newspaper column, this is not your book. What Nathaniel Pearlman has put together here is a collection of first-hand accounts from people who have actually built a reputation, deserved or not, for on-the-ground knowledge in one aspect or another of the political technology world. I say deserved or not, because I don't know all of them (it looks like almost half of them are Republicans, anyway).

I do know that a party's political technology infrastructure makes a difference. When I assumed the Democratic National Committee chairmanship in 2001, we were way behind, and it had cost us dearly. The Republicans, who had the benefit of a succession of RNC chairmen who made long-term investments in their party, were far ahead. They had built, for instance, a huge, state-of-the-art database that they could mine for donors. We had nothing like that. We had a brochure-ware Web site, a tiny e-mail list, and not a single voter file at the DNC. In fact, as I wrote in my own bestselling book *What a Party!* "We had such a variety of outdated software and hardware, it was like we had our own low-rent technology museum."

As a businessman accustomed to thinking about return on investment, I began in 2001 a multiyear technology infrastructure project to close the technology infrastructure gap and modernize the DNC. We upgraded state voter files and cleaned and corrected bad information that was wasting real money in mailing costs. We built an e-mail infrastructure and TV and radio studios. We rebuilt the computer and telephone systems, created a new Web site, and established online fundraising systems. We raised money and worked hard and moved the party light-years ahead and into the modern age.

Before, during, and after my service at the DNC, the political technologists and Internet strategists and entrepreneurs that Nathaniel has brought together for this book were also working away on their own tracks. Their experiences and adventures and the lessons they learned are well worth a read, even if they have varying degrees of accuracy.

I know that Nathaniel and his contributors from across the political spectrum have worked hard on this volume, and I hope that you will pick it up and learn a little about how politics works from the inside.

Terry McAuliffe
Former Chairman, Democratic National Committee

Acknowledgments

Much appreciation to my Dad—a real writer—for helping me on this project. This editor needed his own editor and he was mine.

Thank you, Connie, especially for the three weeks you let me work on this book in Vermont while you single-parented the two kids in DC. Can I do it every summer?

Thanks to the other contributors! I know that I hassled you a lot, but we got it done!

I could not have done this without the executive team at NGP VAN, especially Mark for his great chapter and Stu for his support of the project.

Great gratitude to all of the employees—and clients—of NGP Software, Inc., past and present, for making the journey possible for me.

Thanks to everyone else who gave me good advice or assistance, including my sister Eve, Stephanie Abbajay for the copyediting, series editor Ray Smith for his help and everyone who touched the project at Praeger/ABC-CLIO.

Introduction

Nathaniel G. Pearlman

The written coverage of political technology—a discipline that has occupied my attention for two and a half decades—is rarely deep or insightful. For the most part, I have read about the same few highlights: either the horse-race drama of online fundraising or the romanticized accounts of the application of specific innovations, such as mobile devices or social networking, to electioneering. Occasionally I come across a thin article about microtargeting models or national voter files.

To partially remedy the deficit in existing accounts of the political technology revolution in progress, I have brought together some of the leading practitioners of political technology to describe the state of the art in their areas of expertise. I have come to know these contributors—either first-hand or by reputation—as a consequence of my own long history in the political software business or as a result of my stint as chief technology officer for the Hillary Clinton for President campaign. I have asked each contributor to put into historical context the innovations he or she has witnessed, employed, or created. I have also suggested that the contributors try to make some guesses about the future. I have undertaken this enterprise because I think that the developments in political technology should be interesting and meaningful to those who care about the functioning of our democracy.

Each contributor to this volume has interpreted the assignment in his or her own way. As a result, the contributions appear in a variety of formats. Some of the writers discuss the shift from older styles of political communication to the twenty-first century options of Web sites, e-mail, political blogs, online advertising, and mobile devices. Some illuminate the less public work that has been developing over many years in the assembly of national voter-file databases, the creation of the software used to manage campaigns, or the statistical analysis of data that helps to direct political campaign resources and campaign strategy. Efforts to improve the methodologies used in each of these areas are continual and constant; the present state of the art, impressive though it might be to outsiders, will soon look as antique as the work that we performed a decade ago.

Though the sophistication in political technology and analytics has taken an enormous leap in recent years, in many areas it is still underdeveloped or unevenly applied. Political technology is in an early stage: consultants, candidates, and companies are still figuring out how to fully leverage analytics and modeling, integrate huge amounts of data, and incorporate distributed campaigning into the familiar and customary strategies for raising money, conveying a message, and mobilizing voters. It is a fact of life among political technologists that whatever works today, technologically or strategically, will be superseded as new technologies arrive, tactics improve, and potential voters become less receptive to last year's style of persuasion.

My hope is that these firsthand accounts will contribute to a better understanding of the ways in which technology intersects with politics. Inasmuch as every contributor to this volume has stood in the eye of a storm of change—working on techniques, some of which are visible but imperfectly understood and others that are invisible to the public—they have, in sum, captured an untold story.

Contributors to this volume tend to write objectively about their contributions and experience, but their style of analysis should not be misinterpreted as lack of passion. Those of us who have entered the world of political technology and have taken a side in the partisan battle do so not mainly for personal reasons or private gain but in order to improve the world.

In their essence, political campaigns in the United States today are still very much like those described in 1840 by the young Abraham Lincoln. Lincoln was a practical politician and a student of the less romantic side—the nuts and bolts—of political campaigning. Eight score and ten years ago he laid out this confidential plan to organize his party:

> ... divide their county into small districts ... appoint in each a sub-committee ... make a perfect list of all the voters in their respective

districts, and to ascertain with certainty for whom they will vote . . .
keep a constant watch on the doubtful voters, and from time to time
have them talked to by those in whom they have the most confidence
. . . place in their hands such documents as will enlighten and influence them . . . report to you . . . the progress they are making, and
on election days see that every Whig is brought to the polls . . . raise
a fund . . . immediately after any election in your county, you must
inform us of its results . . . let no local interests divide you; but select
candidates that can succeed . . . we go to the work of organization in
this State confident of success.[1]

Lincoln concluded that, "we have the numbers and if properly organized
and exerted, with the gallant Harrison at our head, we shall meet our foes
and conquer them in all parts of the Union."

Today's campaigns simply employ new tools to implement old strategies. Whether aided by information technology or not, the principal elements of the job are still fundraising, organizing, tracking supporters,
persuasion and communication, and getting out the vote. That these elements are so recognizable underlines the continuity of our politics and
the durability of the concepts behind our typical campaign practices.
And yet the day-to-day implementation of these traditional techniques
has been so altered by new technology and by the professionalization of
political consulting that even those of us who have been at the forefront
of implementing the innovations cannot help but find the degree of
change to be astonishing.

The revolution in communication technologies has had dramatic
effects on political campaigning. When Lincoln wrote about placing
in the hands of voters "such documents as will enlighten and influence
them," he had no way of anticipating the many ways in which modern
tools would allow interaction with voters. Will Robinson, a long-time
Democratic media consultant with an enduring interest and expertise
in technology, deals with these complexities every day. Will surveys
the vast changes in the communication technologies that have swept
the media landscape and buffeted his profession. Will is the founding
partner of the New Media Firm, which is a full-service political media
consulting and advertising agency that specializes in the integration of
traditional and new media for Democratic candidates and progressive
organizations. As Will explains, because campaigns must communicate with people of various degrees of digital aptitude, the successful
modern media consultant must be a communications triathlete. Will
shows how recent technological changes in the postbroadcast world

are driving a return to individualized communications in political campaigns.

One aspect of that return to individualized communication is the ability of candidates to use Web-based tools to captivate and engage voters and inspire their public participation. Mindy Finn and Patrick Ruffini, who are partners at Engage, a Republican political Web-strategy group, are prominent Internet consultants in Republican circles and experts in mobilizing an online following. Mindy and Patrick have held senior new media roles on two presidential campaigns (Bush-Cheney 2004, Romney 2008), at the Republican National Committee, and at numerous state-wide campaigns and policy initiatives. In 2011, they worked for the presidential campaign of Tim Pawlenty. Mindy and Patrick give us an insider's account of the development of Internet strategy and tools on the Republican side, with a focus on message, money, and mobilization.

Voters who become engaged online can be tapped to fund a campaign. Nicco Mele was the Webmaster for Howard Dean during Dean's run for the Democratic nomination and was therefore at ground zero during the explosion in online fundraising that took place in the 2004 presidential contest. Nicco tells how he impulsively quit his job, drove to Vermont, joined the Dean campaign, and assisted in building its initial Web presence. After the Dean campaign, Nicco launched his own company, Echo-Ditto, which has thrived as a community-building and Web-technology consulting company. Nicco also holds a lectureship at Harvard's Kennedy School of Government. He shares his knowledge of the history and practice of online fundraising.

The Dean campaign was also the first to make successful use of the blog to generate grassroots energy. Liz Mair has made a profession out of helping campaigns manage their relationship to the blogosphere. She is an independent consultant who was formerly vice president at Hynes Communications and before that online communications director at the Republican National Committee. Liz explains why campaigns ignore blogs at their peril and analyzes the uneasy integration of blogs and online media into modern campaign communication operations.

Campaigns also communicate by advertising. The chapter on Internet marketing—the practice of creating and placing online ads—is authored by Andrew Bleeker and Nathaniel Lubin. Bleeker worked for the Hillary Clinton for President campaign in 2007 and then with Lubin on Barack Obama's 2008 Internet marketing team. After providing online marketing services to the Democratic Party in 2008, Bleeker founded Bully Pulpit Interactive and has since become a leading consultant on digital marketing to progressive campaigns, nonprofits, and corporate social responsibility efforts. Lubin has now returned to the 2012 Obama campaign as the campaign's in-house lead for digital marketing. Bleeker and Lubin provide an insider's view on how political advertising increasingly moves online.

Many feel that the next communications medium to be employed by campaigns will involve mobile technology. Julie Barko Germany, vice president of digital strategy at DCI Group, an international grassroots public affairs firm, and former director of the Institute for Politics, Democracy, and the Internet at George Washington University, has specific expertise in this area. Julie has authored chapters in *The Routledge Handbook of Political Management*; *Campaigning for President 2008: Strategy and Tactics, New Voices and New Techniques*; *Voting in America*; and *Rebooting America*. Julie offers a knowledgeable assessment of the role of mobile communications in campaigns.

Lincoln's admonition to "keep a constant watch on the doubtful voters" manifests itself today in various methods of polling and information gathering. As the director of policy research at The Winston Group, a DC-based Republican polling and strategy firm, Kristen Soltis monitors and explores the relationship between the campaign and the voters. She provides political analysis for outlets such as MSNBC, CNN International, *Politico*, the *Huffington Post*, and Bloggingheads.tv. Kristen writes about the ways in which technology has altered the work of the professional pollster.

Elected officials also attempt to communicate with voters. Ken Ward, CEO of Fireside21, provides online software for U.S. House offices on Capitol Hill that allows members to track their interactions with constituents. Communicating with the electorate in the modern world is complicated and difficult. Ken shows how twenty-first century politicians can build closer relationships with constituents by using the latest technologies and strategies.

Lincoln wanted to keep a perfect list of all the voters in order to keep a constant watch on them, ascertain which side they were on, make sure that they were contacted and that the proper documents were placed in their hands, and ensure that they were brought to the polls. Huge investments have been made to bring this idea to fruition in a nation that has grown to more than 300 million people. A number of the contributors to this volume have been in the forefront of these efforts.

Bob Blaemire, for example, was an early practitioner of the art of compiling and distributing electronic voter files for use in campaigns. His company, Blaemire Communications, was at one time the leading voter-data vendor to state Democratic parties. Bob helped to invent the voter-file industry and advanced the delivery of voter data from tangible products like mailing labels and printed lists to the Web-based world of data and analytics. Bob's story helps explain why the market for voter data is structured as it is, at least on the Democratic side.

Josh Hendler was technology officer at the DNC when the national party committee made two major decisions: to choose a common vendor across the states for voter-file technology and to build the national voter file in-house. Josh started in politics as a professional software developer when he joined the presidential campaign of General Wesley Clark in 2003. He then led the Kerry 2004 internal software efforts, specializing in the intersection of technology and the modern field campaign. His career shows just how much has changed in the last eight years. Josh urges closer collaboration between political technology engineers and organizers.

Mark Sullivan's work revitalizes Lincoln's admonition to "keep a constant watch on the doubtful voters, and from time to time have them talked to by those in whom they have the most confidence." Mark, the founder of the Voter Activation Network (VAN), describes his company's rapid ascent from a two-person firm serving Democrats in statewide races in Iowa to its current position as the dominant supplier of Web-based voter-file management software not only to the Democratic Party but also to unions and progressive nonprofits. The application for which he is responsible, the VAN, is now ubiquitous on the Democratic side, where it facilitates canvassing operations involving thousands of simultaneous users.

The next chapter helps make the connection between the voter file and other Internet-based technologies and is also written by an industry veteran. Michael Turk, a senior Internet strategy consultant on the Republican side, describes his party's adoption of new technology over the past two decades. Turk managed Internet operations for three presidential campaigns—Fred Thompson 2008, Bush-Cheney 2004, and Quayle 2000. He served as the Republican National Committee's first e-campaign director. Turk is a founder and partner of CRAFT | Media/ Digital and has worked for years at the intersection of politics, public policy, and technology. Turk uses his chapter to describe the evolution of data-driven politics and to take on what he sees as the conventional wisdom that the Republican Party has run behind the Democrats in its use of new technologies.

Turk refers in his chapter to the practice of microtargeting—the use of statistics applied to large collections of data on voters to predict and influence their behavior. Two knowledgeable contributors, one Republican and one Democrat, help explain why the campaigns employ these methods.

The first, Alex Lundry, is vice president for research at TargetPoint Consulting, a large Republican firm with a special emphasis on microtargeting. Lundry works as a political pollster, data miner, and data visualizer. His client list includes the RNC, Senator John McCain, Governor Mitt Romney, Governor Chris Christie, Congressman Dave Camp, Resurgent Republic, and American Crossroads. In his chapter, Alex explains how Republicans have used mathematical models to influence and persuade potential voters.

The second, Aaron Strauss, represents the Democratic side of political targeting. Aaron is senior analyst and director of decision analytics at the Democratic polling firm the Mellman Group. Aaron—who recently earned a PhD in government from Princeton University—has worked in the political analytics revolution as part of the targeting efforts of Gore 2000, Kerry 2004, Clinton 2007, and Obama 2008. Aaron discusses how and why decision making in political campaigns has become increasingly data driven.

My own chapter is about my adventure in the world of political technology. The company that I founded in 1997, NGP Software, Inc., which provides political fundraising and compliance tools to Democrats and their allies, grew from a one-man shop into an important part of the Democratic Party's technology base. NGP recently merged with VAN to form the 130-plus person firm NGP VAN, Inc. NGP's current clients include the Obama campaign, the Democratic national and state party committees, the campaigns of most federal and many state-level Democrats, and many others. The growth of NGP parallels that of the political technology market generally and illustrates how expectations for technology have risen over time.

Another software company with aspirations to change the political technology market was cofounded by Edward Saatchi after the Obama 2008 campaign. Saatchi's company grew out of an online tool that was originally designed for the Obama campaign's field operation in Georgia in 2008. NationalField's software is a private social network that encourages and tracks the efforts of the campaign's field operatives. Ed's story shows how much room there still is for new entrants into the political technology market. It remains to be seen if NationalField's product will be widely adopted by political technologists.

In his campaign plan, Lincoln asked that, "immediately after any election in your county, you must inform us of its results." Stephen Ansolabehere, now professor of government at Harvard University, writes about the intersection of political campaigns and the world of voting technology. The U.S. electorate learned in the year 2000 with the Bush versus Gore mess that the accurate counting of votes is a task that is not always straightforward. Voting technology itself is occasionally what makes the difference between victory and defeat. Steve, who is a political methodologist and author of several books and numerous articles about U.S. politics, was formerly professor of political science at MIT, where he led the Caltech/MIT Voting Technology Project.

Collectively, the writers of these 17 chapters paint a full picture of the revolutionary changes in the use of technology in the U.S. electoral system. I believe that these accounts are both more revealing and more compelling than the headlines. The casual observer may have heard that one candidate ran a smooth and modern campaign, but the practitioner knows, and the reader of this book will learn, that he has bumbled through a world of imperfect data, immature tools, rejiggered models, data integration failures, undelivered e-mail, crashed programs, and a chaos of perpetual, daily, and sometimes momentary reinvention. Observers and even the candidates themselves may be impressed with an account of the application of one specific technology to a campaign, but they may not realize that practitioners have tested and refined their improvised systems over the course of many campaigns. While casual observers might think that political technology is a mature discipline, practitioners recognize that it's barely out of infancy.

CHAPTER 1

The Digital Revolution: Campaigns and New Media Communications

Will Robinson

My perspective on U.S. campaigns and elections ranges over 40 years in politics, and the shifts in major dynamics of elections during that time have been vast. I started out as a volunteer for a congressional race in one of the most marginal districts in the nation—Bob Edgar's campaign in Pennsylvania's Seventh District. That 1974 campaign looked more like John Kennedy's first campaign for Congress than any campaign for Congress run today. As I progressed through my career, I continued to see technology dramatically change U.S. campaigns and how they communicate with voters. Changes in technology and the breakup of AT&T helped create the massive direct mail and paid-phone campaigns of the 1980s. Campaign finance changes allowed the rise of TV campaigns, and now the Internet has changed it all again. It's ironic that the skills I learned working as a field organizer may be more important in the new era than anything I learned as a media consultant.

I grew up in Delaware County, Pennsylvania, a bedroom county located in the western suburbs of Philadelphia. It was and is still the home of the "War Board," one of the last Republican political machines left in the United States. So when Bob Edgar, a young Methodist minister, ran for Congress in 1974 as a Democrat, his campaign was willing to take help from anyone, including a teenage boy (me) who had to do his homework in the back of the campaign office before he could work for the evening.

Edgar was an outsider, and he benefited from the anti-Nixon landslide that swept the country that year. He ran a classic insurgent effort, spending less than $40,000 on his first race. His campaign was mostly a field operation consisting of literature drops, door-to-door canvassing, phone calls, parades, and neighborhood coffees. There was no paid television or radio advertising and no mass mailings. While the local newspaper covered the race, the major newspapers and Philadelphia TV stations gave it scant attention.

The campaign didn't have access to an electronic voter file. In fact, the entire voter-contact operation was run from boxes of lists of registered voters printed out in street order by precinct. Most of the summer was spent getting volunteers to look up the phone numbers by hand and write them next to each voter's name—by hand. Favorable voters were individually identified through door-to-door canvassing and phone calls made at home or at phone banks located in labor halls or businesses we could use at night. Supporters received get-out-the-vote (GOTV) phone calls, and—when we could—we recontacted the undecided voters. None of the voter IDs was ever put on a computer, and rarely were they carried over for use in the next election.

Bob Edgar's campaign budget was much smaller than the typical campaign of the time. In 1972, the average amount spent on congressional races was $318,000.[1] Back then, making a hands-on connection with voters was the dominant vehicle for campaigns. Things changed in 1978 when Representative Edgar ran for reelection and encountered an opponent who actually had enough money to go on television, a rare occurrence in Philadelphia at the time. Edgar had a fairly substantial lead going into the race, with initial polling showing him 13 or 14 points up, but when his opponent went on television, Edgar's lead evaporated. The campaign's field director described the dramatic reversal as if the Edgar campaign were relying on cavalry while the opponent had gained sudden access to jet airplanes. Edgar, with the power of incumbency and a continuation of his strong "ground game," was ultimately able to prevail in the race, but he only won by a little more than 1,300 votes.[2] In subsequent races, including the 1980 race that I managed just out of college, Edgar spent a considerable amount of money on broadcast television. The shift of strategy and tactics in the Edgar campaigns mirrored changes in U.S. politics at that time.

THE EVOLUTION OF CAMPAIGNS INTO THE 1980s AND 1990s

Since those early days, we have seen a dramatic evolution in political campaigning. Where 1970s campaigns were grassroots driven, campaigns of the 1980s were driven by large media budgets and large direct-mail campaigns. The 1980s also saw the expansion of canvassing and phone banks. And while those paid operations were effective and increased the capacity of campaigns to contact voters, they also served to dampen the grassroots elements of campaigning by supplanting the role of volunteers in the race.

The decline of the grassroots campaign and the expansion of big-money elements were exacerbated by the launch of independent expenditure (IE) campaigns. These IE campaigns—like those by the National Conservative Political Action Committee[3]—spent large amounts of their money on television, forcing campaigns that were being attacked to choose between funding grassroots activity and going on TV. It was not a tough choice; they went on TV and continued the drive toward media-driven and far more expensive campaigns. By 1992 the average congressional campaign budget was $735,000.[4]

The big media-driven campaigns suited the culture of the time. In the 1980s most people still watched broadcast television.[5] A typical voter arrived home from work in time to catch the 6 p.m. news while eating dinner and would spend a typical Thursday watching NBC all evening—from the national news, through the full prime-time lineup, until the late-night news. Cable was just getting started, and there was no such thing as satellite television. The Internet really did not exist. If you wanted to know the weather or the sports scores, you would watch your local TV news.

Campaigns built their broadcast television buys around these local news broadcasts, particularly what we call news adjacencies—the time right before the news. This drove the cost of those prime advertising slots up. Television ads doubled in price from 1972 to 1992 and doubled again from 1992 to 2002.[6]

For campaigns, however, cost was still king. With the rise in television advertising costs in major media markets, campaigns began to move money from broadcast-television buys into direct-mail campaigns.

In fact, the budget reality for a congressional race in Los Angeles was in total similar to a congressional race in Des Moines because what you would spend on television in Des Moines you would move over to direct mail in Los Angeles. Back then, people actually read their mail. And they weren't paying credit cards or bills online so every envelope that came through the slot was opened and reviewed.

Rising television costs also prompted the expansion of other campaign tactics. Even though newspapers were on the decline, people still read them, and newspapers still set the agenda for broadcast news and other outlets like radio. Also, back then, people still had phones that plugged into the wall, and they answered them. The first functional answering machine wasn't invented until after the AT&T breakup in the early 1980s.

Campaigning in the 1980s, I was an early adopter of the expanded range of new computer technology. I spent those years hauling around 26-pound Kaypro computers. They each had two internal 5-1/4" 195K "floppy" drives. The computers primarily had come to replace the boxes of handwritten IDs and hard-copy street lists that we had used in that early Edgar campaign. Each floppy could hold part of a caucus list, but it took multiple floppies for just one congressional district voter file. The computerization of campaign contacts would open a whole new world of opportunities that made campaigns both more efficient and more expensive. As voter files became computerized nationally, the volume of direct mail and direct-mail fundraising increased.

The Republicans led the field in utilizing this new technology and data for fundraising. President Reagan hosted a national television program that drove voters to call in and donate to his campaign via a toll free telephone number. In the 1980s Republicans also dramatically increased their fundraising through the mail using techniques pioneered by individuals like Richard Viguerie, who built up huge computerized lists of conservative donors.[7] Ironically, on the Democratic side most of the money being raised by mail was from senior citizens—loyal FDR Democrats. In 1990 the average age of the top 100,000 Democratic donors was 74.[8] Until Internet fundraising reached a critical mass, the majority of Democratic donors were over 50 years old.

In the 1980s, I worked primarily as a field organizer and Democratic campaign and party operative. As the technology changed, field campaigns relied less on volunteer organizations and more on paid operations. Volunteer phone banks and volunteer canvasses were replaced by paid phone banks and paid canvasses. The invention of the phone autodialer made it even easier to flood an area with hundreds of thousands of phone calls. While the paid operations were efficient, they lacked the connection and persuasiveness of grassroots volunteer operations. This flood of lower-quality voter contact would soon encounter technological and legal barriers that would make them less and less effective.

While grassroots campaigns certainly existed in the 1990s, the last full-scale volunteer campaign I worked on was Doug Wilder's race for governor of Virginia in 1989. He used extensive volunteer canvassing and phoning and ultimately won by less than one vote per precinct. In the 1990s, more campaigns relied on paid media and waves of direct mail and paid phoning, which made voter contact more of a vote-harvesting operation. Campaigns identified voters over the phone, mailed the people who were undecided or lived in persuadable precincts, and made GOTV phone calls to identified supporters as Election Day neared.

2000: THE INTERNET AGE COMES TO CAMPAIGNS

Fast forward 10 years. Campaigns and the cost to wage them continued to escalate thanks to bigger, better technology. Mass media, mail, and other paid programs continued to expand the reach of candidates to the electorate while new technology was bringing the voters even closer to the campaign. Before our eyes, the Internet was revolutionizing campaigns and the way voters interacted with candidates.

In 1998, I worked with Tammy Baldwin's campaign for Congress in Wisconsin's Second District. The first openly lesbian woman to run and win a congressional seat, we took advantage of what was then the leading edge of Internet technology. For starters, the Baldwin campaign had an active Web site, which was unusual for a congressional race at the time. On the Baldwin campaign we took it a step further and used the site to give people the ability to look up their polling place. And we produced a TV ad that we posted online even though the commitment it took to see the ad was significant since very few people had broadband access. Slow and steady dial-up was the norm of the day.

We made these investments because one of the campaign's key strategies was to reach college-age voters who were the earliest adopters of Internet communications. In a tight primary, moving quickly to engage this audience was a key to winning. Through the Web site, we gave them a vehicle to learn about the campaign and the information they needed to turn out for Baldwin.[9] Groundbreaking for the time, we sent e-mail to young people, and our TV commercials had a phone number they could call to find their polling place. We even went out with a digital camera and took pictures of the off-campus polling places. These efforts worked, and that campaign helped set a new dynamic for congressional races.

But the real beginning of the Internet Age was the 2000 presidential campaign. In 1999, Bill Bradley's campaign for president asked the Federal Election Commission to allow contributions made by credit card through a campaign Web site to be eligible for federal matching funds in the same manner as donations by check.[10] The FEC agreed, and "Dollar Bill" Bradley raised the first ever $1 million online.[11] The floodgates were now open. Bradley's haul was soon surpassed by John McCain, who raised $7 to $9 million dollars online. Campaigns started communicating using Web sites and e-mail, and accumulated online lists. It was a long way from reams of paper lists in boxes. The Internet precipitated a whole new culture in campaigns.

At the same time broadcast TV was becoming less dominant. Twenty years earlier, in the 1980s, the majority of TV viewing was on broadcast, but now, in the early 2000s, less than half of TV viewing was on broadcast networks while 35 percent was on cable.[12] Additionally, regular, "snail" mail usage was dropping off.[13] People, especially younger voters, were beginning to pay their bills online and toss out envelopes without opening them.

Then, in 2003, a federal "Do Not Call Registry" was created.[14] Even though polling calls and political calls were exempted from the letter of the law, it still had an impact as people increasingly viewed any unsolicited phone call as intrusive. At the same time, an increasing number of people acquired cell phones. People weren't cancelling their landlines yet, but more and more were using their cell phones to communicate.

All of this technology was beginning to permeate into field operations. In 2004, Democratic canvasses used Palm Pilots to store voter lists and record voter preferences at the door. Short videos were also put on the handheld devices and played by the canvassers in an attempt to be more persuasive.[15] When the video played at the door carried a similar message as the television advertising airing locally, the overall campaign message was reinforced and additional voters were persuaded. However, this type of contact was still not as effective as when voters heard a campaign message directly from someone they knew personally.

Throughout the rest of the decade, Internet communication increased and mass media continued its gradual decline, although political campaigns continued to spend vast amounts of money on broadcast television. By 2008, the Internet truly began to dominate political communication.

The change in communications in politics was very similar to what happened to the music industry in the United States. It used to be that we heard music after listening to the Top 40 songs on the radio and then going to a record store to buy the record. A regular record store had 7,000 to 8,000 records, and the megastores might have had 20,000 titles. That was pretty much it. However, if you wanted to listen to independent or alternative music or groups that weren't part of the Top 40 culture, you had to buy it through the mail or go to specialty stores. Once music started moving online, more and more musicians who weren't mega groups were able to attract listeners and buyers of their music. Relatively quickly, we went from radio (and actual records and CDs) dominating the music industry with a focus on just the Top 40 songs, to as many as a million different pieces of music available online.

The same thing happened with media in the United States. When broadcast television stations dominated the media, your choices for watching something on television were limited to four or five broadcast stations. Then television started becoming available in other formats—initially cable, and then you could record the TV on your VCR. Now television has moved to the Internet where Netflix, Hulu, and other services offer content with few, if any, commercials. As broadcast television become less and less dominant, in politics we needed to figure out what other forms of media we needed to buy to make up for those lost eyeballs. Of course, the decline of the media meant millions were going to the Internet for more political information, which provided an opportunity for the Obama presidential campaign to organize them there and raise hundreds of millions of dollars online.

THE SCOPE OF MODERN CAMPAIGN COMMUNICATIONS

Today, we are in a period of incredible transition. There are now three sets of people in U.S. politics, each rooted in the media environment of the last three decades. Seniors really represent the end of an era of the viewing behavior and technology that we saw in the 1970s and the 1980s. My 87-year-old mother still gets up in the morning and watches all four hours of the "Today Show." She goes out to the curb to get her newspaper and mail. She reads her mail, and she regularly corresponds with her friends through letters. She watches some TV at night, and she'll wait for the 10 p.m. or 11 p.m. news to find out what the weather might be and other news in her community.

At the other end of the spectrum are the 20-year-olds, the Millennials, who have never owned a record, don't watch broadcast television (except maybe for sports), don't read printed newspapers or magazines, and don't have a phone that plugs into the wall. They think that e-mail is something that you use to communicate with your grandparents. They talk to their friends via texts and social media, and they get their entertainment and news on the Internet. In focus groups, voters in their 20s and early 30s admit to not checking their snail mail for months at a time.

In the middle is everyone else. Depending upon your age, you use some combination of broadcast, Internet, cell phone, and other communications vehicles. The growing diversity of new communication tools is matched by the pace at which traditional tools are disappearing. Newspapers are cutting staff, and outlets are vanishing; the amount of money being spent on political advertising in print is diminishing. We're also seeing a parallel, glacial implosion of the U.S. postal system with the greatest decline in usage since it was established shortly before the Revolutionary War. With more and more Americans using e-mail and paying bills online, they require less and less of the traditional postal service.

Political campaigns can no longer rely solely on the traditional ways of doing politics. Standard TV buys are less effective because they are still targeting mostly broadcast. Those who are doing cable work now find that substantial percentages of the West have very, very low cable penetrations. Even in some Midwestern and Eastern states the urban areas and suburban areas may have high cable penetrations but the exurban and rural areas do not. Greater numbers of people cannot be reached by phone because of the filters of caller ID and answering machines, making it harder for phone campaigns to reach and identify voters. Traditional telephone polls also are now having a difficult time reaching voters, and polls without cell phone users are increasingly unrepresentative of the population.

In this period of transition, campaigns now have to figure out—depending on whom their intended audience is—what combination of old media and new media to use to effectively talk to voters. They must look down the road to trends that are reshaping political communications, including these seven:

1. The Fall of Broadcast Television

The first of these trends is the fall of broadcast television. Broadcast television is now down to its lowest ratings ever. In a growing number of local markets less than 25 percent of households are watching the late night local news. Instead, viewers are now watching ESPN, Comedy Central, or Netflix at night. They are getting their news, sports, and weather from other sources. This also means they are no longer targets for traditional TV buys that have been built around local news and news adjacencies. For those of us who do political communication for a living, this dramatically changes how we need to communicate.

2. *The Rise and Fall of Cable*

The second trend is the rise—and beginning of the fall—of cable television. Currently cable television has roughly 60 percent penetration of U.S. households. However, cable penetration reached its peak in 2008 or 2009 and has declined ever since.[16] The recession certainly plays a role, as families cut back on unnecessary expenses, but the increasing availability of television programs online plays a significant role as well.

Satellite television, on the other hand, has continued to grow, but it presents a different problem for political advertisers. Satellite systems do not sell local advertising, only national advertising, which isn't very useful in politics unless you are running for president. Cable also is being undermined by people who are beginning to buy their television through their telephone company. Verizon FiOS is eating into cable's market share. AT&T now has direct TV that it offers to thousands of households. In many ways, cable's expansion in the 1990s brought with it the seeds of its own destruction. The companies sold their cable service bundled with broadband, so at the same time that people are buying cable they also have the ability to watch TV online via Hulu, Netflix, and YouTube.

3. *The Rise of Internet Television*

At the time of this writing, about 63 percent of households in the United States have access to high speed broadband Internet, a virtual prerequisite for watching video online.[17] Internet television has already had winners and losers in this growing area. Emerging content providers like Hulu may have hit their peak and now have an uncertain future. Hulu has been put up for sale, and a small but loyal group of people basically use Hulu as their digital video recorder. Netflix, however, is still growing in leaps and bounds, despite the recent setback it suffered when it angered its subscribers by abruptly announcing dramatic rate and plan changes. In the spring of 2011, Netflix video streaming service accounted for nearly 30 percent of all U.S. Internet traffic in the evenings. CEO Reed Hastings now considers online streaming video the core of the Netflix business model.[18]

For political campaigners trying to figure out what communication tools we're going to use to reach people who are no longer watching cable and no longer watching broadcast television, it becomes clear that an increasingly large amount of money needs to be spent communicating with people who are watching video online.

4. *The Rise of DVRs and the Death of Commercials*

Digital video recorders also contribute to the problem of reaching voters through broadcast television. TiVo was invented in the late 1990s, but now both cable companies and satellite companies offer digital video recorders. About 40 percent of U.S. households have DVRs that allow people to fast forward through commercials.[19] The likelihood that viewers will skip over television ads in this context is dependent on the nature of the recorded programming and the time lag between the original airdate and the viewing of the recorded program. For example, when watching sports, consumers are more likely to watch the commercials. However, when someone records a first-run episode of *Grey's Anatomy* and watches it with a group of friends three days later, there's a good chance they're going to speed past every commercial.[20]

5. *The Rise and Fall of E-mail*

Another piece of the evolution of political communication is what's happening to e-mail. There is a trend, especially among younger people, to use e-mail less in favor of social networking sites.[21] As of this writing, Facebook usage has surpassed e-mail and other Internet usage in the United States. Additionally, text messaging is replacing e-mail among younger users. A growing percentage of Americans are now seeing their e-mail traffic as spam. Industry standards for message-open rates have declined drastically.[22] Less than 20 percent of political communications by e-mail are opened. However, text messaging still has a 97 percent open rate in the United States, prompting campaigns to expand the use of text messaging in their communication.[23]

Social media now dominates for a huge sector of voters. When Barack Obama ran for president in 2008, Facebook was just getting started, yet by 2011 Facebook had become the most popular Web site on the Internet.[24] It's also the largest photo repository in the world, and more people are referred to video from Facebook than any other online source. Facebook now gives advertisers the ability to target ads to individual users using nearly any piece of personal information stored in its massive databases.

6. *The Rise of Mobile Communications*

Mobile devices are becoming a primary means of communicating with voters. More than 300 million cell phones are in operation in the United

States, which would translate to nearly 96 percent of the population if the phones were distributed evenly among every man, woman, and child in the country.[25] Twenty-five percent of households are cell phone only, and many more are *functionally* cell phone only, meaning that they still have landline phones but conduct most of their business through their cell phone.[26]

The number of smart phones is growing by leaps and bounds; by the summer of 2012 over half of the United States will have smart phones.[27] The rise of mobile communications is having an impact in several ways. First, a very high percentage of people, nearly 44 percent, are using their smart phones to connect with the Internet. Second, we're beginning to see that consumers are willing to watch video on their smart phones. Where a family might once have gathered on the sofa to watch a show, individuals are now multitasking—watching television at the same time they are online, talking with friends on Facebook, or sending and receiving text messages.[28]

In addition to finding other new and effective ways to reach voters beyond television, we need to figure out how we reach voters who are doing two or three things at once, which may require a television ad, combined with an online ad, and now—increasingly—ads targeted to mobile devices.

7. The Rise (or Return) of Personalized Communications

Voters' online behavior already has allowed campaigns to place online ads that are more finely targeted to a voter's demographics and interests. As we steadily move away from broadcast "appointment" media, consumers will be able to select what they want to watch, when they want to watch it, on whatever device they have with them. Soon we will be sending tailored communications to more tightly defined sets of voters across a whole array of media platforms, including smart phone devices. The logical conclusion of this technology will be sending targeted video messages to individual voters as we do direct mail today. This will allow us to use the same types of real-time performance metrics for video as we use for banner ads or search ads, allowing real-time changes to flights of online media.

The increasing use of social media as a voter's online portal means that a campaign's communication with the voter will become increasingly interactive, whether it is two-way communication between the voter and the campaign or group or discussion of the message or requested action within the voter's own online social network. As in old-time campaigning, the source of that communication will play a big role in its credibility and trustworthiness. Already, millions of younger Americans are relying on their personal Twitter networks to make consumer choices, and both Twitter and other social media will play a starring role in 2012. In late 2011, Facebook began experimenting with social television. Right now, Google TV is the closest thing to what paid new video media may look like. Currently Google TV has no local advertising inserts and is limited to a small number of cable channels on a few satellite networks, but its access to billions of pieces of consumer data and proven behavioral reporting technology puts it first at the starting line.

This does not mean that broadcast TV is going away completely. Radio didn't disappear when TV was invented; it changed. While the radio is no longer the focal point of the U.S. household, during the course of a week most Americans still listen to some radio, even AM. Political professionals need to be prepared for the opportunity to communicate with individual voters with video messages and the ability for those voters to answer back.

NEW POLITICAL COMMUNICATION— BACK TO THE FUTURE

The only thing that's really certain about the future of politics is uncertainty. A lot of the trends that started in the early 1980s have been accelerated through the early 2000s and are really at a fever pitch. Campaigns that are less likely to adapt are going to have a harder time reaching voters.

As we move forward, more of the population will be digitally adept and more likely to use new technologies to communicate. Social media gives campaigns the ability to use those networks to connect with people personally, send them targeted information, make personal appeals for them to join a campaign, and send them tailored advertising spots.

Being a modern media consultant is really like being a communications triathlete. We need to figure out how to use traditional media to reach seniors, new media to reach Millennials, and a hybrid of communication to reach everyone else in the middle. Recently my firm has been experimenting with "iceberg" media buys. Iceberg campaigns have small broadcast TV components with heavier targeted layered cable, online, social media, and mobile advertising "below the surface." All of the platforms deliver the same message in different formats and lengths. The message may be carried by a 30-second TV commercial, 20-second Web or mobile video, banner ads, and search advertising. The e-mail, text, and social media make the campaign interactive, where voters can sign a petition, take action like making a phone call, or just send feedback. The social media allows them to send our message to a friend or involve them in the campaign.

Sometimes the use of old media helps increase the effectiveness of the new media campaign. A well-situated billboard can reinforce a Web site or text campaign to commuters, or canvassing can reinforce the message to Millennials who don't have phones, read papers, or own a TV. These had dramatic effects, especially when used to target specific demographics like younger or single women.

In some ways we're going back to the future. We are returning to where I began with a very personalized campaign that didn't rely on sweeping tactics like broadcast media and large-scale mail or phone programs. We are beginning an era of "connecting" political campaigns where communications will be as diverse as the populations to whom they are speaking.

I was taught as a young political operative that the single most persuasive form of communication was your candidate, and the second most persuasive was a friend, family member, or a neighbor leaning over the back fence or sitting at a coffee table and saying, "You know what? This candidate—I really trust her. I think she's a good person." This kind of discussion is now happening every day through Facebook and Twitter. As we move away from campaigns with large broadcast TV buys to more individualized campaigning through social media and other technology, the connection between the candidate and voter will once again become paramount.

CHAPTER 2

The Quest for Victory: Campaigning Online for President

Mindy Finn and Patrick Ruffini

It was a day like many others at Bush–Cheney reelection headquarters in Arlington, Virginia, in the early summer of 2004. The first wave of staffers—not counting the overnight shift in the War Room—would arrive at 6:00 in the morning, not to leave until 8:00 that night.

The department where we worked—the e-campaign—was no exception. Early mornings would see staffers scurrying about the building, getting in the faces of senior staffers to get them to sign off on a national e-mail to go out that day, multiple blog posts drafted and posted to the blog, microtargeted e-mail sent to small segments of the "file," and the latest TV ad posted to the Web site, with graphics optimized from multiple rounds of "heat map" analysis showing what drove more clicks.

The more formal dress code of earlier in the campaign had become relaxed as more field grunts came aboard. On this day, we were advised to dress up. For many staffers, the first inkling came with a Fox News breaking-news alert: President Bush was en route to campaign headquarters for surprise visit. A nervous energy pulsated throughout the building. Despite working on behalf of the most powerful man on earth, it's not like he made it to the office every day—or ever, until today.

Staff lined the edges of rows upon rows of cubicles as President Bush made his way around with his campaign manager, Ken Mehlman. It was suddenly our turn. "Sir, this is the e-campaign," said Mehlman, for an introduction. The president looked puzzled for a moment, then said, "Oh, GeorgeWBush.com! I've been saying that a lot."

After an awkward pause—we were not the most outgoing group—Mindy Finn piped up: "We know sir, and every time you do, the traffic skyrockets," making a checkmark with her finger. "Does it really?" replied the president in an "Aw, shucks" way. "I'll keep saying it then."

With that, he swiftly pivoted away from us and continued down the walkway with the sharp motion and posture of an army general.

FINDING OUR PLACE

In those early days, there wasn't a neat little box marked "Internet" on the organizational chart of most campaigns. Despite the media boiling down the Internet into a sound bite (massive e-mail lists! blogging! social media!), the truth is that even very early on, the Internet team did a lot of everything. We were in charge of the Web site, the e-mail marketing, online content like the official blog, video, online chats, flash games, and real-time debate rapid response. We also built activism tools, like self-organizing event modules and call-from-home applications. We sought an identity. Were we tech people or communicators? Organizers or fundraisers?

Sometimes, what we did broke through, and the higher-ups "got it," like the time when we spent weeks crunching data to e-mail voters with individualized maps and driving directions to polling places, and received reports of several voters walking into the polling location with the printouts in hand. Or the time when we doubled our goal with 4,000 online-organized house parties, engaging hundreds of thousands of attendees and generating coverage in hundreds of media outlets.

What started out as a two-person shop housed in the press operation grew to be its own department with a senior staff–level director. The eventual decision to create an e-campaign department in the Bush campaign was an early admission that the Internet represented the campaign in microcosm—equal parts message, money, and mobilization. (This was a lesson GOP campaigns later would unlearn at their peril.) With the advent of social media, and with major campaigns playing themselves out much earlier in the election cycle in an online-driven news cycle, the Web has become the central nervous system of the modern campaign.

As early as 2004, it was clear that neither of the presidential nominees' campaigns could have functioned without the Internet. For the Bush campaign, it was recruiting the vast majority of its volunteers online. For the John Kerry campaign, it was the imperative to raise money to compete with an incumbent president. The Kerry campaign would end up raising $80 million online—half of its entire haul from March to the Democratic convention.

In 2008, the Internet's impact would be supersized. Without the Internet, Barack Obama would not have become the Democratic nominee. The $500 million he raised online showed that it is possible to get more done on the Internet than previous "outsider" campaigns could get done with traditional channels of populist discontent. The Internet creates a larger space for opposition to established front-runners to form, in no small measure because the insurgents can be competitive financially and organizationally on day one. A curious feature of the 2012 Republican primary race is how much earlier in the cycle dark-horse insurgents seem to catch on in the polls.

From the moment John McCain collected $2 million online after his 2000 New Hampshire primary victory to today, the Internet has gone from bit player to big player. In many ways, it is now the stage on which the presidential campaigns play themselves out, particularly in the early phases of the race. And it's a transition in our own personal stories, too. We've gone from being misfit junior-level press staffers, to senior staff on presidential campaigns and national committees, to advisers to candidates brought on long before media consultants, all within a few years.

Candidates and strategists at all levels are haunted by a vague awareness that this thing called the Internet could make or break them, yet they can't fully control it. Oftentimes, success or failure online is dictated by factors frustratingly beyond the tactical decision-making realm of most campaigns, elemental stuff like, Are you genuine? Likable? Fiery? Inspiring? A threat to the political establishment?

Campaigns usually fail by trying to reverse engineer these qualities into their candidate. If candidates are Internet friendly to begin with, the job of the campaign and of the digital staff is to get out the way, first by letting the candidates be who they are in a way that will win them votes, and second by getting out of the way of supporters who want to help that candidate by providing meaningful and productive ways for supporters to organize online—and offline—for the campaign.

Beyond these basic strategic guideposts lie 1,001 tactical decisions. While the capacity to generate an online following may be inherent in the candidate and the message, only the online team can capitalize on it by optimizing the Web site to leave no potential volunteer or donor on the table or by building the tools to replicate the offline campaign at massive scale online. Bush's manager, Ken Mehlman, was fond of saying that "Lots of little things add up to one big thing." Successful campaigns build a data-driven culture that sweats the details, and this is reflected in the very best online teams.

In setting up a system that works, integration is key. Kerry Internet director and Hillary Clinton adviser Josh Ross summarized it by saying, "The Internet Director must know everything the campaign manager knows, and they need to know about things like databases." It is no surprise then that the Obama 2012 campaign calls the top digital staffer on its payroll the chief innovation and integration officer and pays him more than the campaign manager.

Successful digital campaigns aren't one-trick ponies. They're not just fundraising, or communicating, or mobilizing. They're all of those. Just as the Internet has become interwoven into all aspects of our daily lives, it's no surprise that it would also become the underlying infrastructure that allows politics in the modern era to function.

THE REELECTION FIGHT

The game was on. As early digital staffers for the Bush reelection effort, we were mindful of the high expectations facing us. John McCain had used the Internet four years earlier to run laps around our candidate. McCain was one of the first candidates to use the Web for organizing, asking activists to use his Web site to call early-state voters and enlisting activists in later-voting states in ballot access programs.

Over on the Democratic side, Howard Dean was McCain on steroids. His campaigners blogged dozens of times daily, flaunting their online grassroots energy. They used the Web to fund their upstart campaign and catapult to the top of the Democratic field. Over 180,000 people were organizing for the candidate on Meetup.com and holding in-person meetings in cities across the country up to a year before the first votes would be cast.

As the primary process concluded, the onus was on us, the digital staffers for an incumbent president, to match or exceed all of these previous efforts. And we had to do it without the key ingredient behind the online political success of McCain and Dean—a passionate antiestablishment message. We occupied the White House. We *were* the establishment.

We did have a few things going for us, however. In the previous two years, the Republican National Committee (RNC) had invested millions of dollars in a crack program to build up the Bush e-mail list from 300,000 to six million. We shifted from building to mobilizing. The first fundraising e-mail by the reelection campaign netted $400,000.

As the Bush campaign waited for the twists and turns in the Democratic primary race to finally result in an opponent, the staff were at work building a technology infrastructure ready for the general election. The master plan for 2004 was written in 2002 by Chuck DeFeo, the RNC's online communications chief. A 30-page memo to the Bush high command outlined tools, tactics, and strategies for the 2004 campaign. The process of selecting the right partner began long before the official start of the campaign, with Ohio-based New Media Communications winning out as the lead Web technology vendor for the party and, eventually, the campaign.

Over the next three years, Bush and the RNC would spend $3 million building campaign tools with New Media. In 2008, the Obama campaign spent $2 million with Blue State Digital, their technology vendor. Though these numbers seem high for a Web site, what was built was more just a Web site; it was the ability for supporters to run and manage their own microcampaigns. This included applications for house parties, phone banks, and door-to-door canvassing, a Karl Rove–devised system for people to manage "personal precincts" so people could spread the word to their personal networks with push-button ease, and a voter registration and absentee ballot system that would enable field staff on the ground to "chase" these voters' ballots.

The Bush campaign's mission was mobilization. In 2000, the Bush team had nearly lost the election because of a poor ground game in the final weekend. In response, Rove instituted the "72-Hour Task Force"—an effort to saturate the ground with local volunteers who were known and trusted by the voters they were reaching. This return to nineteenth-century, grassroots, shoe-leather politics would have an unlikely ally in technology. In no sense would a purely online campaign replace traditional grassroots, but, even in those early days, online tools turned out to be surprisingly crucial to the overall campaign.

Volunteer goals at Bush–Cheney headquarters were tracked on a county-by-county level by massive Excel spreadsheets capable of stumping a quant geek with advanced MBA training. Every Saturday, the political department held a conference call with each of its state directors to go over the numbers. The call lasted 10 hours.

The campaign's national vote goal was 55 million (it received 62 million). Of those, it was hoped that 2 percent, or 1.1 million, would become campaign volunteers. The Web site was the primary driver of this activity: approximately 70 percent of all volunteer sign-ups came in online, and the campaign exceeded its overall volunteer goal with a total of 1.4 million.

Once on the site, the goal was to give these volunteers something meaningful to do—online and offline. The campaign wanted to avoid the mistake of not following up with or thanking volunteers. Once signed up, a volunteer's view of the Web site changed almost completely. Content areas were collapsed, and the largest element on the home page was a dashboard measuring a volunteer's progress toward key goals: encouraging five people to register to vote, recruiting 10 more volunteers, or hosting a party. Volunteers who completed these goals were awarded prizes—a printable picture of the president, an exclusive screensaver, and finally, a Bush-signed certificate that was mailed out for completing every task.

Ultimately, the campaign's primary goal was to move people offline, into the field—and nowhere more so than in the swing states. While GeorgeWBush.com was designed to provide a "sticky" online experience, with a heavy use of online games and videos, the site's highest goal was to supply the boots on the ground to execute the 72-hour plan in its 19 target states.

DeFeo, who later moved over to the campaign, tells the story of his mother-in-law, a casual Republican in Missouri who bookmarked the site and visited a few weeks after he gave her a guided tour. In the upper right-hand corner of the homepage—a placement strategically selected because eye-tracking studies suggested that was the spot users looked to first—was a short snippet of text alerting her to a phone bank that night in Kansas City. These short alerts—"the 140 characters of 2004," DeFeo called them—were automatically displayed for logged-in volunteers and geographically targeted at the county level. These alerts became a minor obsession for Patrick Ruffini, who worked late perfecting personalizations to dozens of microsegments, like the Polk County Farmers or Duval County Small Business Owners. DeFeo's mother-in-law ended up attending the phone bank and a half dozen more like it. The goal of this feature, as DeFeo explained, was to use online prompting to "hook" people into the more "professional" side of the campaign.

Democratic campaigns also found online and offline strategies playing off each other in surprisingly effective ways. Josh Ross tells the story of when the Kerry campaign shifted the focus of online phone-calling campaigns from contacting voters to volunteers calling other volunteers. Under the direction of technology director Josh Hendler, Ross estimated that the move doubled the productivity of field staffers by crowdsourcing volunteer recruitment in swing states. The experience was also a much more pleasant one for activists. "Have you ever been to a phone bank? It's horrible," observed Ross, noting how volunteers frequently face hostile reactions from disinterested voters on the phone. "It's a much more rewarding experience to be calling other volunteers in battleground states," said Ross. "We were getting ten times more calls done. This made it fun."

In 2008, the Obama campaign made the heart of its online campaign the social network myBarackObama.com, or MyBO, where anyone could create a local grassroots group with built-in listservs. This self-organizing technology paid dividends during the primary when upstart volunteers began creating groups like "Idaho for Obama" in later-voting caucus states, when the campaign itself was focused solely on Iowa. The result? When the campaign *needed* those tiny caucus states to prevail in the long slog against Hillary Clinton, it had a powerful head start. Obama won Idaho by 79 percent to Clinton's 17 percent with just 20,000 votes cast, netting Obama a larger shift in the all-important delegate count than many larger states.

Sometimes, the goal of getting people to organize offline was explicit and best expressed in the motto of Meetup.com founder Scott Heiferman: "Use the Internet to get off the Internet." In 2004, the Bush campaign launched a "Parties for the President" tool that saw more than 30,000 parties created with an estimated 500,000 attendees. A huge "Ah-ha" moment for the staff came when, within minutes of the first online invitations being sent out, a map on the campaign's internal dashboard began to light up with dozens, then hundreds, then thousands of parties.

The campaign was always pushing the envelope of what was technically doable. We were obsessed with proving to ourselves and to the world that the Internet worked for mobilizing votes. One feature of the party tool allowed hosts to invite up to 50 nearby volunteers also active on the Web site to their events. This effectively doubled RSVPs, according to our tracking and anecdotal reports. And perhaps the most grueling task was the millions of e-mails sent to swing-state voters containing maps and driving directions to each voter's polling location. It was a weeks-long, computationally intensive process that could have been completely derailed by one bad batch of data.

The Bush technology effort married the 24/7 culture of a start-up with expectations of Fortune 500 performance. The bug list for the initial Web site build numbered 500. Between July and October of 2004, a tracking spreadsheet identified 927 bugs, issues, or questions resolved. Given the extreme time and budgetary limitations inherent to most campaigns, it's a miracle that the tools worked at all. Those running campaign tech teams see their share of successes but must also confront myriad software bugs, patchwork solutions, and other departments breathing down their neck wondering why the cool new toy you promised them isn't ready yet.

LESSONS LEARNED, 2008

In the following years, our journey would take us to senior roles at the RNC for one of the most expensive, hard-fought Senate races of 2006 and to respective presidential campaigns in 2008 (for Mitt Romney and Rudy Giuliani). In that time, we mediated bureaucratic turf fights among political, communications, and finance departments for control of the Internet. The tenuous coexistence that characterized the 2004 campaign gave way to a tunnel vision about the Web—seeing only the role for communications and fundraising.

At least in those two areas, the Romney campaign innovated ways to encourage person-to-person, supporter-driven activity. The first "digital" hire for the Romney campaign, Stephen Smith, director of online communications, led initiatives to encourage supporters to blog and for bloggers to join the Romney blog network. His task list included the successful launch of the first full-fledged campaign Web site to coincide with the campaign announcement in February 2007. The Web site, the most robust of its time for the GOP primary field—with features like MittTV, a specific section to promote campaign videos, and a blog—gave the impression of a well-organized, sophisticated campaign, one that did not plan to cede digital dominance to then-front-runner John McCain.

The impression and reality conflicted, however. While the McCain operation had a head start building robust grassroots fundraising and field tools, the Romney team's digital effort stopped at communication's edge. Angst over the lack of digital operations permeated Romney headquarters. We received calls from three different members of Romney's team in one week, all expressing the same desire: to hire an experienced digital director. (The McCain team had signed a conglomerate of digital staffers and vendors with presidential campaign experience, including New Media Communications). In retrospect, the fact that these calls came from the directors of the finance, strategy, and administration departments foreshadowed a lack of integration among the individual fiefdoms within the campaign, and revealed that in the hierarchy no division came close to finance's power.

Finance won the battle of "owning" the Internet, based on the argument that only a jaw-dropping fundraising number would be enough to catapult Mitt Romney safely into the top tier. With a promise that the role would sit in the finance department but encompass the overall digital strategy and that the team would spin off into strategy or its own division after the second fundraising deadline on June 30, 2007, Finn joined the Romney campaign as director of online strategy. Concurrently, the campaign hired a chief technology officer from the private sector to oversee both internal IT and database and product development.

An assessment began to determine what was "under the hood" of the apparently robust Romney technology operation. Two easel-sized white papers that adorned the wall of the online strategy director's office served as constant reminders of a major growing challenge for the campaign— multiple databases operating independently. One sheet showed the current state of data, nine circles scattered across the page. The other represented the ideal, a central data store through which the other data sources flowed. In order to build the tools to empower grassroots supporters to meaningfully aid in voter contact, persuasion, and turnout, the ideal—or something close to it—must be reached.

To the finance division's credit, it embraced the idea of rolling out an online action center with a toolset to empower and motivate supporters to act. It had already earned accolades from the major bundlers and donors, as well as the media, for the development of a system for managing fundraising downlines through the use of a complex coding system. This system had its debut at a national "Call Day" after the campaign announced its exploratory committee in January 2007. The Call Day entailed hundreds of the campaign's most ardent money men and women converging on Boston for a telethon-style day of making calls to potential donors and inputting the donations into the system, termed "COMMITT."

The political department, meanwhile, had no plans and little interest in an online action center akin to the Bush 2004 tool set. They had invested in a VoterVault "lite" system for accessing voter data and had their sights set on administrative tools for use by campaign staffers only.

Yet based on experience that showed the value of these tools, the online strategy and technology teams embarked on the development of one anyway. They knew that by the time of the Iowa caucuses—which the Romney campaign believed it would win—the campaign would face a grassroots tool deficit if it held off on development until the general election.

The platform would integrate directly with MittRomney.com and include a progress bar that rewarded everything from filling out your profile to recruiting friends and making donations. It would include a call-at-home and personal precinct module. The strategy and finance teams supported the development of this toolset, and the political department reluctantly got on board too.

The first real opportunity to test whether the Internet could catalyze the integration of campaign activity among divisions came toward the end of the first fundraising quarter. The online team—then still technically part of the finance division—suggested having a virtual event, a hub to direct momentum towards and showcase the Romney campaign's grassroots strength in the midst of party angst over front-runner John McCain's lack of popularity among activists. The finance team, naturally, believed this event should focus specifically on fundraising, with some type of gimmick to follow on the success of Call Day.

Armed with data that showed the campaign would net more supporters and likely more money if it lowered the barrier to entry, the online team persuaded the finance team to make the virtual event sign-up focused. "Sign Up, America"—a name meant to double as the objective and the directive of the minicampaign—was born. With a goal of recruiting 24,000 supporters in 24 hours, the organization came from the top but tapped the ideas and resources of the entire Romney operation, from field staff in Iowa, New Hampshire, and South Carolina to the state finance directors and entire communications team. The theory: the campaign would not reach the tipping point of inspiring the broader grassroots-activist base without empowering its most invested supporters first—its staff and professional volunteers. All were given Web-based tools (cobbled together in three weeks) for activating their personal networks by e-mail, through event management, and by simple personalized tracking links.

Video updates throughout the day, media promotion, and a telethon-style baseball "mitt" that filled up as the sign-up number escalated toward 24,000 contributed to momentum. Most importantly, the candidate himself appeared at campaign headquarters in the final hour of Sign Up, America to tout the progress of the initiative and stood in front of a big screen while a realistic video overlay of himself—dubbed the "mini-Mitt"—encouraged Web visitors to sign up. The tools, a light version of their 2004-era predecessors, did the trick, with the campaign recruiting 31,000 supporters as the 24-hour deadline hit.

The robust Romney campaign Web site, fundraising systems, and Sign Up, America–type events held promise for the Romney campaign and its digital operations. Yet its intentions for organizing tools, like the action network, for example, never met their potential, and Romney lost Iowa and New Hampshire and dropped from the race in February 2008 before Super Tuesday.

With Romney's departure, the general election was effectively set between Barack Obama and 2000's online hero, John McCain. While McCain began his campaign with high hopes of online success, hiring a virtual armada of online advisers, its reversion to scrappy underdog in mid-2007 meant that most Web development floundered. The McCain online team had aggregated best practices of the previous two presidential cycles to finally do digital right. The problem? The campaign had not caught up. Limp fundraising met with boundless spending and internal squabbling, and the McCain campaign imploded by summer 2007. The frontrunning campaign that promised to be Bush 2004 reloaded found itself broke and running on fumes.

By the time the McCain campaign revived after the New Hampshire primary in January 2008, there was little hope of building an online infrastructure to compete with the Obama campaign. The team that remained embraced blogger outreach, Web video, and digital advertising, but that was mostly it. The McCain team was advised internally, months before Obama would do the same, to announce its vice presidential pick online, yet the suggestion was swiftly rebuked as "undignified." When the Obama campaign did the same, earning between one and two million new mobile opt-ins, it left many GOP digital politicos scratching their heads, hoping for better luck in 2012.

AND NOW, 2012

This marks the third presidential election cycle in a row that the Internet had made its impact known. As the use of that technology has grown more and more essential, it has also faded into the background as an essential pillar of the organizational structure rather than the stuff of breathless, gee-whiz media accounts.

On April 4, 2011, BarackObama.com opened its doors for the 2012 campaign. Instead of the feature-rich spectacle that greeted visitors on the day Obama announced in 2007, complete with the MyBO network, the 2012 site was simple and direct, greeting visitors with a simple question: "Are you in?" and inviting users to connect with Facebook to share the announcement with friends.

Two weeks earlier, Governor Tim Pawlenty, the candidate for whom we worked early in the 2012 cycle, made news by becoming the first presidential candidate to announce on Facebook. A simple Facebook application counted down to the timed release of an announcement video, as fans were encouraged to "Like" the page to be the first to get the news.

His campaign Web site opened its doors with an action center—built with our firm's technology—incorporating game mechanics and a connection to Facebook to inspire people to take more and more action, from recruiting others, to sharing on social media sites, to pledging to travel to swing states.

Digital politics is being boiled down to the essentials, and it is going social and mobile. Social media holds the power of allowing campaigns to create personal, one-to-one connections with voters tied to their real, social identity. It also has the potential to solve one of the central problems with digital campaigns today: that you only ever preach to the choir. Senior strategists are still deeply skeptical of how it moves votes.

Facebook and other social media sites are creating an online public square where people are exposed to politics through their friends—the most trusted referral source. Share a story about politics, and your apolitical friends won't be able to escape it. With social media, every opinion expressed in a comment thread becomes a "signal" to be captured and analyzed. Which campaign will be the first to seriously conduct sentiment analysis on tweets as a complement to traditional polling? Online data can give campaigns a granular and real-time view of how they are doing, and we will probably see an explosion in sentiment-analysis technology in the next few years. Beyond better qualitative analysis, social and mobile data could unlock information about implicit voter behavior: when do people vote, when do they decide, and who influences that vote?

Election Day 2010 featured two experiments in the use of data stores powered by social media that provide glimpses into the future. Foursquare's "I Voted" project visualized real-time mobile check-ins at more than 100,000 polling places across the country. More important than the raw numbers (50,416 check-ins) were the trends—visualizing for the first time in a public, real-time format what times of day people voted (overwhelmingly, it is after work).

That same day, Facebook asked its 140 million U.S. users if they voted and got 11 million responses—arguably history's biggest exit poll. A few days after the election, Facebook's data team released numbers showing GOP users far more likely to cast a ballot in 2010. These findings tracked with the final results and opened the possibility that insights about voter behavior culled from social media could be the polling of the future.

Our experiences helping shape cutting-edge political technologies in 2004 led us to build Engage, the firm we cofounded in 2008, around the idea of empowering activists with technology. We applied this principle early on in the 2012 cycle with a social action and data tool we call Multiply, deploying it for presidential campaigns and for organizations eager to mobilize fans like political campaigns do.

Campaigns shouldn't build technology for technology's sake. Yet, as the stories in these pages illustrate, political technology has the power to captivate and engage, to bring people who would have never met around a common cause, and to inspire public participation in political campaigns at levels never imagined by the political bosses of yesteryear.

CHAPTER 3

Skyrocketing Numbers: Online Fundraising for Political Campaigns

Nicco Mele

In 1983, Democrats were facing an incumbent Republican president who was enormously popular, an incredible communicator, and a movie star to boot. But the front-runner for the Democratic nomination was Walter Mondale—a candidate who did not stir up much excitement. Mondale was a long-time establishment leader of the Democratic Party, having been a governor, senator, and vice president of the United States under Jimmy Carter. He had spent much of his public life preparing to run for president, working his way up the Democratic Party food chain. He was widely considered, according to conventional wisdom, to be unbeatable for the nomination, mostly because he had locked up the party's fundraising machinery and most of the critical endorsements. But he remained an uninspiring figure who was widely regarded as unable to mount a credible challenge to Ronald Reagan.

Because Mondale appeared to have the force of the establishment behind him, other challengers in the Democratic primary struggled to raise money and pick up endorsements. Mondale easily won the Iowa caucus, but then to everyone's shock he lost the New Hampshire primary to a young upstart senator from Colorado—Gary Hart, a charismatic and handsome senator who had finished in Iowa with a respectable 16 percent. Suddenly, Democrats across the country who had been resigned to Mondale as the nominee got excited. They started to send money to Gary Hart in the hopes that he might defeat Mondale.

But there was a problem. This was 1984, long before the Internet; the only way to contribute to a presidential candidate was to write a paper check. And then there was the problem of where to *mail* the check. Gary Hart's campaign was not even six months old and didn't have an office address you could look up in the Yellow Pages. Democrats across the country wrote checks to Gary Hart, put them in envelopes, and addressed them to "Senator Gary Hart, Washington DC."[1] Hart's Senate office had to forward this flood of mail to the campaign office in Denver, Colorado.

The campaign office suddenly had a problem. There were boxes of envelopes that needed to be opened and thousands of checks that needed to be endorsed and deposited. And then the campaign had to wait two to four weeks for all these out-of-state checks to clear before the money was available to them. Gary Hart literally couldn't get the money in the bank fast enough to spend it in order to effectively challenge Mondale in subsequent primaries. Mondale was able to quickly outspend him and consequently lock up the Democratic nomination. Mondale went on to lose 49 states to Ronald Reagan in the 1984 election.

Now let's fast forward to 2007. The Democratic Party had an establishment front-runner who had spent her entire adult life in Democratic politics. She was in the White House for eight years as the first lady. She had one of the best political fundraising operations ever seen, honed by decades of fundraising for Democrats around the country. Her husband was the ex-president. She appeared to have the nomination locked up. Almost every elected Democratic African American official in the country had endorsed Hillary Clinton over Barack Obama. But many Democrats had reservations about having another Clinton in the White House; after all, if she won reelection, then for 28 years the United States would have either a Bush or a Clinton as the head of the executive branch. Nevertheless, Hillary looked unbeatable, so the crowded primary field had trouble raising money and landing endorsements.

Even Barack Obama, the young, charismatic upstart, was having trouble raising money on a scale competitive with Hillary Clinton. But Obama was able to use the Internet to build a parallel fundraising operation outside of the establishment. And so when he won the Iowa caucus, defeating Hillary, he was able to take advantage of the enormous outpouring of support that materialized when it was evident that he was a credible challenger to the establishment. Once there was a crack in the Clinton armor, Democrats all over the country started to send money to Obama, but this time, unlike in 1984, the challenger was able to raise the money to win not only the primary but the general election as well. That's the power of the Internet for political fundraising: it allows candidates outside of the establishment to raise money fast, cheap, and with great impact.

IT ALL STARTED WITH BILL

The story of online fundraising does not begin with Obama. In many ways, it begins with Bill Clinton. Clinton's impeachment inspired Joan Blades and Wes Boyd to start MoveOn.org. Now a pillar of the Democratic establishment, MoveOn was, in the early days, at best a fringe curiosity. While it still retains its name from the impeachment—"Censure and Move On" was the rallying cry—few could have imagined the enormous impact MoveOn would have on the political system. In many ways, it invented online political fundraising.

The vast majority of online fundraising is done through e-mail solicitation. It is remarkable: e-mail has not changed substantially in 15 years, and e-mail fundraising has remained remarkably consistent with clear best practices established over the last decade or so. Besides e-mail fundraising, there are three other methods of online fundraising that have emerged in politics, many of them as old as e-mail fundraising, including peer-to-peer, crisis, and platform fundraising.

MoveOn.org started as a personal e-mail to friends that went viral, creating a nationwide movement for Americans fed up with the impeachment process. Recognizing the power of their growing e-mail list, Blades and Boyd began to make plans to use their list to raise money to defeat Republicans and conservative Democrats who persisted in their support of the impeachment when so many people in their districts wanted them to "move on." Although MoveOn.org was founded in September of 1998, it wasn't until June of 1999 that it set up its own political action committee, the MoveOn PAC, and started raising money online. The success MoveOn found with online fundraising was exceptional, raising $250,000 in its first five days of operation and $2 million over the course of 2000.

The early use of e-mail solicitation to drive online activity was not new. E-mail was, from the early dawn of the Internet, the "killer app." Even today, most Internet users do five things online: shop, search, use social networks, watch videos, and access their e-mail inbox.[2] And they spend a significant chunk of their total time in their e-mail inbox. If you are not sending them e-mail, you are probably not reaching them.

MoveOn.org established and refined the model of building an e-mail list around hot-button issues that resonate, then using the e-mail list to raise money for candidates through carefully crafted e-mail messages with powerful narratives and conversion analytics. During the 2000 presidential primaries, the Bill Bradley campaign petitioned the Federal Election Commission (FEC) for permission to raise money online through Web-based credit card processing and then went on to raise over $1 million online. In the 2004 presidential primary campaign, the Howard Dean campaign (where I worked) built an e-mail fundraising option modeled explicitly on MoveOn.org, to the extent that we would call MoveOn staff begging for advice and help. That campaign raised more than $20 million online,[3] rocking the political establishment with the power of its online fundraising operation. And four years later—a mere eight years after the FEC approved online fundraising—Obama went on to raise close to *half a billion dollars* online.

Howard Dean—like Obama—was driven to online fundraising out of necessity. Dean had not spent decades cultivating and building a network of major donors to the Democratic Party. Nor did Dean have the budget or the time to build a direct-mail fundraising machine. But the Internet was fast, cheap, and ready right now. The real question was whether or not it was possible to raise any substantial sum of money online.

There was some evidence in the spring of 2003 that Dean could raise money online. The first-quarter online fundraising response had significantly exceeded its modest expectations, and Dean's online reach through Web site traffic, blog activity, and Meetup.com activity was growing exponentially. Even if the campaign was able to harness just a small part of the online activity, it would be able to raise a staggering sum of money online.

WHERE I COME IN

At about this point my life collided with the story line of online fundraising. While I was in high school, I had started doing tech work. It was fun, and it paid a lot better than waiting tables. While I was in college, I worked in Washington, DC, as a technical consultant for a wide range of organizations. One of the places I worked was Common Cause, at the time one of the largest grassroots advocacy groups in Washington, DC.

Common Cause was founded in 1970 by John W. Gardner as a "citizens' lobby" to "hold power accountable." Over the years, Common Cause had become focused on the role of money in politics. Major donors and fundraisers enjoyed more and more access to our political leadership on both sides of the aisle, creating a culture of influence that was making it harder and harder for ordinary Americans to shape the direction of our government.

It seemed to me that the role of money in politics was key. Pick almost any policy issue you cared about and you would find a well-financed interest (frequently a major corporate interest) wielding undue influence over the issue's fate in Washington. (Elizabeth Drew has written eloquently and convincingly on this subject in books like *The Corruption of American Politics*.) My obsession with politics—and the role of money in politics—led to a job offer from Common Cause upon my graduation from college. I was tasked with building an online presence for them, managing their Web site, and growing an online activist base that they could use for various advocacy actions.

But after a couple of years fighting the good fight at Common Cause, I was restless and frustrated. U.S. politics seemed impossibly corrupt and the prospect for change remarkably distant. I moved to New York City and took a nonpolitical job with the International AIDS Vaccine Initiative, a nonprofit vaccine research institution. I loved living in New York, but watching the presidency of George W. Bush take the country into war in Iraq was deeply upsetting. I began to spend my evenings surfing the emerging political blogosphere, lurking on sites like MyDD.com. And it was there that I first encountered the story of a nonpolitician, a medical doctor, who was running for president of the United States— Governor Howard Dean.

In March of 2003, one of my friends was getting very excited about Dean and invited me to a big event at the Essex Lounge in Manhattan where Dean was supposed to speak. I arrived fashionably late only to find that the venue was packed, with a line snaking out the door and down the block. I waited around for a while and then decided to head home. I was never going to get inside in time to hear Howard Dean. But now my curiosity was piqued. The energy of the crowd outside the Essex Lounge was intoxicating, and I had not encountered anything like that in Washington, DC.

I went home and Googled "Howard Dean." I found an enormously flattering *New York Magazine* profile, "The Unlikely Rise of Howard Dean." It got me even more fired up about him. I decided I would make a contribution to his presidential campaign—the first politician to whom I had ever contributed financially. But then I ran into an odd problem: I could not find his Web site to make the contribution. It was not coming up in a Google search and it wasn't anything easily guessable, like "HowardDean.com," "DeanForPresident.com," or even "Dean04.com." I finally found it buried in the search results—DeanForAmerica.com. Once I found the Web site, I could not find the "donate" button; it turned out that to donate you had to click a button inexplicably labeled "A Pre-scription for Change, Click Here." Instead of giving the Dean campaign a contribution, I decided to throw them a bone and make it a little easier to find the campaign Web site. I bought a Google AdWord so that any-one who searched for "Howard Dean" or "Dean for President" would see a little box pop up to the right of their search results that said, "The Official Web site of Gov. Howard Dean's presidential campaign: DeanForAmerica.com."

I cannot remember what kind of daily budget I put on the Google AdWord; it was ample but not dramatically generous (I was living on a nonprofit salary in New York City, after all). But I know that I bought the ad and immediately forgot about Howard Dean and the Google ad I had bought until a couple weeks later when my credit card bill arrived. There was a whopping charge from Google. I logged on and saw that the search volume for keywords relating to "Howard Dean" was skyrock-eting. The graph looked like a hockey stick, with a slow initial start and then a sharp upward angle.

Sitting at my desk at work, I excitedly called the campaign. After wait-ing on hold for an eternity, I asked to speak to whoever was running the Web site, and got transferred to a woman named Zephyr Teachout. I told her I was running the Google ads. She said, "Oh, I wondered who was doing that." I explained that I could not afford to keep buying the ads but that someone on the campaign should. "I think you can raise some money online this way to easily offset the cost of the ads," I explained. Zephyr was unimpressed. "We're pretty busy," she said. "We don't have anyone here who knows how to do that. If you want to do that, you should move up here and do it."

I remember I stared into the phone incredulously. She wants me to move to Burlington, Vermont? To be a volunteer on the campaign, run-ning Google ads? Does she think I'm crazy? I politely concluded the con-versation and hung up.

About 10 days later, I packed my car and moved to Vermont. Zephyr's words had stayed with me. It had long been an aspiration of mine to join a presidential campaign, and with the wars in Iraq and Afghanistan escalat-ing I felt a particular urgency to change the course of the country. And what the hell—it sounded like fun!

I showed up in Burlington at the headquarters midday on a Saturday. I cleared off the end of a creaky desk and set down my alien-shaped flat-screen iMac. Within an hour of arriving I was working with Zephyr Teachout, Bobby Clark, and Matt Gross on overhauling the Web site. They seemed stunned that I could actually make changes to the Web site without calling anyone. Prior to my arrival they had been call-ing a Web company in another state for every single edit to the site. Soon my hours on the campaign were impossibly long as the Web site became the hub of the campaign's activity, requiring constant care and feeding.

The truth is that I arrived in Vermont ignorant of online fundraising. I had the right combination of technical and design skills—jack-of-all-trades, master of none—to take the campaign's online activity up a notch. But I still had no idea what I was doing; it was mostly reactive. The cam-paign manager, Joe Trippi, had been following the rise of MoveOn.org. He was convinced that MoveOn had a secret that we needed to learn in order to raise money online. He had us carefully follow them, tracking their model of e-mail acquisition through online petitions followed by well-crafted e-mails to the petition signers designed to convert them into political donors.

Trippi began to court MoveOn aggressively, asking them for advice and help. The folks there were assiduously evenhanded. They did not want any accusations that they favored one candidate over another in the presidential primary. MoveOn eventually offered all the presidential campaigns help, and we gratefully took them up on it. Zack Exley, a MoveOn senior staffer, visited our campaign headquarters and helped us understand how to raise money online.

FIRST YOU ACQUIRE, THEN YOU CONVERT

Online fundraising begins with e-mail acquisition. Unlike direct mail, you cannot rent or buy an e-mail list; that is tantamount to spam. You must build your list organically, acquiring new subscribers by appealing to the cause at hand and capturing them when they casually visit your Web site. In a well-run campaign, e-mail acquisition is baked into every single part of the campaign. When you enter the campaign office and talk to the receptionist, he or she will ask you to write down your e-mail address.

For the Dean campaign, e-mail acquisition became an obsession. At the height of the campaign, Trippi would call me at all times of the day or night and demand to know the net new number of e-mail subscribers since his last call. A little icon on the Web site ticked up every day as the campaign continued to grow. In an explicit attempt to mimic MoveOn.org, we began posting various petitions. One of our first and most successful was an online petition in response to a withering attack from the DLC (a conservative Democratic think tank) immediately following one of the first candidate debates in May 2003. The petition went viral, bringing thousands of new sign-ups to the campaign.

If online fundraising begins with e-mail acquisition, it comes to fruition with conversion. Online fundraising is like direct mail in one respect—a lot of it is about math: how many people did you send the e-mail to? How many opened it? How many clicked on the link? Did one subject line perform better than another? But online fundraising is different from other fundraising because to build a successful online fundraising campaign you need to craft a coherent narrative over time. It is almost as if each e-mail you send is the next installment in a serialized novel, growing with intensity and engagement over time. The most compelling narratives draw their power from the real world, from the political dynamic or the programmatic activity of the campaign. In other words, a good story that is complete fiction will not fare well, but if the story is about the real-world work, about the impact the campaign is having, then it will carry a strong punch. That's the conversion.

In the case of Howard Dean, the compelling story line was there from the start: Dean was the outsider, the only Democratic presidential campaign not headquartered in Washington, DC, the only Democrat with the courage to stand up to Bush on issues like the war in Iraq and the sorry state of health care in this country. With the end of the quarter approaching, we needed to convert the online excitement around Howard Dean into cold, hard cash; otherwise, Dean would continue to be ignored by the mainstream media and the political establishment.

A clear, common goal with some urgency attached about reaching the goal is a staple of fundraising from well before the Internet ever existed. In a twist on the classic thermometer, we created a baseball bat and announced our intention to raise more than $500,000 in four days before the end of the quarter.

The baseball bat changed colors as donations came in. In many ways simply announcing our progress toward our goal was a thunderclap in traditional political campaign fundraising because traditional campaigns closely guarded their fundraising totals over the course of the campaign as an important part of playing politics.

Soon we blew past our original goal of $500,000 and decided to set our sights even higher, on the absolutely outlandish second-quarter fundraising goal of $7 million. But as crazy as the goal was, supporters understood that reaching this goal depended on *them*. Consequently, they poured energy into reaching that goal and then justly felt as through they, acting individually in a collective manner, had accomplished something great. Each individual $50 or $100 contribution combined together is the recipe for success in meeting the much larger, stunning total.

Dean's progress toward the goal became a riveting political drama in part because it dramatized the role of the Internet in allowing an insurgent candidate—Dean—to meet and then beat the establishment candidates—like John Kerry—at the "money primary." A narrative about overcoming impossible obstacles to become the front-runner for the nomination to be president of the United States—what could be more exciting? Donating to Dean online meant that you were part of the most exciting story in Democratic politics in decades.

The story of the bat to this day gives me flashbacks. I had hoped to go to a minor league baseball game on Friday night. Instead I was tasked by Larry Biddle, a senior member of the fundraising team, with creating a thermometer baseball bat for the campaign's final fundraising push for the second quarter. But the bat quickly took on a life of its own, growing well beyond the original $500,000 goal to a final total of over $7 million.

As the only technical Web staffer, I updated the bat graphic myself, using a graphics editor program to manually fill up the bat pixel by pixel. Demands for more frequent bat updates came closer and closer together, and my sleep deprivation accelerated. Jim Brayton, a campaign volunteer who soon joined the campaign as staff, came in to spell me for periods so that I could sleep, shower, and eat.

We raised a shocking amount of money in the final days of June 2003. The Internet team was able to significantly staff up, investing in new technologies and new staff to grow and expand our reach and operations. We managed to move beyond manual updates to the bat graphic, allowing future bats to be deployed without the round-the-clock hands-on maintenance required the first time around. The promise and opportunity of small-dollar online fundraising resonated across the political establishment with a resounding crack of the bat, fueling a new generation of tactics and strategies bringing together online and offline activity for maximum impact.

And then, of course, it all came crashing down. Despite the Dean campaign's meteoric fundraising, we managed a distant third place in Iowa. The national news media kept Howard's "scream" on constant rotation, making it hard to pull the campaign out of the nosedive. We soldiered on—all the way through Wisconsin—but on a sunny day in March, Howard Dean announced he was pulling out of the presidential race.

I was on the campaign almost exactly 12 months. When I arrived, I was the only person able to update the Web site, but over the next 12 months,

as the Internet became critical to the campaign's success, the online team
grew and grew. At its height, we had approximately 35 people on the
Internet team at headquarters. Out of those 35 people grew several companies that have had a lasting impact on the field. One of those companies
was my own, EchoDitto. Our first client was a little-known state senator
from Illinois who harbored big ambitions, a man with a name that would
appear to have doomed his electoral ambitions from the start: Barack
Hussein Obama.

ONLINE BECOMES THE NEW NORM

The companies that grew out of the Dean campaign have dramatically
shaped the landscape. The largest—Blue State Digital—went on to provide the strategy and technology for Obama's 2008 presidential campaign. Blue State was acquired in 2011 by WPP, a large advertising and
marketing conglomerate. Others remained small but influential, like
Chapter Three, a Drupal consultancy that grew out of a Drupal-based
open-source project called "DeanSpace" that the Dean campaign had
nurtured. Another, Advomatic, has built hundreds of Drupal Web sites
for political causes and candidates. The innovation and game-changing
experience of the Dean campaign proved too good an opportunity to
resist for a generation of entrepreneurs in technology and politics.

That was certainly my experience. As it became clear in February of
2004 that Dean's chance at the nomination was fast evaporating, the job
offers started to pour in. I kept them tallied in a spreadsheet and wondered at the amazing variety of opportunities being presented to me, from
more politics to other Internet start-ups to big advertising agencies. But
the truth is that I was a true believer, and the prospect of losing was
almost impossible for me to absorb. If I thought too hard about what
I was going to do next, well, that meant Dean wouldn't win. When Dean
finally pulled out of the race, I was bewildered and unable to let go of the
dream. I stuck around, helping to organize a fire sale of all of the office
equipment and furniture and then vacuuming up the empty office.

Finally, I called together about 10 people from the campaign and
invited them to meet me at a local coffee shop. We had built something
incredible together. It was now up to us take what we had learned during
the Dean campaign and share it with a wide range of organizations.
I called up many of the organizations that had offered me a job and tried
to convince them to hire us as a company instead. Remarkably, many of
these calls proved successful. Our work was then—and remains today—a

combination of technical implementation of open-source software (with a special expertise in Drupal) and strategic advice rooted in the perspective of the social Web.

Starting a company is a special kind of misery, requiring absolute focus and significant sacrifice. For the first 9 or 10 months of the company—the remainder of 2004—I did not have a permanent place of residence and instead sofa-surfed, taking advantage of the kindness of friends. When I finally did rent an apartment, I neglected to get any furniture beyond my inflatable mattress. Joe Trippi's wife, Kathy Lash, took pity on me and offered me a mattress they had stored in their barn out on their farm on the eastern shore of Maryland. I strapped it to the top of my ancient Honda Civic, drove it home, and then rented an upholstery cleaner to get rid of the barn smell of hay and animals. (I went on to sleep very well on that mattress for years.) My complete and entire focus was making sure the company survived and our clients thrived online. I made many, many mistakes as I learned how to manage clients, manage cash flow, and keep my team energized and engaged. But I will never forget the feeling of watching a client's project blossom online to incredible success, like the Service Employees International Union's "Since Sliced Bread" campaign or the World Food Program's "Walk the World" day of action.

For our first two years, immediately following the Dean campaign, the bulk of our work was with political candidates and campaigns, but we moved out of political candidate work and into working with nonprofit and corporate clients. As much as I love politics, my earlier frustrations with the role of money in politics became magnified as I waded deeper into the heart of U.S. politics. I remain very much committed to reducing the influence of money in politics, and I believe that the rise of small-dollar online donors has thus far proved the most potent antidote to the poisonous culture of influence in Washington, DC.

In the wake of the Supreme Court's Citizens United decision, which ruled that corporations are allowed to spend as much money as they want to influence election outcomes, it is clear that a legislative solution for campaign finance reform is unlikely in the current climate. How can ordinary Americans possibly combat the huge sums of money corporations can marshal to influence election outcomes? Small-dollar donors can be organized online cheaply and easily, providing some hope of countering U.S. politics overrun by corporate interests.

Online fundraising has moved well beyond the primitive bat updates that fueled the Dean campaign's meteoric rise. There are now a plethora of tools and a wide range of consulting firms built around online fundraising. While there are some other models, the vast majority of online fundraising continues to follow the basic MoveOn.org model—e-mail acquisition on the one hand, e-mail conversion on the other. Barack Obama's 2008 presidential run perfected the MoveOn model down to a science, tracking every conceivable metric and testing and tweaking every variable to maximize performance: which subject lines and which senders lead to higher open rates? Do certain photos or donation premiums (like mugs or t-shirts) increase the response rate or the average gift? What other online or offline behaviors increase response rates?

The amount of ground covered between the 2004 Dean campaign and the 2008 Obama campaign is staggering. In those four short years, Facebook, YouTube, and Twitter all arrived on the scene with incredible velocity. The amount of video produced by the 2008 Obama presidential campaign—and the tens of millions of Americans who consumed it through YouTube and other venues—was unimaginable in 2003 when I was on the Dean campaign. The complexity and sophistication of our online lives have grown in ways that were unimaginable just a few years ago, and politics continues to seek the tactical advantage in technology in order to win elections.

CHAPTER 4

Ignore at Your Peril: Campaigns and the Blogosphere

Liz Mair

In June 2011, progressives congregated in Minneapolis for the sixth annual Netroots Nation Convention. Among the political paraphernalia sported by attendees—many of them bloggers, online commentators, Twitter users, and reporters for left-leaning Web sites—were buttons designating the wearer a member of the "Professional Left," a reference to former White House press secretary Robert Gibbs' less-than-friendly remark about various liberal activists, including prominent online media figures.[1] These were people broadly perceived as having helped deliver the Democratic nomination to Barack Obama, defeating then-Senator Hillary Clinton, and as having helped propel him to the White House, defeating Senator John McCain. Obama owed them.

On Friday morning, *Daily Kos* associate editor Kaili Joy Gray welcomed White House communications director Dan Pfeiffer to the convention by saying, "Thank you for joining us here with the Professional Left."[2] In a form that Gibbs might view as typical of that demographic, Gray proceeded to press Pfeiffer on the matter of a jobs bill, when the military would stop discharging openly gay members, and Obama's stance on gay marriage.[3] The sense of disappointment about his administration from attendees was palpable. The enthusiasm that had motivated many people in the room had declined sharply. As Gray put it, "We're all Democrats, and we understand the importance of making sure Democrats are in power. But they might not turn out in the same way that they did in 2008. You know, some people are saying, 'I'll show

up on Election Day, but I'm not going to knock on doors. I'm not going
to make phone calls. I'm not going to donate money' . . . What's in it for
us in a second term?"[4]

The fact that such a question could be asked and be treated seriously
speaks to a reality in politics today: bloggers and online media now play
a significant role in politics; they can help make or break you, and campaigns ignore them at their peril. Obama knows this. Clinton knew it.
And those running for office today had better believe it. Blogs and online
media matter more than you probably realize, and for multiple reasons.

In the aftermath of the 2008 presidential race, Brian Rogers, a spokes-
man for McCain's campaign, told *Politico* that "*HuffPo* and [*Talking
Points Memo*] really are the assignment editors for many in the Washington press corps—particularly the cables. . . . That's not just a Republican
hack saying it—that's speaking as a press guy fielding calls and e-mails
daily from the MSM that start with, 'Did you see this thing on *Huffington Post?*'"[5]

As a Republican National Committee (RNC) staffer who worked with
both outlets during 2008, I was acutely aware of the impact that online
media—including *TPM* and the *Huffington Post*—had and how it had
grown. When I began blogging, first as the editor of the moderate
Republican site *GOPProgress* and then at my own site in 2007, *TPM* and
the *Huffington Post* were still developing as media outlets. By 2009, when
I began advising former Hewlett-Packard CEO and U.S. Senate candidate Carly Fiorina as well as Fortune 500 companies and trade associations, their influence was firmly established. As Rogers's quote suggests,
a major reason that online media and blogs matter is because they are
read by members of the traditional media—reporters, news producers,
and so on.

BLOGS AS GAME CHANGERS

On April 11, 2008, *Huffington Post* writer Mayhill Fowler published a
piece reporting on comments that then-candidate Obama made at a San
Francisco fundraiser before the Pennsylvania primary.[6] Fowler quoted
Obama as saying,

You go into some of these small towns in Pennsylvania, and like a lot
of small towns in the Midwest, the jobs have been gone now for
25 years and nothing's replaced them. And they fell through the
Clinton Administration, and the Bush Administration, and each

successive administration has said that somehow these communities are gonna regenerate and they have not. And it's not surprising then they get bitter, they cling to guns or religion or antipathy to people who aren't like them or anti-immigrant sentiment or anti-trade sentiment as a way to explain their frustrations.[7]

Subsequently dubbed "Bittergate," the comments did not stay on the *Huffington Post*. Mainstream publications, talk radio, and cable news picked them up. The episode became a testament to the fact that online media coverage can beget mainstream news and radio coverage, as well as cable news coverage. Online media matters.

According to a 2009 George Washington University/Cision study, 89 percent of journalists utilize blogs for online story research, compared to 65 percent who use sites like Facebook or LinkedIn and 52 percent who use microblogging tools like Twitter.[8] This trend is evident in the realm of political reporting, and outside it, too. A spring 2011 Brunswick Research study[9] showed that two-thirds of business journalists said they have written a story that began with blogs or social networking sites, with blogs most likely to form the basis of a published piece.

The results of neither survey will surprise those who have watched online media evolve, and who have perceived mainstream media to have followed the lead of online media and blogs with regard to matters including the Monica Lewinsky scandal, and the "macaca" story involving then-senator George Allen (R-VA), which was broken by the Virginia left-of-center blog *Not Larry Sabato*[10] and subsequently covered by mainstream reporters.[11] In the case of the Anthony Weiner scandal, multiple news outlets covered a story initiated by Andrew Breitbart's *Big Government*. On just one MSNBC prime-time show over the course of several nights in June 2011, by my count, at least 50 percent of the stories covered had been broken or blown up by the *Huffington Post*, *TPM*, or *ThinkProgress* earlier in the day. And if you watch a lot of cable, you will notice that online media is not just breaking the news, but more and more they are delivering and analyzing it, too. Dana Loesch, the editor of Breitbart's *Big Journalism*, is a contributor to CNN, as is *RedState*'s Erick Erickson. Online media personality Cenk Uygur of *The Young Turks* for a time hosted the full 6:00 p.m. hour on MSNBC, a channel dotted with appearances from bloggers.

Some of these individuals' opinions are particularly noteworthy, however, because they garner the attention of political activists, both the original talent pool for prominent conservative and liberal political bloggers and the bulk of the readership among the bigger ideological sites.

This provides another reason why, in an age when there is heightened recognition of the impact that a party's base can have on its electoral outcomes (think the Tea Party and the Anti-War Left), blogs matter.

This development has been evidenced in a couple of ways. First, more so on the left than the right, the backing of a candidate or committee by a prominent activist blog or blogger can trigger substantial money flowing to that person or organization. As reported by Personal Democracy Forum's *TechPresident* blog in March 2011, Wisconsin's State Senate Democratic Committee had banked $725,000 to fight recall elections, "much of it [coming] through externally-directed national bundling by MoveOn and *Daily Kos*,"[12] both opponents of labor law changes pushed in the state.

Second, on both ends of the ideological spectrum, backing for a candidate—or active opposition to his or her opponent—can swing more generalized, nonfinancial support and signal or help build grassroots strength.

Ahead of the 2006 midterms, the progressive netroots congregating at activist left-of-center blogs had lost tolerance for Senator Joe Lieberman given his apostasy on the Iraq War. They targeted him for defeat, boosting Connecticut businessman Ned Lamont's candidacy as a primary opponent. Lamont, benefiting from extensive netroots support, beat Lieberman in the Democratic primary (though he went on to lose to Lieberman in the general election). In 2010, prominent netroots figures including Jane Hamsher attempted to expand upon these efforts, recruiting into the race and backing Arkansas Lieutenant Governor Bill Halter against incumbent Democrat Senator Blanche Lincoln. While Halter did not win the nomination, he did hold Lincoln to 44.5 percent in the primary, forcing her into a runoff.[13]

But the 2010 cycle really belonged to conservative online activists. Erickson, the biggest name in that game, was deemed by the *Daily Telegraph* to be the 69th most influential U.S. conservative in 2007.[14] That was not long after *RedState* readers had helped bring down immigration reform legislation after front-page writers at the site inveighed against it. But in 2009, that clout—and that of his fellow *RedStaters*—was on display in an electoral context.

Unhappy with the backing of the National Republican Senatorial Committee (NRSC) of moderate Republican and former Florida governor Charlie Crist's Senate campaign, in May 2009 Erickson called on *RedState* readers to donate "not one dime to the NRSC."[15] Crist wound up leaving the GOP and losing a three-way race to his former primary opponent, Marco Rubio.

Dede Scozzafava also found herself in *RedState*'s firing line. Nominated as the Republican candidate to replace outgoing Republican representative John McHugh, the National Republican Congressional Committee (NRCC)'s backing of Scozzafava—viewed as too liberal by many conservatives—elicited a strong response. RedState urged opponents of the decision to make their views known. The site also touted the candidacy of Doug Hoffman.[16] Scozzafava wound up exiting the race before the election, which the Democrat, Bill Owens, won by a small margin. For Erickson though, it was a victory—and a precedent had been set for *RedState*'s engagement in many GOP primaries in the midterm cycle.[17]

But blogs and online media matter too because of Google's dominance within the online search market. Google tends to serve up on page-one results from sites like those name-checked here. That means their content is often seen by members of the public who are researching a given subject online. That's also the case with, say, *Daily Kos* and *RedState*—blogs generally recognized as very ideological—because links may be e-mailed or otherwise shared by readers with their larger networks. That means that voters, even those who do not typically read blogs, are being influenced by them.

Of course, as anyone who has read John Heilemann and Mark Halperin's book *Game Change* knows, blogs and online media are also read by candidates and their families. For example, Elizabeth Edwards "would stay up late scouring the Web, pulling down negative stories and blog items about her husband. . . . "[18] This process is aided by the use of Google alerts, in addition to the now-standard inclusion of blog clips (and tweets) in campaign war room alerts, in many cases as the work product of a dedicated staffer. This is another way in which online media matters.

REACHING OUT TO BLOGS

Former Democratic National Committee (DNC) chairman and Vermont governor Howard Dean is the figure most commonly associated with early blogger engagement at the presidential level. Dean's team helped develop a virtual army of pro-Dean bloggers who would advocate for him. Additionally, they engaged Markos "Kos" Moulitsas Zuniga of *Daily Kos* and Jerome Armstrong of *MyDD* to advise on running a netroots-savvy campaign.

Little of this was by conscious design at the outset of the campaign, however. The Dean folks focused on bloggers and took them seriously in part because campaign manager Joe Trippi was of the same world as online activists. Likewise, bloggers rallied around Dean organically, boosting his candidacy, excited by his status as the only major antiwar Democratic candidate. Dean's campaign identified a base that had naturally developed and naturally existed; then, the campaign actively nurtured it and leveraged it to propel Dean forward, with Trippi often taking the lead himself.

But as much as lore treats Dean as the only candidate who cared about blogs and blogging back in 2004, his blogger engagement efforts were not, in fact, unique. John Kerry's campaign also undertook blogger engagement efforts that merit attention. Peter Daou, best known as Hillary Clinton's Internet director during the 2008 campaign and a prominent blogger in his own right, worked with bloggers on behalf of Kerry during the 2004 cycle.

Right-of-center bloggers, meanwhile, played a role in the "Rathergate" controversy, questioning the authenticity of certain documents that might charitably have been described as "damaging" regarding former President George W. Bush's Air National Guard service. The episode demonstrated the importance of the blogosphere to campaigns, cementing in some Republican operatives' minds the importance of closely integrating online communications operations with other campaign efforts.

In 2008, all major presidential campaigns, the DNC, and the RNC hired staffers or consultants tasked with interacting with bloggers and online media; however, the extent of their remit, their seniority, and the nature of their efforts varied.

Daou served as Clinton's Internet director. A substantial portion of his remit was mitigating criticism of Clinton, the only top-tier Democratic candidate in 2008 who had voted in favor of the Iraq War and had not apologized or recanted. While there were prominent pro-Hillary bloggers writing and advocating, many of the big progressive blogs exhibited an anti-Hillary bias. That constituted a significant challenge that could only be met by someone with a background as a blogger himself, with well-established relationships that enabled him to work with bloggers to ensure his candidate's side of the story was being heard. In order to accomplish this, Daou blogged about the race himself, at the *Huffington Post* and *Daily Kos*.

More commonly, the person handling online communications worked directly under or with the communications director. This was the situation at both the RNC and the McCain campaign. At the RNC, as online communications director, I reported to e-campaign director Cyrus Krohn but worked closely with communications director Danny Diaz.

Patrick Hynes, McCain's online communications strategist, worked directly with the communications director and larger team. In both cases, we were empowered to issue quotes and speak on the record in interviews, something I did regularly, acting as a surrogate, including on radio, on camera, and even in a debate at a blogger conference. Along with other, much more high-profile surrogates, I also ran guest blogs under my name.

Hynes also did radio interviews, including one live from the Minnesota State Fair ahead of the convention, for which we had worked to ensure credentials were offered to about 200 bloggers. More typical, however, was Hynes arranging for bloggers to speak to McCain directly, weekly or fortnightly—a vast commitment of time that some campaigns might have balked at. Not McCain: as Hynes put it to the *Washington Times* in 2008, "During the unpleasantness, whenever Senator McCain put himself in front of reporters, the question was always, 'How much did you raise today, when are you dropping out.' And then we'd put him on the phone with bloggers, and they'd want to talk about Iraq, and pork and chasing down al Qaeda."[19] Per the campaign, that direct dialogue with bloggers offered McCain a "tremendous positive psychological" lift.[20] According to Hynes, it took "a great deal of sting out of the criticisms" regarding immigration and other issues where McCain was out of step with the party base.[21]

Republican outreach was focused on a great diversity of writers. In addition to pitching and responding to conservative and center-right online media, we communicated with writers at left-of-center sites including *TPM* and the *Huffington Post*, encouraging them to participate in calls with McCain and high-profile McCain backers. "The McCain campaign was very diligent in getting us on their conference calls," Greg Sargent, a blogger with *TPM* during 2008, told *Politico* in 2009. "It helped us do the job better. It made more sense for them to reach out because they got their point of view in our stories."[22]

Republicans also reached out to publications like *Glamour* and *BlogHer* as well as mommy-bloggers. We focused attention on issue-specific blogs writing about everything from health care to the environment to technology, putting high-profile, expert backers of McCain like Carly Fiorina on the phone with them. We even integrated outreach to overseas online media into our work.

Kombiz Lavasany—a blogger himself and former conservative turned progressive—was tasked with besting these efforts at the DNC. Recognized along with Daou as one of the best in the business, Lavasany and his team pummeled McCain over his now-infamous "100 years" remark regarding U.S. troop presence in Iraq and the "fundamentals of our economy are strong" statement, for example.

When Palin emerged on the scene, Lavasany's job got more interesting. Negative chatter about her began bubbling online organically, as did media demand for information on the governor. The McCain campaign had little jump on the Democrats when it came to research on Sarah Palin (only a handful of campaign staff even knew the identity of the vice presidential pick ahead of her unveiling); the blogosphere was where the juiciest information—accurate and not—could be found. Much of the most accurate but worst information regarding Palin—in many cases grabbed from the blogosphere—passed through the hands of Lavasany and his team. Lavasany remains modest. "If I did anything," he said to me by e-mail, "it was finding good true stories and facts about her and making sure that other people were seeing it."

Jon Henke, Fred Thompson's blogger outreach consultant then in the employ of New Media Strategies (NMS), says he operated differently, with NMS reporting not to one specific official but rather to the campaign manager and various division heads. Henke was empowered to speak on the record but preferred to avoid acting as a spokesperson, working on background. Henke sees his job differently than a press secretary would. "I am a messenger, not part of the story," he emailed for this essay.

Other campaigns during the 2008 cycle integrated blogger outreach into their work, but in some cases, other endeavors took precedence over online communications or drowned out successes in that area. For example, MyBarackObama.com earned widespread praise from online activists and new media figures across the political spectrum; however, the campaign itself was generally regarded as less robust when it came to online media outreach as such.

By the 2010 cycle, online communications had come to be seen as a sufficiently established campaign function that many prominent candidates for governorships, the Senate, and the House of Representatives had integrated it into their operations, in some cases making it a significant focus of attention.

On the right, the rise of the Tea Party—activists who get much of their news and information from conservative blogs—made blogger outreach arguably even more critical. *RedState*'s Erickson, for example, had targeted multiple Republicans he viewed as moderate or establishment for defeat. He opposed the reelection of Pennsylvania senator Arlen Specter—who switched parties, from Republican to Democrat—and Utah Republican senator Robert Bennett, as well as the Senate campaigns of Florida

Republican governor Charlie Crist and Delaware Republican representative Mike Castle. None of these men today sit in the United States Senate, in three cases having been succeeded by their more conservative rivals, and in one case having been succeeded by the Democrat. Erickson also opposed the candidacies of former Colorado lieutenant governor Jane Norton, Gresham Barrett, Andre Bauer, and Henry McMaster in South Carolina, and senator Kay Bailey Hutchison running for Texas governor. Not one of these individuals won the Republican nomination for the office they were pursuing.

Some Republicans viewed as more establishment or more moderate did prevail in their contests, including Fiorina (in the Republican primary), and Indiana senator Dan Coats. Other candidates lacking real primary opposition but expected in some quarters to face a rougher general election, like Missouri's Republican senator Roy Blunt, were ultimately elected. These campaigns took the business of running seriously; one of the important things that they identified early on was online media outreach and blogger engagement, which was handled by a reasonably senior person.

WHAT'S NEXT FOR ONLINE OUTREACH

As of the time of writing, with the 2012 cycle underway, prioritizing online communications and assigning a staffer or consultant with deep experience in this area to handle that work is still not fully standard practice.

However, the DNC continues to employ a staffer tasked with online communications—Greg Greene. Former Utah governor and ambassador Jon Huntsman's deputy national press secretary, James Richardson (the RNC's online communications manager in 2008 and previously a blogger himself at *RedState*), communicates with bloggers as well as conservative media generally. Texas governor Rick Perry announced his run for president at the 2011 *RedState* Gathering, after having been introduced by Erickson, and maintains an online media outreach team. As for Obama, Pfeiffer, as noted, appeared at Netroots Nation in 2011. The *Huffington Post*'s Sam Stein was among the reporters to ask a question at Obama's first press conference after being sworn into office.[23] Jesse Lee serves as the White House's director of progressive media and online response.[24]

These individuals face a media environment that has changed in several respects since 2008. First, where blogs were a cutting-edge thing in the

2004 cycle, and Twitter was a cutting-edge thing in the 2008 cycle, both are now well established. Twitter plays a significant role in influencing coverage and enabling activists to communicate information about candidates quickly, broadly, and extremely easily. If your candidate screws up during a debate and gets trashed for it prominently on Twitter, it can negatively impact postgame buzz. Ignoring Twitter or failing to populate it with information that advances your cause either directly or via prominent tweeters, presents risks.

Second, online media and blogs have arguably become *more* important, not less. *Huffington Post*—much of whose political reporting remains philosophically tinged—now regularly attracts more than 20 million unique monthly visitors according to Compete.com. Moreover, the distinction between blogger and reporter has in some cases diminished and become muddied.

Garrett Graff, editor-in-chief of the *Washingtonian* and former deputy press secretary to the Dean campaign, says he saw this coming years ago when he first posited that in the future, "the best blogs would look like the best newspapers, and the best newspapers would look like the best blogs." Now, certain major political news outlets, both locally and nationally, have veered in that direction. When *Politico* launched in 2007, some of its writers were described as "bloggers," some as "reporters," and different people categorized different writers in different ways. Today, the *Washington Post* carries ideologically driven blogs; the *New York Times* carries Nate Silver's blog *FiveThirtyEight*.

This situation raises a question for campaigns relevant to who deals with whom: are political authors at the *Washington Examiner* (much of whose writing is done via a blog), whose writings have ideological undertones and who also offer their opinions, bloggers or reporters? What about the authors at *Real Clear Politics*? Who deals with Jim Geraghty at *National Review*? Who deals with Josh Marshall or Benjy Sarlin or Evan McMorris-Santoro or Eric Kleefeld at *TPM*? Who is in charge of communicating with ideologically tinged reported sites that have cropped up as mainstream press has atrophied in particular states?

Working well with bloggers has tended to be contingent on the staffer or consultant in question being or having been part of the blogging community and sometimes being willing to give out more information than a mainstream communications operative would ever consider desirable. Per Daou, "[it is] a completely different animal from traditional media." Bloggers tend to want information; mainstream reporters often want quotes. The convergence of blogging and reporting has made staffing responsibilities somewhat trickier; it is no longer always obvious where lines can or should be drawn. It now may be more critical to ensure that a relatively senior staffer or consultant—preferably with experience as an ideologically driven writer and with established relationships—is handling authors with identifiable bloggy sensibilities. This is part of what has made 2008's online communications veterans from the DNC, the RNC, and the campaigns of Clinton, McCain, and Thompson sought after, as well as figures like Ben Tribbett, Soren Dayton, and Kevin Holtsberry.[25]

The final and most basic way in which the media environment has changed since 2004 and 2008 is the expansion in stories taking off minutes after they are thrown up online or initiated via tweeting. News cycles really are 24 hours a day now; clutter has increased, and for many, filtering is the new priority item. Breaking through the noise while staying on message presents an ongoing challenge for some candidates. The growth of online media, and the convergence of traditional media and blogs, has arguably led to more professionalism in political ideological expression. It has also arguably made it tougher to grab meaningful headlines. Politics can look less like *Meet the Press* and more like *The Real Housewives of DC* (or Iowa, or New Hampshire, or South Carolina).

Of course, what was being written on blogs and online media was influencing what was on *Meet the Press* five years ago. Also, and for a long time, critics might argue politics needed a bigger dose of scrutiny and transparency—as opposed to professed neutrality and objectivity—which online media arguably provides. Ultimately, the challenges presented by the modern media landscape, in which blogs and online media exercise the influence they do, will need to be met head on, full force, and with the right personnel.

CHAPTER 5

Growing Power: Digital Marketing in Politics

Andrew Bleeker and Nathaniel Lubin

Like many in our field, we have spent the last several election cycles banging on the door (or as some would say, crashing the gate), hoping to be brought in. Digital marketing was always the stepchild, a nice idea but one we could not afford. Even the 2008 Obama campaign did not set out to run a digital campaign. They would be the first to admit that they knew that they needed to run a "different'" campaign, and they were open to ideas if they could be proven. We all spent 2007 fighting for every dime we could find for online advertising, conducting small tests here and there, and shouting from the rooftops about the return on investment.

And then Iowa happened. We remember just hitting the computer screen, hoping it would refresh and not crash anything. In one night, both the Obama and Hillary campaigns made more money through online ads than any campaign before them. From there it was a long but steady climb, reporting our spending and performance each and every day. In the general election, the campaign placed our team directly across from the chief financial officer's office so they could keep an eye on us. But by the final weeks of the election, we had proven that there we so many things that we could do online more efficiently and with more scale that we were up nights worrying about how we would spend all the money we had! Alas, that trend has not continued.

THE TRANSITION TO DIGITAL

Just like the world of corporate marketing, the political world is under-going a transition to digital. But the political space has its own set of structures and incentives that have slowed the adoption of new techniques despite their advantages.

In just a short period of time—only two to three election cycles—digital marketing has gone from a novelty to a recognized and growing power in political communications. As Americans spend more and more time online, and as the Internet becomes the primary vehicle for getting information and keeping in touch with others, political campaigns have increasingly turned to digital media as a platform for paid political advertising.

Online advertising has several advantages over competing communications platforms, particularly television. Digital marketing is hugely adapt-able, changing to meet the goals of specific campaigns and easily scalable to reach any size audience a budget allows. Digital campaigns can be highly targeted—using an array of contextual, geographic, demographic, and other proxies to qualify audiences—and can be launched much more quickly than traditional advertising channels. They can also be ramped up on short notice to capture the peak of a target audience's interest. For example, in the period immediately prior to an election when many voters are actively searching for voting information, perhaps for the first time in the race, marketers can scale digital operations to meet the increased vol-ume. We have gotten many a phone call the Saturday before an election where digital was the only way to still get a campaign live in time.

Perhaps most importantly, digital marketing operations are account-able. The tangible outcomes of online advertising campaigns can be directly measured, enabling optimization to any of a political campaign's central goals, including each of the three M's—money, mobilization, and messaging—paving the way for growth in almost all aspects of political operations. Yet, at the time of this writing, this field is still in its infancy. Only a few firms and organizations have made serious investments in dig-ital advertising, and there is still a long way to go. We have seen inconsis-tent levels of buy-in from cycle to cycle as well as uneven partisan commitments.

Due to the reputation of Obama 2008, the corporate world believes that politics is a hub of sophisticated digital innovation. While this is true in some respects, paid political online marketing actually lags many years behind Madison Avenue. Some of the explanation for this is institutional difficulty with evaluation—everything winning campaigns do is seen to be a success, while anything a losing campaign did must have been a waste. For example, we cited an innovative example to a sitting governor only to hear, "Yeah, but he lost." And since campaigns are usually reticent to share information even after an election, pundits and observers are often forced to judge the success of a campaign by the flashiest, most creative, or newest tactic, not the actual effectiveness of the program.

Moreover, the political industry faces a tremendous lack of institutional memory as campaigns disband immediately after the election without having time to analyze results or write anything down. With staff scattered, it takes us longer to learn what really works, one reason why innovation and strategy tend to be driven by consultants rather than campaigns. And while budgets still tend to be determined by senior consultants who make their money on television commissions, it has only been in presidential campaigns that the scale and incentives were there to really innovate. Today, there are a handful of senior strategists in both parties who actually believe in digital marketing, and many more who like the idea so long as it doesn't have to come from their media budget.

As we move into the 2012 cycle and beyond, both parties appear poised to make significant commitments in the online space. We are excited by these changes, not only with respect to the attention paid—and budgets allocated—but also by the improvements in technological precision and efficiency. As active participants in this field, we look forward to watching the digital political world grow as we expect it will over the next two years.

Below, we outline a brief history of the trajectory of digital advertising over the last few electoral cycles and some of our expectations for 2012 and beyond. This is a field that is changing extraordinarily quickly, and we have no doubt that the comments and categorizations offered here will soon be out of date. Nevertheless, we offer some of our perspectives on the digital arena on the eve of what we expect to be by far the largest paid digital effort in political history: the campaign to reelect President Barack Obama.

THE EARLY DAYS

Though online ads first started popping up in the 2000 race, where they were really just flat banners, the first real use of political online advertising occurred in 2004. In the days before Facebook and Google came into their own, political online advertising more closely resembled gambling. We would place online ads much like their traditional counterparts—signing insertion orders for $50,000 or so and hoping for the best. We were barely able to see how anything performed.

In 2004 and 2006, campaigns tended to focus on many of the early mainstays of traditional online advertising units, especially banner display ads and even dreaded pop-ups. These types of ads can be effective for message delivery, but then as now tended to require cost-per-impression pricing models. As a result, direct-response campaigns were few and far between. Instead, digital operations tended to be evaluated in terms of reach and creativity, with little regard for the immediate consequences of digital appeals. Landing-page actions were limited, and there was almost no real optimization to lifetime value.

One exception to this rule was Yahoo. Prior to the rise of Google and before the existence of Facebook, Yahoo was one of the premier early players in the political space. The Kerry and Bush campaigns—helped, respectively, by Michael Bassik at MSHC Partners and Eric Frenchman at Connell Donatelli—extensively used banner ads through Yahoo and even produced some successful return on investment. Whether it was asking for $50 to "Topple King George" or buying the ad space of major news sites just after a debate finished to remind voters "Kerry Finishes Strong—Ready to Lead," these campaigns set the stage for things to come.

BARACK, HILLARY, AND Mr. McCAIN

As the 2008 cycle began, a new digital structure quickly began to take shape. The ultracompetitive primary season had tremendous implications for the entire political landscape but particularly for digital marketing. Primaries offered test cases for new tactics and opportunities for demonstrating localized success. Over time, as digital marketing proved its worth, particularly on the Democratic side, the role of online advertising and the budgets allocated to it increased.

Early in 2007, Michael Organ, an accomplished marketer with more than 20 years' experience in the field, convinced Joe Rospars, the new media director of Obama for America (OFA), to appoint him to a previously unheard-of position in a political campaign—director of online marketing. Organ built a whopping team of two tasked with employing a full arsenal of digital advertising tactics to help Barack Obama win the Iowa caucuses.

After his stints with Kerry, the coauthor of this article, Andrew Bleeker, was fortunate enough to start off running digital marketing for Hillary Clinton (with slightly less campaign support) and then to succeed

Organ as the digital marketing director for Obama in the general election. As he did for Bush in 2004, Frenchman ran online advertising for McCain, and the duel continued. (While we only told him about it afterwards, we enjoyed reading his blog throughout the cycle.)

Our responsibilities grew along with budgetary authority by moving toward clearly defined metrics. Early on, each of the major Democratic campaigns made the shift from direct fundraising appeals to e-mail list building, establishing new best practices in the political space. We found that we could simply raise more money by getting more people on our list and walking them up a ladder of engagement rather than simply asking for money at the get-go. And if this was true for a candidate on national TV every night, it was even more so for state races. This remains one of the least recognized aspects of the OFA online marketing apparatus: the campaign raised more than $500 million online, but almost nobody ever saw a fundraising ad (except for some brief test campaigns to validate this approach).

The rise of Google was critical to this shift. For the first time in the political space, Google provided a single platform capable of delivering qualified advertisements on a pay-per-click pricing model that could be bought at small volumes and provide large bang for the buck. As these early campaigns demonstrated success, leadership buy-in for digital marketing grew. This development allowed for budgets that could be extended well beyond those initial buys, enabling the testing and evaluation of countless display and banner networks.

List-building campaigns allowed marketers to bring new people into the organization at a much lower point in the funnel, leaving the heavy lifting of fundraising to a dedicated e-mail team that had weeks and months to craft specific appeals designed to convert new acquisitions into donors. More than 6 million of the 13 million e-mail addresses on the OFA list were entered via paid online advertising, an investment that produced an enormous reward.

At the same time, field-related activities took a place in digital marketing for the first time. During the early caucuses, OFA pioneered a caucus ID tool for reaching and enabling further messaging to localized segments of the population that were most susceptible to the message. We also tracked our ability to help turn out voters in each of the primaries and caucuses, establishing benchmarks for how to scale our operations as voter interest increased heading into the election.

In the general election, the role of online marketing grew even further, and the metrics for evaluating both field and messaging goals became more clearly defined. Using core direct-response tactics, for example, more than 500,000 new voters were registered in battleground states from online marketing campaigns leading to the Obama campaign's voteforchange.com registration portal. On Election Day, more people found their polling information in certain states through online advertising than was the margin of victory. Sadly, it was really only the presidential campaigns that invested in digital marketing that cycle; the major state races were largely stagnant.

TEA PARTIES, DEMOCRATIC DECLINE, AND MARK ZUCKERBERG

The year 2010 marked a sea change in the political digital advertising space. Whereas Democrats' digital marketing efforts outspent Republicans by more than five to one in 2008 overall and more than ten to one in the 2008 presidential race, the balance of power reversed in the two years following. Republicans realized that they could not afford to abandon the digital space, and their candidates used online marketing to take advantage of Tea Party enthusiasm early and often. Ultimately, their online marketing budgets reached levels roughly twice as large as their Democratic counterparts.

But on both sides of the aisle, for the first time, statewide candidates across the country consistently made at least minimal commitments to online marketing. These candidates tended to focus small but highly efficient campaigns on the core marketing platforms of the previous cycle, like Google, as well as one particular new kid on the block—Facebook.

Facebook represented the single biggest new player in the 2010 landscape. Despite the press it received, Facebook had only a small place in 2008 advertising, owing largely to the very limited advertising platform initially available (it is, in fact, still quite limited, although much improved). By the end of the cycle, Facebook commanded the strong second-choice platform position behind Google, with budgets growing and showing no sign of letting up.

As the use of paid digital media grew in the 2010 cycle, so too did the demand for specialists to manage it. But maybe the same kid doing the Web site and approving Facebook friends shouldn't also be running the marketing strategy. Following the successes of 2008, the first dedicated online marketing shops grew to fill this new niche. With the added buying power and sophistication afforded by these shops, campaigns were able to employ more personalized and more local online advertising efforts. As a result, almost every major 2010 campaign employed digital advertising in some form or another, with quite a few transitioning from the "check the box" approach and moving toward making online advertising a more integrated part of broader programs.

Scott Brown's campaign in Massachusetts in particular earned early praise for employing a series of targeted campaigns around the opening of campaign offices situated around the state. In addition to serving the Brown campaign's direct response and messaging needs, these efforts augmented earned media in the local Massachusetts press and reinforced Brown's "local guy" narrative.

WHAT COMES NEXT?

The 2012 election cycle is already poised to blow prior campaigns out of the water. The first major event of the cycle proved this clearly: President Obama's reelection kicked off with a significant online advertising push in order to reengage key members of the president's base. No television buy was placed.

Yet the presidential campaigns remain an exception. At a time when corporate America believes online marketing should represent upwards of one-quarter of all media spending, politics still lags far behind. Many campaigns still will not place any online marketing, and most that do will allocate a mere pittance.

For the more serious operations, digital marketing in 2012 will be much more connected to broader messaging and strategic priorities than it was in the past. Rather than serving as a distinct tactical bucket through which to respond to the discrete goals of other parts of the campaign, digital will likely take on its own center of gravity, enabling coordinated campaigns designed to achieve benefits of scale from the start and reinforcing the various electoral priorities that all campaigns must balance. Unlike before, every major aspect of the Obama campaign—including infrastructure building, fundraising, field outreach, persuasion and message testing, and early-vote and get-out-the-vote efforts—will take advantage of significant online marketing campaigns.

To achieve success in these various campaign goals, marketing operations will be much larger than ever before, with defined teams tasked with fulfilling each individual responsibility. E-mail acquisition still looks to be the constant, the backstop that helps pay for and justify the rest of the program. Political campaigns across the board appear to be moving toward a more precise evaluation and tracking of the success of all programs, and online marketing will be no different. Every dollar spent on each paid media channel will need to be earned and justified.

But some of the catchwords of earlier cycles will actually become mainstays of this cycle. We believe that three themes will define the growth of marketing in 2012: (1) local, (2) mobile, and (3) video. While each had larger roles in prior election cycles, especially in 2010, all are poised for explosive growth in 2012.

With larger budgets and staff, campaigns will be able to employ and scale customized messaging at levels even finer than the designated market area or cable-zone specificity used in television advertising. Thanks to the detailed targeting data available to modern political campaigns, digital marketers will be able to craft media plans and tactical approaches that reach people at the zip code or even, in some cases, the individual level at scale, bringing custom solutions to the table that will match distinct messages to specific audiences.

And in that effort, campaigns will move their outreach increasingly away from the PC and toward the phone. Key demographics in 2012, especially Hispanic audiences, spend a disproportionate amount of their online usage on mobile devices. Political campaigns on both sides will not hesitate to advertise to key audiences where they already spend their time, especially when it means reaching people when they are on the go and cannot escape marketing appeals.

Last, the increasing connectedness between digital and traditional media is poised to be reinforced by a large growth in the reliance on digital video communications. Campaigns are already able to take advantage of the benefits of 15- and 30-second spots; the benefits of targeting, tracking, and specificity in this space will command increasing attention. And with the addition of geolocation and behavioral data, we can increasingly communicate with ever more relevant and targeted messaging.

The 2012 election is very likely to be incredibly tight. Again, there will be relatively small numbers of critical swing states and unprecedented amounts of money from all quarters pouring in to flood the media markets. Winning messages are going to be the ones that cut through the clutter—not just with memorable creative work but also by being tailored to key segments and able to keep supporters engaged throughout the campaign cycle. And as the presidential contest absorbs all the money, even in statewide races the difference between winning and losing may be how campaigns can stretch their dollars, ensuring they are reaching their exact audience with precisely the best message at the best time.

FIVE RECOMMENDATIONS GOING FORWARD

To get more tactical, here are five specific recommendations applicable to most campaigns based on the outcome of dozens of elections won and lost:

1. *Have a Goal*
Digital marketing can accomplish many objectives but not all at the same time. Whether it is raising money, registering voters, or delivering a message, the more specific the goal, the more effective the campaign will be. The types of tactics and media placements that work for one objective are unlikely to be best for another. And the more specific, the better: for instance, working on a goal of a three-to-one financial return on investment from fundraising dollars is far easier to optimize than simply wanting to grow an e-mail list. All advertising should stem from this same goal and, again, be as specific as possible.

We also need to be realistic about what online advertising can and cannot do. A simple banner ad is unlikely to make a lifelong Republican suddenly realize he should vote Democratic. However, it can provide new pieces of information that change the way someone considers a question and frames a debate. An ad that says, "John Smith—the only candidate endorsed by the NRA," is likely to be more effective for messaging in a Republican primary than simply a smiley photo of the candidate asking you to join the campaign.

2. *Think Like Your Audience*
Sun Tzu said, "If ignorant both of your enemy and yourself, you are certain to be in peril." So too in advertising. The biggest risk is to fail to understand the audience you are trying to reach: not just who they are—their demographics, zip codes, and so forth—but how much they know about the race, whether they care, and what might actually matter to them.

Why should someone click on your ads? What one fact might actually cause someone to reconsider his or her stance? What would actually get someone to stop her busy day, take out her wallet, and make a donation? Or, much harder, go out and volunteer for a candidate? These questions are at the heart of our profession and critical to the success of any digital marketing campaign.

The question to ask with any ad is, "What is my value proposition?" If you cannot answer it, then trust us, neither can your audience. Yet every group has a reason for its existence, and every candidate a reason to run. But why should someone help you? Why should they join your e-mail list if they are already on everyone else's? There is only so much advertising can do. If there is no difference between your online community and every other campaign's, there is really no reason for someone to join. And, as our audience gets ever more jaded, we must articulate our value propositions even more clearly.

Similarly, making a $5 online contribution is totally irrational by some measures. Doing so will not cause the candidate to remember your name, enhance your status among your peers, or have any chance of tipping the outcome of an election. So why on earth should someone give? A small donation only makes sense if donors believe that there are tons of other people out there just like them doing the same thing at the same time. We need to make them feel the sense of community and urgency to provide this clear motivation.

So, what to do? The subsequent points add further color, but in practical terms this often means using a "hook" or proxy to encourage action. We are more successful with ads that accomplish our goals (collecting e-mail addresses, raising money, conveying messages) while providing a clear value to the user. Rather than asking supporters to simply donate or join, perhaps we may be more successful asking them to RSVP for an event, receive insider updates, or be the first to know. In all cases, the best ads provide something users want.

3. *Understand the Plan*

While digital marketing is slowly increasing its share of campaign dollars, often these initiatives are still left to young junior staffers who operate in isolation. Yet campaigns are most successful when they are truly integrated, using digital media to support what is happening on the ground, in the press, and in other paid media.

Campaign goals naturally evolve over time. Most of the campaign is spent raising money and doing the occasional press stunt. As such, most of the digital marketing campaign should likely be spent growing the online supporter community as efficiently as possible. This is best done by investing early. While the bulk of fundraising occurs toward the end of the cycle, the success of a campaign is dependent on the size and activity of its e-mail list. Thus, waiting too long to build the community can be devastating.

As the election nears, these activities can grow in scale with public interest. Typically, campaigns start to actively pursue field-related activities (volunteer recruitment, voter registration, and early or absentee voting) in the last weeks before the relevant deadlines. Pure message-delivery advertising often comes last, reaching its peak in the final weeks leading up to the election.

In terms of tactics, media planning is a mix of art and science and should be based on as much data as possible to reach a specific campaign goal. However, some basic concepts tend to hold true. In most cases, if we could only spend one dollar, we would spend it on search marketing. Because people have already shown interest by searching for something, they are the people most likely to take action. However, even if you are the president of the United States, there are likely not as many people searching for you and your topics as you would like. As we scale campaigns, we must move up the ladder of efficiency. Each level adds additional reach and higher-impact techniques but reduces the likely efficiency (moving away from a cost-per-click and pay-as-you-go model, for instance).

4. *Capitalize on Moments*

Political campaigns are not static things that slowly ramp up as the election nears. Rather, engagement is highly driven by the news of the day, spiking during key moments and plateauing with the public's attention span. Thus, when looking ahead at a campaign calendar, we are best served by building around events.

There are two types of moments—organic and manufactured. Organic moments are those that naturally occur in the course of a campaign—announcements, debates, filing deadlines, registration deadlines, fundraising deadlines, conventions, and, clearly, election days. Getting people to do anything for a campaign is hard enough in person, let alone through a passive online ad when they are in the middle of doing a million other things. People only tend to act from strong emotions—excitement, fear, lust, or greed (topics for a completely different chapter). Not surprisingly, the best fundraising day President Obama had in 2008 was the day Sarah Palin addressed the Republican National Convention—a true organic moment.

But how campaigns leverage these moments is as important as the moments themselves. We recognize that what people are actually interested in is not just another e-mail but knowing something particular, such as who will be the Democratic vice presidential nominee. Rather than simply leaking the name to a reporter as it has always been done, campaign management was supportive of the idea of using this moment for acquisition. We told our supporters about the choice via e-mail and text messaging first. The "be-the-first-to-know" campaign was wildly successful, adding millions of supporters to our list for only a trivial cost.

Yet those high-profile moments are relatively few and far between. So, while digital campaigns may be built around these events, what do we do during the intervals between them? How do we create moments? By creating artificial events, that's how. Goals are a classic example, as in, "Let's reach 1,000,000 supporters!" Who really cares about the millionth supporter? No one, but it provides urgency and ties back into the feeling of community. The same is true of contests. The Dinner with Barack contest was one of the most successful ongoing fundraising campaigns (though legally not a contest). Like a goal, it provided a deadline and a clear value proposition.

What experience teaches is how to lay out such a calendar, filling gaps between organic moments with artificial or created ones, without overwhelming our audience with more campaign activity than they could possibly be interested in. After all, if they are still not paying attention by Election Day, it doesn't much matter.

5. *Test, and Then Test Again*

Unlike other forms of advertising, the good and the bad of digital is that once the ads go up, the real work is just beginning. There are very few truly good or bad ideas in digital marketing. There are, however, many very poorly optimized campaigns. Digital campaigns work on the concept Michael Organ has called "micro failure." It's okay to try many things that fail, so long as we learn those lessons cheaply and are willing to invest heavily in what succeeds.

Often, the difference between one variation and another is not a 1 or 2 percent difference. Indeed, we have seen seemingly small differences make a campaign perform many times better than a very similar counterpart. The devil is in the details, and the good campaigns are the ones that never stop testing. In our larger campaigns, we are constantly pulling reports and making optimizations every day.

But optimization is only as good as the campaign goal. After having confused many sitting statewide officials, we have learned to speak to campaigns in terms of offline goals. That is what the campaigns care about anyway—votes, dollars raised, volunteers recruited, and so forth. (We do not recommend trying to explain that the campaign is going well because 1 percent of the audience has clicked on our ads.) To do this, tracking is very important. Whether with source codes or pixels, it is critical to consider tracking when launching the first campaigns so that you can track lifetime value down the line. All of your systems need to be integrated so that you are tracking the right conversions rather than simply clicks and impressions.

Optimization must occur at all levels of the campaign. This begins with the ads themselves (search, Facebook, banners, video, mobile, etc.). What should they say? What color should they be? What is the call to action? What is the button copy? Which size units should we use? All of these are important factors to the ads' performance.

Optimization must continue beyond the ad unit. Based on performance and audience demographics (usually measured by comScore or the like) we must carefully choose which sites to target and precisely where on those sites to appear. Given the sensitivities of politics, we never recommend working with blind networks; we feel that it is always worth knowing where your ads could appear. And, after the click, we must then optimize the landing page itself, clarifying the ask and how to get more people to take it.

While we could continue with more advice, the most important thing is to realistically assess your own abilities. Learning the basics of online marketing is relatively simple—take $50 and start playing around on Google and Facebook. But if all of a sudden the campaign is on the line, please do not wait until Election Day to call a specialist. There is only so much they will be able to do at that point.

Looking forward, we see the boundaries between online and offline disappearing every day. We choose to call our profession digital marketing, not online marketing, because everything is becoming digital. Whether it is radio bought through Pandora, television bought through Google, interactive billboards, or ads in taxis, all marketing is becoming digital marketing. For campaigns, this means the potential for greater segmentation, interactivity, and optimization. But for practitioners, it means traditional media is no longer exempt from the findings of a direct-response campaign. The future of political advertising belongs to the innovators.

CHAPTER 6

You *Can* Take It with You: The Evolution of Mobile Politics

Julie Germany

Mobile has become a buzzword in the field of digital political communications. From text messaging campaigns to mobile applications, from mobile search and Web sites optimized for the mobile Web, the craft of reaching people over mobile devices with a political message has become a young but potent tool in electoral and advocacy campaigns.

Mobile is new. It feels special, as if deploying a mobile tactic instantly makes our campaign more savvy or connected. Voters are now connecting on their mobile devices, and political consultants are building tools to reach and mobilize them. The digital politics industry is often faced with a difficult choice: implement mobile tactics before we really understand the audience and the role mobile technology can play in political strategy, or wait and risk falling behind.

After the U.S. Senate election in Massachusetts between Republican Scott Brown and Democrat Martha Coakley, a *Boston Phoenix* headline read, "Walking Edge: The iPhone App That Killed Coakley."[1] Brown won 52 percent of the vote on Election Day, compared with Coakley's 47 percent. In the months after the election, pundits credited the Brown campaign's technology strategy, including the campaign's use of mobile technology, with helping win the election.

The "Walking Edge" mentioned in the *Boston Phoenix* headline refers to a mobile application that used the Global Positioning System (GPS) capabilities found in most smart phones and a voter database to assist with canvassing and voter outreach. Campaign volunteers used it at polling stations to check off voters from the database after they voted. Canvassers then avoided their doors and focused their time and effort on those who had not yet voted. This kind of mobile-enabled get-out-the-vote campaign enables a more efficient use of campaign resources—particularly during high-profile races.

Can a mobile communications tactic win an election? Or is it the kind of tool that will reach its full potential only after a number of election cycles? Today, mobile communications still feels like a very young medium. Campaigns know they want to use it, but they don't always budget for it, and they don't quite incorporate mobile communications into campaign strategy early on. Successful, sophisticated mobile communications, like any new political tactic, will require a period of experimentation, trial and error, and testing before we see its adoption on a massive scale by political campaigns.

Today, political campaigns sit in the midst of this experimentation period, sometimes adopting new techniques and tactics but not fully committing to a large-scale mobile strategy. For some, that might mean building a text-messaging list and using it to organize volunteers. For others, it means building mobile applications with information, like events and news updates, catered to an audience of supporters. For others, it means tailoring the resources on their Web sites for the mobile Web. Campaigns invest in new technologies because they hope they will help raise money and win elections. Text messaging is an exciting but not quite tested tool, and therefore some campaign managers will not invest heavily in mobile tactics until they see that other candidates have used mobile as a tool to win elections.

This process of cautious experimentation has increased in intensity over the last few election cycles. Mobile political communications tactics have evolved beyond text messaging to include mobile applications like Walking Edge, mobile social tools, advertising, and utilizing mobile Web browsers and search engines. In this sense, "mobile politics" does not simply refer to a particular device or mobile handset. The true spirit of mobile politics focuses on delivering resources and tools that inform, enable, and engage voters everywhere, at any time, and on any device, from tablets and smart phones to laptops and the technology of the future.

THE NEW RULES OF MOBILE

I first became interested in mobile while serving as the deputy director of the Institute for Politics, Democracy and the Internet at George

Washington University. I had the opportunity to analyze the way presidential campaigns used the Internet to reach and mobilize supporters in 2004. At the time, mobile politics meant taking Blackberries door-to-door while canvassing and then uploading data about voters at the end of each day. Over the last six years, my interest in investigating, analyzing, and doing mobile outreach has led to the publication of one handbook—*Politics-to-Go: A Handbook for Using Mobile Technology in Politics*, the first such guide—several events, many client projects, and a conference called the mCitizen Summit, which launched in the spring of 2011.

Three fundamental aspects of mobile politics have a central focus in most successful mobile efforts, both on the campaign trail and off. First, mobile is a highly personal medium. We keep our smart phones with us all the time, even when we sleep. This means that political campaigns should temper the desire to use mobile tools, especially text messaging, as the more modern equivalent of blast e-mail and limit engagement to highly targeted, relevant, immediate, and useful information or calls to action.

Second, when it comes to mobile interaction, trust is imperative. Mobile users aren't going to take an action, send a text message, or download an application unless they trust the company or person pushing it. Users will turn you off and report you as a spammer if you abuse the privilege of connecting with them over a mobile device.

Finally, with mobile communications, pull is almost always more effective than push. In other words, using mobile to engage and pull voters into your campaign tends to be far more successful than pushing mass, impersonal text messages to them. Mobile phones are not e-mail or direct mail. Using them to send a mass text message push is a waste of money, and it ends up really irritating people. Mobile strategies that are effective in the long run produce useful content and tools for their users.

Mobile politics has changed and increased significantly since I published *Politics-to-Go* in 2005. Back then, we struggled to find good examples of mobile technology deployed in electoral campaigns because the voters were to a great degree not yet connected by mobile devices. Today, there are 303 million mobile phone subscribers in the United States, and we send 2.1 *trillion* text messages a year, according to CTIA—The Wireless Association.[2] The user base and audience for mobile politics is growing and engaging.

Smart phone and tablet use throughout the day have more deeply connected us to news, information, political coverage, shopping, and each other, according to a 2011 white paper from Ericsson.[3] Instead of checking on the news during our morning commute, then again during lunch, the commute home, and in the evening, mobile users receive news and information at steady intervals throughout the day from mobile applications and their mobile browsers.

Burson-Marsteller and Proof Integrated Communications released a study, "The State of Mobile Communications," that argues that mobile will soon be the primary digital means of access. Researchers found that 80 percent of the U.S. population had a mobile device in 2010, and 35 percent of U.S. adults use mobile devices for wireless Internet access. In fact, smart phone usage of mobile Web browsers and applications increased 110 percent in the last year. Furthermore, the study found that mobile engagement isn't just relegated to the young: 82 percent of seniors use their mobile phones for information and learning.[4]

Smart phone usage in the United States is growing, According to a 2010 comScore report, 43.7 percent of the U.S. population used a mobile Web browser, accessed applications, or downloaded content. Another 21.3 percent used their mobile phones to access social networking sites and blogs, 27.9 percent checked their e-mail, 22.5 percent played games, and 17.2 percent used instant messaging. Compare this with the around 67 percent of Americans who use text messaging, which still reigns as the most-used mobile tool.[5]

Mobile usage in the United States is part of a global revolution in how people get information and interact with each other. That interaction now includes multimedia, social tools, and mobile Web browsers—not just text and e-mail. Mobile Future's 2010 video, "Mobile Year in Review 2010," notes that, globally, users downloaded five billion mobile applications in 2010 and watched 100 million YouTube videos on their mobile devices. Twitter usage increased 347 percent, and Foursquare gained 500 million new members.

How did voters use these tools to engage in the 2010 election cycle? In a postelection survey of U.S. adults by the Pew Internet and American Life Project called "Politics Goes Mobile," authors Aaron Smith and Lee Rainie reported that 26 percent used their cell phones to participate in or get information about the 2010 midterm election. Around 14 percent of U.S. adults used their cell phones to tell other people that they had voted (6 percent said they reported conditions at the local voting station, like delays or low turnout, over their cell phones), and 12 percent used their cell phones to keep up with news and information about the election. Ten percent sent text messages about the election to their friends and family, 4 percent used their cell phones to monitor election results, and 3 percent used their cell phones to take election pictures or videos and share them with family or friends. Only around 1 percent of those surveyed used election-related mobile apps to receive updates from candidates or political groups, and another 1 percent donated to a campaign, party, or political group via text message.[6]

Pew Internet calls the members of this group "mobile political users," and they tend to be highly engaged and technologically savvy. In 2010, mobile political users went to the polls in larger numbers than the rest of the population: 71 percent of mobile political users said they voted in the 2010 election, compared with 64 percent of all adults. Mobile political users tend to be more male than female, and they tend to be slightly younger, more financially well off, and better educated. Around 36 percent of mobile political users are African American, 25 percent are white, and 25 percent are Hispanic, according to Pew.

They also tend to be more technologically engaged than the rest of the population. Again according to the Pew study, around 92 percent of mobile political users have broadband Internet at home (compared with 60 percent of all adults), and 81 percent of them go online every day (compared with 72 percent of all Internet users). Almost three-fourths of mobile political users (72 percent) use social networking sites, and they often use their cell phones to engage in social networking, send e-mail, browse the Web, use instant messaging, and send text messages.

The Pew report suggests that the rise of mobile politics was one of the biggest campaign trends in 2010. Smith and Rainie note that the partisan leaning of this group of mobile political users resembles that of the general population: 27 percent say they are Republican, 35 percent say they are Democratic, and 32 percent say they are independent. Around 44 percent of mobile political users said they voted for a Republican congressional candidate in 2010—the exact same amount that said they voted for a Democrat. While Democrats and Republicans use their mobile phones in similar ways to engage in politics, Democrats were more likely to send text messages to others about the election and use text messaging to inform others that they voted.

MOBILE CAMPAIGNING IN 2010

Since 2010, "make this mobile" has become the new "make this digital" or "make this a Web site" or "make this a Facebook page." Mobile is the current "big thing," and, as a result, many federal campaigns and large political organizations have started to incorporate mobile tactics into their communications, volunteer, and get-out-the-vote activities. Sometimes they have done this without understanding the larger strategic function that mobile communications can serve in political campaigns.

What many campaigns have learned is that consistent, strategic use of mobile communications is important. Over the next few election cycles, political campaigns need to decide how they will incorporate mobile tactics into campaign strategy to avoid what mobile marketer Kenny Hyder calls "abandonment valley": peaks and spikes in an organization's use of mobile that can result in supporter drop-off. Hyder spoke on a panel called SMS: Simple Messaging Solutions at Blogworld Expo in 2010. Hyder's points mesh well within a broader conversation about campaign strategy: What does the campaign want to accomplish with mobile technology? Who does the campaign need to reach over mobile? For many campaigns, the answer to that question is "committed volunteers and decided voters," the people who are most likely to sign up for a mobile campaign rather than the "undecideds." What does the campaign need to do to reach them? What do we want them to do (tell their neighbors to vote, report from their polling location, sign up to volunteer, etc.)? How will the campaign integrate mobile with other channels?

TEXT MESSAGING

Some political campaigns in 2010 tried to use text messaging as if it were the new e-mail, pushing messages with little relevance or context to "get messages out" rather than engage supporters in key campaign activities. Smart mobile strategists, however, knew that text messaging is not the new e-mail. They used text messaging as a useful tool to inform their supporters, organize volunteer opportunities, and run get-out-the-vote campaigns. Among left-of-center groups, Revolution Messaging has honed the craft of using text messaging to target supporters and encourage action.

Jason Rosenberg of Revolution Messaging noticed a marked increase in text messaging as a campaign tactic in 2010. "The 2010 election cycle was a pivotal point for campaigns to incorporate text messaging into their tactical toolboxes," he said. "Organizations used it to maintain activism, for list building, and to encourage supporters to take an action" (In person interview, May 15, 2011).

Eric Berto, a mobile strategist at Waggener Edstrom, recommends focusing on creating mobile content that causes people to take an action. That means developing simple, succinct, focused, and shareable messages that use active voice, contain actionable content, speak to the common audience, and are structured in short, tight paragraphs with no wasted words or phrases.

However, before most campaigns can begin writing messages, they must build a robust mobile phone list. The Mobile Marketing Association and most mobile phone carriers require what is called a "double opt-in" process before any organization, even a political campaign, can send mass text messages. Double opt-in refers to the process of confirming a mobile subscriber's interest by asking him or her to opt in twice. He or she might sign up for a text message campaign, but then the campaign must receive a second confirmation—usually by text message—that the user wishes to remain on the list.

Some 2010 candidates used text-messaging campaigns to engage voters in surprising ways as a part of their list-building initiatives. For example, Meg Whitman's gubernatorial campaign in California ran a trivia contest about the College World Series and gave away free hats to increase its mobile list. Former Wisconsin Senator Russ Feingold asked Milwaukee Brewers fans to predict over text message which mascot—Bratwurst, Polish, Italian, Hot Dog, or Chorizo—would win a mascot race on opening day over text message.

In Missouri, Republican Senator Roy Blunt painted his campaign RV with the words "Text JOBS to BLUNT." His opponent, Democratic Senate candidate Robin Carnahan, placed humorous signs in bathrooms that read, "Text FLUSH to Robin" and "Text WASH to Robin" to help increase mobile-list size. In an interview with Associated Press reporter David A. Lieb, Carnahan emphasized the impact that text campaigns can have: "From a campaign's perspective, texts are great, because there's a really high open rate for those. They pop up on your phone, so it's really easy to communicate with people quickly and know that they're seeing that piece of information," Carnahan said.[7]

We do not know if this kind of list building will prove to be of any value over the long term, but we do know that these same aspects of text messaging—the way it feels so personal and immediate—can also become liabilities. When text messages start to feel like mass e-mail campaigns and lose their immediate, personal, highly relevant, information-rich attributes, the public will tune them out or report them as spam. In 2010, mobile subscribers in 11 states (California, Colorado, Delaware, Florida, Illinois, Minnesota, Missouri, New York, North Carolina, Pennsylvania, and Virginia) complained about text message spam sent by political groups. In the hours leading up to Election Day, Revolution Messaging founder Scott Goodstein reported that Republican-leaning groups were likely the culprits, according to *RCR Wireless News.com*.[8]

MOBILE BROWSERS AND MOBILE SEARCH

As a few political campaigns began to realize in 2010, mobile communications does not begin and end with text messaging. Today, the
mobile browser possesses a high level of utility for on-the-go users
who do not always carry a laptop with them or cannot afford to own
one in the first place. According to Dave Fleet, a mobile marketer at
Edelman, searches made over mobile browsers accounted for 16 percent of Google traffic in 2010. Over 54 percent of mobile browser
users use search on their mobiles. During campaign season, it is highly
likely that mobile searches on candidates and polling locations will
increase rapidly, particularly considering the ease with which many
smart phone owners use their phones' GPS and mapping tools to get
directions.

In fact, in 2010 we started to see some political campaigns begin to
implement tactics for mobile browsers. Katie Harbath, the former new
media director at the National Republican Senatorial Committee
(NRSC), reported that mobile visitors accounted for 3.5 percent of all
Web traffic to their site in 2010. During the last four months of the
2010 campaigns, that number grew to 6 percent. On Election Day,
mobile visitors accounted for 10 percent of all traffic to the NRSC site.
The mobile traffic numbers Harbath gathered from the NRSC site in
2010 illustrate the kind of growth in mobile, election-related searches
that we can expect to see as more voters rely on their mobile devices,
instead of their laptops, for on-the-go news and information.

Harbath reported that most of the NRSC's mobile Web visitors,
46 percent, used iPhones to access the site. Another 21 percent reached
the NRSC on Android handsets, 19.7 percent used iPads, 7.8 percent
used their iPods, and 5.4 percent accessed the site on their Blackberries.
Not surprisingly, the most popular NRSC content was the homepage
and the polling place locator.

Over the next few years, we can anticipate greater emphasis on writing
content for the mobile Web and improving mobile search results through
on-page search engine optimization (SEO) title tags, header tags, keywords, link building, local search, and predictive text. ActBlue, an online
clearinghouse for contributions to Democrats, tweaked its mobile donation page during the 2010 election cycle, making it easier to navigate
and complete on a mobile browser. *TechPresident*'s Nancy Scola reported
that those small optimizations led to a 160 percent increase in the donor
conversion rate.[9]

We can also expect to see a rise in mobile advertising, from banners on mobile Web sites to advertising within the mobile applications of major media and entertainment organizations. When it is targeted and designed with an emphasis on relevance and usefulness, mobile advertising will have the potential to reach and engage voters just as powerfully as traditional display ads, if not more so. For example, Katie Harbath reported that the NRSC's 2010 Election Day mobile ads to help voters find their polling place received a 6 percent higher click-through rate than desktop ads and were 39 percent cheaper. In general, mobile advertising is a growing trend. In June 2010, comScore reported that mobile advertising more than doubled over a two-year period.[10]

PLANET OF THE APPS

Mobile applications, or apps, are tools that are built and downloaded onto your mobile device for a specific purpose—a game, a buying guide, a social network, a media outlet, a recipe index, and so forth. A year ago, developers had produced 100,000 applications for just one type of smart phone, the iPhone. It is a $2 billion industry. The mobile industry is growing so much that *PC Magazine* recently reported that the tech industry is facing a shortage of mobile app developers.[11] Many Beltway organizations—from media outlets like *Politico* and the *Washington Post* to political parties, organizations, and campaigns—experimented with mobile apps as a tool to inform and engage supporters in 2010.

The 2008 presidential election saw the rise of the first mobile application built on behalf of a national candidate. The Obama campaign developed and launched its iPhone app a little more than a month before Election Day. The app focused on the same kinds of information-rich tools that supporters could find on the Obama Web site, including newsfeeds, policy information, video updates, office locations, wallpaper, ringtones, and campaign photos. Two of the app features focused on engaging voters in electoral activities—a volunteer information tool and a tool that accessed each user's address book to help them call friends and remind them to vote for Obama. Around 500,000 people downloaded the Obama campaign's iPhone app by Election Day. They used it to stay connected with the campaign and to remind their friends and family to vote.

In October 2009, U.S. representative Eric Cantor, the then minority whip in the House of Representatives, launched a mobile application for iPhone and Blackberry called WhipCast. The app delivers text, audio, image, and video updates to users, as well as Republican talking points, policy discussions, polling information, and floor schedule updates. It was designed to inform and organize Republican members of Congress, but it was also used by Republican supporters to stay informed and on message. While Cantor's office cannot give us exact numbers, we know that the WhipCast app has been downloaded hundreds of thousands of times by Republican supporters across the United States.

In May 2010, the NRSC became the first party committee to launch an iPhone app. Organizing for America released an iPhone app that summer and made the announcement through a Web video. The DNC also launched another iPhone and iPad app this year. It includes an election center, alerts on breaking news, an event location, discussion points, photos and video, and the ability to call Congress and report back on your interaction. The Voter Activation Network launched miniVAN, an iPhone canvassing app similar to Walking Edge that streamlines the get-out-the-vote process. In an interview with the *Daily Beast*, Josh Hendler, the DNC's director of technology, said, "Traditionally, people got a clipboard, they got paper. They'd go to an office, then go around with their paper, write everything down, then go back to office, and finally, enter the data."[12] Today, he noted, canvassers can upload all of that data from applications on their smart phones and tablets.

Sam Brownback's gubernatorial campaign in Kansas launched a SamforGov app, which contained basic bibliographical and issue background on his candidacy, news from the campaign, e-mail sign-up, and a list of campaign events—the same kind of content visitors would likely find on a campaign Web site. The John Kasich for Ohio gubernatorial campaign launched a similar app, Kasich for Ohio, which was built using a tool called appmakr, a relatively quick and affordable way to turn Web content into a basic, customizable iPhone app. Felton Newell's campaign for the House of Representatives in California's 33rd District released Newell for Congress. Like other apps, Newell for Congress had the same feel as an extension of the campaign's Web site.

Moving forward, one of the first questions political campaigns should ask themselves before building a mobile app is whether their voter audience will actually use it. The answer depends on how useful, entertaining, and easy to use the app is. Mobile apps with highly useful information and tools are used more than applications that push out old messages. Today's mobile users are savvy; that means campaigns must plan for human resources over time to update the app with new, relevant information and incorporate ideas for their mobile apps in regular strategy meetings.

Another aspect to consider is the type of device. Most political campaigns and organizations developed their mobile apps for iPhones. These apps reach a large portion of the smart phone–using population, but they do not reach everyone. As the number of handsets increases, smart phone users will also turn to other types of devices, like Blackberry and Droid. When building a mobile application, campaigns should remember that there is not just one version of the iPhone or one type of Droid or Blackberry. Think, for example, about the success of Amazon's Kindle. Amazon has extended the reach of its book reader by allowing other mobile devices in addition to their own to read their digital books. Users can buy a Kindle device, or they can download the Kindle app on most smart phones or tablets, reaching as many potential Kindle users as possible.

MOBILE SOCIAL TOOLS

As the world of mobile political communications continues to evolve, the intersection of mobile technology and social media will produce some of the most engaging, headline-grabbing tools over the next few years. Look at the mainstream, consumer-driven competition already on the market, like Foursquare, Gowalla, and Localmind—the kind of applications that garner cover stories in major tech magazines about once a month. Mobile social media refers to online social networks that are accessible on mobile handsets and share content via social channels. They connect mobile sites and apps with social networks, have location-based check-in services, share or stream content, and use social gaming.

360i's *Mobile Marketing Playbook* suggests that mobile social media will continue to be an important part of how we communicate with each other because it taps into consumers' intrinsic motivation to connect and sometimes compete with others. This process, argues David Berkowitz, one of the authors, enhances our self-esteem, drives our feelings of altruism and competition, fuels our intellectual curiosity, and entertains us.[13]

These intrinsic motivators all add some degree of meaning to our lives. Think about the mobile possibilities of a political tool like Engage's Multiply app, which allows campaigns to award points and badges when supporters take an action, like telling their friends, volunteering, or helping with get-out-the-vote efforts. Multiply accesses its users' social graph—the people they are connected to—on Facebook to make sharing with friends simple.

Political campaigns are just beginning to tap into the potential of integrating a social tool like Multiply with a mobile outreach program. Engage developed one of the first mobile social get-out-the-vote programs, called iVote, with Foursquare, Jess3, and the Voting Information Project. Foursquare users who checked into 108,000 polling locations

on Election Day received the first-ever virtual "I Voted" badge. While we
have little research to suggest the badge increased turnout, it served as a
social, patriotic reminder about the important of voting.

Tools like these already have a built-in audience, as increasing numbers
of mobile phone users across many demographics access their profiles over
a mobile device. The 2010 Burson-Marsteller report found that of Facebook's more than 500 million users, 100 million of them access the site
through their mobile device.[14] Further, according to Nielsen's "Global
Faces and Networked Places" report, the use of mobile social networking
applications has increased 249 percent since 2009. Around 60 percent of
all mobile Internet usage is spent on social networks.[15]

LOOKING TO 2012

We are not going to see an election cycle in 2012 where mobile tactics
are the lead story, but we are getting close. As the mobile space continues
to evolve and the number of people reachable on their mobile devices
explodes, the ways in which campaigns incorporate mobile tactics to reach,
inform, and mobilize supporters will grow. In fact, we do expect to see
mobile tactics—from text messaging to mobile advertising to apps—have
a major impact on communications and outreach during the 2012 presidential election cycle. While some campaigns will view their mobile presence as trendy "brochure-ware" or an extension of their Web sites, others
will develop comprehensive strategies to integrate mobile with some of
the core activities of their campaigns—from volunteer organizing to rapid
response to get-out-the-vote efforts. Adherence to command-and-control
messaging, a reliance on tactics that worked well in the past, and cost will
hinder the adoption of better mobile tactics.

Successful campaigns will incorporate mobile tactics in a way that per-
sonalizes their communications with constituents and pulls supporters
into real campaign activities that meet the fundraising, communications,
and mobilization goals of the campaign. For some, mobile technology
will be another way to push out content, like issues statements and candidate biographies. For others, mobile politics will become a race to
develop the most sophisticated, integrated tactics that will intensify the
art of political campaigning and enable relevant, targeted voter outreach.

The campaigns that succeed will be the fastest to emerge from this
period of experimentation and trial and error with a concrete grasp of
how mobile communications can enhance political strategy and an understanding of how their voters use mobile technology.

CHAPTER 7

Blessings and Curses: How Technology Is Changing Polling

Kristen L. Soltis

Campaigns do not happen in a vacuum. The forces of the media, the opposition, and external events all constantly shape the relationship between a candidate and his or her prospective voters. The campaign pollster's job is to monitor and explore that relationship, to quantify it, and to offer strategic guidance on how best to maximize a campaign's chances of victory.

Research allows a campaign to sort noise from reality, to "keep a finger on the pulse" of the electorate, and to have a clear picture of the situation in which a campaign finds itself. From that foundation of knowledge, a campaign can create a plan for cultivating support and can review and reassess if the plan is "moving numbers" enough to reach the necessary vote goal.

As a pollster, my job is to help clients understand the real world in which they operate. For the last six years, I have worked with political, nonprofit, and corporate clients, and yet despite the vast differences in the objectives of each client, my role has been the same—to advise clients on how to communicate based upon data that *accurately* represents their audience. The firm that I work for, The Winston Group, is a Republican polling firm that serves both Republican and nonpartisan clients. There are many firms on both sides of the aisle that cater to political campaign clients, offering opinion research services. Our primary job is to use a survey or focus group to simulate a campaign environment as accurately as possible so that a campaign's desired narrative and messaging can be evaluated and tailored before going public in a press release, a Web video, or an expensive ad buy.

When it comes to winning a political campaign, having the right pollster matters. The "right pollster" means hiring someone who creates reliable, accurate, useful data, as well as someone who effectively evaluates those results. Good polling provides actionable guidance that lets a campaign make corrections and adaptations in response to external changes and threats. It can tell you when your campaign is on the wrong topic, when your message has started to resonate, or when an opponent's line of attack has started to change voters' minds. By the same token, polling that misses the mark or is skewed risks encouraging a campaign to make the wrong decisions.

HOW POLLSTERS DEFINE AND REFINE

A pollster has three primary roles to play in a campaign: First, to identify *where* a campaign can get the votes necessary to win; second, to advise on *how* to get those votes; and third, to monitor what progress is made toward that goal. There are a variety of types of survey a pollster may conduct for a candidate during a campaign in order to fulfill that role, including a viability survey, a benchmark survey, a follow-up survey, and a tracking survey.

If a candidate is not likely to be well known to voters, a campaign will first field a *viability survey*. This survey tests a small sample of voters in order to find out if a potential candidate has a realistic chance of winning an election. In a viability survey, we ask voters if they have a favorable or unfavorable impression of the various candidates in the race in order to observe how well known and well liked the potential players are. With this, we can guide a potential candidate through deciding whether or not to enter a political contest. In one instance, I conducted a viability survey for a potential U.S. Senate candidate. The potential challenger assumed the incumbent was vulnerable and widely disliked, only to find the incumbent was viewed favorably by 64 percent of voters, making a challenge unlikely to succeed. (The challenger ultimately decided not to run.)

Once a candidate decides to run, he or she will field a *benchmark survey*. This is the longest survey and is fielded to the largest audience. In a benchmark survey, we try to create knowledge about a number of critical items, including but certainly not limited to the following:

- *General political environment.* Do voters think the country is on the right or wrong track? Do they approve of the job that the president, governor, senator, or incumbent congressman is doing?

- *Opinions about candidates, groups and key figures.* How many voters know of our candidate? How many voters *like* our candidate? What types of voters are unsure about our candidate? What do people think about our opponent? Do voters have a favorable or unfavorable view of other major political figures that might endorse us or endorse our opponent? What do voters think about the political parties?

- *Issue importance and issue handling.* What are the most important issues to voters? What do they care about strongly? Do they think that our candidate's political party is best to handle the issues they care about the most?

- *Message testing and contrasts.* Do voters like what we have to say about our candidate? Do they believe the things we have to say about our opponent? Do they believe the negative things our opponent might say about our candidate? When you match up our arguments against theirs, who wins?

- *Ballot tests.* If the election were held today, who would win? After voters hear the messages from both candidates, does the result change at all?

Surveys also ask demographic questions so that the results can be broken out and analyzed by individual subgroups such as ideology, age, income, and gender. One of the reasons why a campaign needs a larger sample for a benchmark survey is so that the "cell size" is larger for subgroups like women or independent voters. It is tough to draw meaningful, statistically valid conclusions from a subgroup of 10 respondents, but is possible to draw useful conclusions from a subgroup of 80. A larger survey means the subgroups will all be larger as well. When survey results are presented as cross tabulations, or "crosstabs" the results are broken out by subgroup.

Crosstabs let me examine, for instance, how respondents who considered themselves Tea Party members felt about issues leading up to the 2010 election and helped my firm produce one of the first public analyses of the demographics and beliefs of the Tea Party. Crosstabs, drawn from a 2010 survey conducted by my firm, look something like this:[1]

In many cases, tracking these subgroups is just as important as tracking the overall results. In the 2010 election cycle, my firm was focused on understanding the issues that mattered most to independent voters. Survey after survey leading up to the election showed that independents cared most about jobs and the economy. House Republicans made the

Generally speaking, would you say things in the country are headed in the right direction, or are things seriously headed off on the wrong track? BANNER 1

	Gender			Age					Gender/Age						Income						White	
	Total	Male	Female	18–34	35–44	45–54	55–64	65+	Men 18–34	Men 35–54	Men 55+	Women 18–34	Women 35–54	Women 55+	<15K	15K–30K	30K–50K	50K–75K	75K–100K	100K+	Men	Women
Base = Total Respondents	1,000	480	520	200	170	230	210	170	90	201	181	110	199	199	93	99	155	160	132	199	365	377
	100%	100%	100%	100%	100%	100%	100%	100%	100%	100%	100%	100%	100%	100%	100%	100%	100%	100%	100%	100%	100%	100%
Right Direction	348	166	182	84	56	73	83	49	37	65	63	46	64	68	32	35	54	56	42	85	102	120
	35%	35%	35%	42%	33%	32%	39%	29%	42%	32%	35%	42%	32%	34%	34%	35%	35%	35%	32%	43%	28%	32%
Don't Know	97	49	48	32	18	15	14	14	15	19	11	16	15	17	11	11	21	15	9	14	35	28
	10%	10%	9%	16%	11%	7%	7%	8%	17%	9%	6%	15%	7%	8%	11%	11%	13%	9%	6%	7%	10%	7%
Wrong Track	556	266	290	84	96	142	113	108	37	118	107	48	120	114	50	54	80	89	82	99	229	230
	56%	55%	56%	42%	57%	62%	54%	63%	41%	59%	59%	43%	60%	57%	54%	55%	52%	55%	62%	50%	63%	61%

right call to focus on asking, "Where are the jobs?" in the 2010 campaign, and, come Election Day, our survey showed that 53 percent of independents trusted Republicans over Democrats on the issue of jobs. Exit polls showed that Republican candidates nationwide won independent voters by 19 points, a dramatic shift from 2008 where Republicans lost independent voters by 8 points.

From a benchmark survey, a campaign should create a plan about what voters they need to reach out to and what messages they should use in order to energize and persuade voters. Every pollster will have a different approach to message testing, but the one that I prefer and that my firm uses is to first test "belief statements" in order to gain a basic understanding of the existing beliefs held by an audience and then to evaluate message contrasts.

For belief statements, we ask respondents if they believe or do not believe simple statements. We then look for areas where voters generally believe a principle that aligns with the candidate's policy goals. In January 2011, my firm conducted a nationwide survey to gauge beliefs about the relationship between spending and jobs. We asked if respondents believed or did not believe that "cutting spending will create jobs." Unfortunately, 56 percent did not believe that statement. However, 52 percent *did* believe that "If Congress cuts spending, this will create a better economic environment that will help promote job creation." The next month, we refined the concept and tested the statement "If Congress cuts spending, this will help end some of the uncertainty for businesses and encourage them to begin hiring again," and found 62 percent of respondents believed the statement. By identifying what people believe and do not believe, campaigns can build messages that mesh with the existing beliefs voters hold.

The second method is to evaluate message contrasts. Again, campaigns do not happen in a vacuum; too often, campaigns (and pollsters) will only consider whether or not their own messages succeed and do not test how their arguments hold up to the opposition. The message contrast lets a pollster use a survey to simulate an exchange between the two candidates. The pollster takes the top four or five messages that a campaign wishes to use and pairs them against the corresponding message from the opposition. I have occasionally encountered clients who balk at testing the opposition's messaging or who want to rephrase the opposition's message in more favorable terms. Unfortunately, this would create useless data that inaccurately reflects the debate. Because of this, when possible, my firm uses the exact language from opposition Web sites or press releases in writing the opposition message to contrast.

Follow-up surveys refresh the data on the general political environment (job approval, direction of the country, etc.) and also update the ballot test to see if a candidate has made progress or lost ground. We also use follow-up surveys as a way to test new messages to see if voters respond well to potential narratives and messages. In the home stretch, as a campaign gets close to Election Day, we may conduct follow-up surveys or *tracking surveys*, sampling a smaller number of voters at frequent intervals (sometimes nightly) in order to see if public opinion is shifting in the final days of the race.

If the pollster's job is to provide an accurate picture of the political landscape, then it is certainly the case that polling goes awry when pollsters fail to accurately measure the election environment. I once came across survey work for a presumed front-runner for a statewide office in the Southeast. The campaign had released a memo of polling results showing their candidate ahead of their opponent by 12 points two weeks out from the primary. The problem? There were more than two candidates in the primary. Due to the omission of the third contender, the poll was not accurately evaluating the true state of the race. On Election Day, that third contender picked up 10 percent of the vote. The presumed front-runner lost the primary. Polling that does not accurately represent the electorate and the dynamics of a race is of little use to the campaign that pays for it.

This sort of unforced error, however, is not the main issue with polling these days. Nowadays, the central problems that pollsters encounter are a direct result of changes in technology. While technology has transformed campaign communication and engagement with voters, for the pollster advances in technology are both a blessing *and* a curse.

POLLING AND TECHNOLOGY

Pollsters today have the ability to leverage new technology to give campaigns knowledge about the electorate they hope to understand. For instance, in 2010, 54 percent of U.S. adults turned to the Internet to get political information or to take action in that year's political campaign.[2] Over 8 out of 10 adults in the United States use a cellular phone.[3] These are tools pollsters can now use to reach and understand respondents. I can now reach respondents on their cell phones while they are away from their homes. I can look at a "word cloud" of Twitter responses to a speech to get an initial sense of what stuck with viewers.

Furthermore, technological advances have presented ways to reduce the cost of survey research. The introduction of automated IVR (interactive voice response) polls allows a pollster to conduct research for a fraction of the price of live interviewers.[4] Online survey research is generally even less expensive than telephone research.[5]

Yet as some doors are opening, other windows into the mind of the U.S. voter are closing. The American Association for Public Opinion Research (AAPOR) notes, "As proportionally more people integrate the use of a cell phone into their daily lives, proportionally fewer people are reachable via a traditional landline telephone."[6] Voters are swapping landlines for cell phones, and the fact that landline surveys do not cover these cell-only voters introduces bias into those survey's results.[7] I have noticed a declining number of young respondents in surveys, and as a result I make sure at least 10 percent of interviews in my national surveys come from cell phones.

Meanwhile, even voters who *do* have landlines are picking up the phone less. Response rates have fallen since the late 1970s and have seen an even steeper decline since the mid-1990s.[8] This development has increased research costs and made polling a more expensive item, as pollsters must spend more trying to reach each individual voter.

REACHING RESPONDENTS

The very first decision I make is *who* to survey and *how many* of those people to survey. As for *who*, political surveys tend to have "registered voters" as a universe. As Election Day draws nearer, pollsters may begin to survey only "likely voters." (The process of determining who is or is not a "likely voter" varies from pollster to pollster.) The pollster must also choose a sample size. For national surveys, 1,000 registered voters is the standard, and for smaller universes like a congressional district, I prefer to interview 300 to 400 individuals.

There are two primary methods that a pollster can use to identify potential respondents. The first is known as random digit dialing (RDD), a process where a computer generates random telephone numbers that are dialed automatically. RDD has advantages for pollsters, in that it does not require that a potential respondent be on a voter list or in a public directory in order to be reached. The *New York Times* requires that surveys meet a certain set of standards in order to be published in their newspaper and requires a probability sampling method such as

RDD.[9] My firm uses RDD for national and statewide surveys because it ensures that households have equal chances of being contacted and does not exclude new registrants or those who vote by registering to vote on the day of the election.

The other method that a pollster can use is registration-based sampling or listed sampling. This involves dialing randomly through a list of those eligible to be surveyed, usually registered voters from the district or state in which the poll is being conducted. These lists can sometimes be retrieved as the voter file from a secretary of state or elections board. For a smaller race such as a municipal or state legislative race, a listed sample may provide a campaign with the ability to more accurately contact those eligible to vote in the desired election.

In local races with very narrow universes, my firm uses a listed sample, often based on the voter file, as a way to avoid the costs of randomly dialing numbers in hopes of reaching an extremely targeted population. This also lets us pair information about a voter's past election history with his or her survey responses, though with the unfortunate trade-off that lists are not always up to date and may leave out newer registrants.

Next, I choose *how* the interviews will be conducted. Primarily, the choice is between live interviews, IVR interviewing, or online research. In live interviewing, there is a human interviewer who typically uses a CATI (computer-assisted telephone interviewing) station that allows the interviewer to input responses directly into a computer. The computer may autodial the telephone number, or the interviewer may manually enter it. The interviewer follows a script based on the questionnaire and records the responses given by the respondent. For IVR, there is no human interviewer. Instead, a recorded voice guides the respondent through a series of questions, instructing the respondent to enter his or her responses into the keypad. Online studies are usually done as panel studies, drawing on a prerecruited pool of respondents, or they are done with a "river sample" where respondents are recruited for a specific one-time survey.[10]

When a survey is complete, the raw data is sent to the pollster. I usually use one or more statistical programs (SPSS, SAS, R, Wincross, etc.) to evaluate the survey results. I provide clients with the data in two ways: as "toplines" or aggregates that give the overall results of the poll, and as a binder of cross tabulations. Once the data is available and consumable, I get to work analyzing the survey. This means poring over the results, looking for patterns, correlations, trends, and anomalies.

A good pollster does more than see how the political winds are blowing. Ultimately, a campaign has a quantitative goal—to win a certain number of votes. My job is to assess where those votes can come from and to advise on how best to obtain them. But getting this right requires having data that accurately reflects the electorate, and the challenge of getting that data makes my job as a pollster tougher each year.

THE CURSES OF EVOLVING TECHNOLOGY

Polling gives campaigns an incredible ability to create a strategy based on solid data rather than instinct and lets operatives and candidates get feedback on their actions in order to reorient their strategy as the race moves forward. Yet with each passing election cycle, the problems with the traditional telephone survey are mounting. A survey conducted using a random digit dialing sample of landline telephone numbers in the United States "will represent less than 80 percent of telephone households and less than 75 percent of all households" according to a report released in 2010 by the American Association for Public Opinion Research.[11] For those aged 18 to 29, some 49 percent are cell only, and 30 percent of Hispanics are as well. This has created a situation where surveys that only contact those with landlines are yielding results that are different from surveys that also include cell phones.[12]

So why can't campaigns just call people on their cell phones, just like they do for landlines? There are a number of legal, financial, and logistical problems with the use of cell phones in the conduct of survey research. First of all, as a result of the 1991 Telephone Consumer Protection Act, it is not legal for a cell phone number to be called with an automatic dialing mechanism.[13] For live interview surveys, this means that the interviewer must manually dial the number rather than use the aid of an autodialer to speed up the process, adding significantly to the cost of a survey. For surveys without live interviewers, it means cell phones must simply be left out. When a campaign or client is looking to do survey research on a budget, they may decide not to pursue cell phone interviews.

Even if cell phone numbers are pursued, there are a multitude of challenges that still face the pollster. For instance, it is difficult to target an audience geographically because of the mobility of cell phones. Someone may have purchased a cell phone in California but may now live in Virginia. That person should not be included in a survey conducted for a California gubernatorial campaign, yet his or her California area code could mean he or she could get a call anyway. There is also the issue of the safety and convenience of the respondent. A California cell phone number could be targeted for a 7:00 p.m. Pacific Standard Time interview, yet the owner of the phone could be living on the East Coast, meaning he or she would be contacted at 10:00 p.m. local time. Someone using a cell phone may be out and about, engaged in an activity that holds his or her attention doing something like driving where survey participation may be dangerous.[14]

Luckily, research has shown that respondents talking to a pollster on a cell phone do not give answers that are systematically lower quality than those over a landline.[15] While cell phone interviews are more expensive (in my experience, at least three times as expensive) than landline interviews, cell phones have begun making their way into political opinion research as a way to ensure that younger voters and minority groups are not underrepresented.

As the need for cell phones drives costs upward, technology is also creating new, less expensive research methods. Some pollsters are taking advantage of online or IVR survey capabilities that remove the need for human interviewers at a significant cost savings. Today, dozens of survey research firms exist in the service of Republican or Democratic candidates and are available at almost any price point. Some campaigns spend large sums on research, yet for a cash-strapped campaign there are firms that will allow a campaign to purchase IVR survey services online, a "basic" election poll that costs $1,500 and asks two ballot tests.[16]

The IVR method allows a pollster to quickly and inexpensively get a read on public opinion. In his analysis of how accurate pollsters were in the 2010 election, FiveThirtyEight.com's Nate Silver found better accuracy in surveys conducted via IVR (by the Democratic firm Public Policy Polling) than in traditional live-interview telephone surveys by CNN/Opinion Research.[17] Unfortunately, IVR research does not include the growing portion of the population that is inaccessible via landline. As Carl Bialik wrote for the *Wall Street Journal* in 2008, "The critics have legitimate complaints about such polls, including that a twelve-year-old boy can convince a computer, but probably not a live interviewer, that he's a thirty-seven-year-old woman. But in these times of slashed media-polling budgets, declining response rates, and the migration to cell phones, most polls are far from theoretically pure. Watching the survey sausage get made isn't pretty" (blog, http://online.wsj.com/article/SB121755195267602989.html).

Online quantitative research is not ideal yet, though it is showing promise. Research has found significant differences in the results of surveys conducted via nonprobability online surveys and probability traditional (usually telephone) surveys, though those differences are actually smaller when the survey subject is political.[18] Online pollster YouGov/Polimetrix conducted a survey of over 31,000 respondents leading up to the 2008 elections and had results that were closer to the final election returns than many major media polls.[19] The methodology used by Polimetrix is known as "sample matching," where a "target sample" is generated, representing a sort of ideal random sample of the population (such as voters), and then from the opt-in online panel a "matched sample" is surveyed, with matches generated based on a large number of variables from consumer or voter databases.[20] Since it is impossible to reach a perfect sample, the sample matching process attempts to construct a sample matched to a target using a very high number of responses in order to generate useful data that might be difficult or expensive to generate via traditional methods.[21]

Some online pollsters use traditional probability samples to reach respondents who are then included in online panels. The American National Election Studies panel research starting in 2008 was conducted via this method through a company called KnowledgeNetworks.[22] These methods have been criticized for "low response rates, high costs, and limitations imposed by small panel size."[23]

This is not to say that online, landline, or IVR pollsters are better or worse than one another categorically. Technological advances have created inexpensive research opportunities but have driven up the price on research that includes "necessary luxuries," like the interviews of the cell-only population. For instance, I presently choose to use live telephone interviews because I believe that the inclusion of cell phone interviews is critical, though some campaigns will choose to go with IVR pollsters because of the lower cost. However, as online research improves, I anticipate using online panels as a tool to help campaigns understand their voters.

THE BLESSINGS OF EVOLVING TECHNOLOGY

Between caller ID, declining landlines, and the logistical and legal challenges of cell phone interviewing, it is a slight relief to pollsters that new methods of research are emerging on the horizon. Online panel research is not the only way that public opinion can be observed using the Internet. Social media monitoring and prediction markets, while not currently widely used by pollsters to monitor voter sentiment, are two examples of where the field may be headed.

A 2009 study by David Rothschild evaluated competitive Senate races and each individual state's presidential race before the 2009 election and compared aggregated polling data with the results provided by Intrade, an online prediction market where investors are able to buy and sell "shares in the outcome of real-world events."[24] Prediction markets like Intrade offer observers the chance to see how much large numbers of investors are willing to wager on a certain outcome as a way of predicting what the likely outcome will be. In his conclusions, Rothschild notes that the aggregated "debiased" polling forecast provided by FiveThirtyEight .com was the "more accurate forecast," with "debiased" indicating that it is drawn from the trends evidenced by a linear regression of the existing polls. He notes that if Intrade's results were also debiased, "they would have provided a more accurate forecast and more valuable information than the best poll-based forecasts currently available, especially early in the cycle and in uncertain races."[25] While different than direct opinion research, prediction markets currently provide the media with information about political winds and could be used by political campaigns to evaluate the campaign's momentum.

Social media monitoring may also evolve as a way of understanding public opinion. Some 79 percent of adults are Internet users, and 49 percent use a social networking site.[26] As pollsters look for new ways to reach potential respondents, it may be that sites like Facebook present an opportunity to conduct methodologically rigorous political opinion research. Twitter is another option since it offers people a chance to broadcast their thoughts and opinions with lightning speed. Currently though, as writer Jolie O'Dell remarked on Mashable.com, "Natural language processing Twitter tools are still rather crude," which complicates researchers' ability to glean meaningful insights from the enormous quantity of data produced.[27]

But social media data is already used as a way to gauge opinion: after the 2011 State of the Union address, NPR asked its Facebook fans to give their reaction to the speech in three words and generated a "word cloud" from the responses, aggregating many opinions together into a consumable visualization. (The largest word? *Salmon*.)[28] As tools are developed to better parse the data generated by a socially networked and engaged public, pollsters may find themselves in a unique position: rather than *asking questions*, they may be responsible for *gleaning answers* out of large quantities of opinion data.

Social media monitoring and prediction markets are still very new and do not provide campaigns with the sort of detailed guidance that a commissioned survey can provide. Neither cell phone research nor online panel research is perfect, either. Each brings with it a host of methodological and logistical problems that have made campaign pollsters hesitant to make the jump from their more traditional landline polls.

There is no such thing as a perfect political poll. Yet pollsters have reason to be hopeful. Even as voters dodge their calls, hang up the phone, and cut free from the landline, they are putting their opinions on the Internet and are reachable when not sitting at home.

Technology is giving campaigns more ways to engage with voters. Similarly, it is giving pollsters more and more ways to *understand* voters. While the challenges continue to grow greater with each passing cycle, unprecedented quantities of data are available to be parsed by the campaign and polling team that are up to the task of digging in.

CHAPTER 8

Serving the People: Constituent Relations in the Digital Age

Ken Ward

In 1931, a young Texan named Lyndon B. Johnson headed to Washington to work in the office of Congressman Richard Kleberg. At 23, Johnson was a recent college graduate with a knack for public speaking and debate, but he also had a keen intellect. Johnson concluded that to be an effective representative one also had to be effective in communicating with constituents. As secretary for Kleberg, the future president ran constituent communications with a tireless zeal uncommon on the Hill in those days. His mantra: letter in, letter out.[1]

When the Kleberg office received a letter from a constituent, a response went out the same day. This may now seem an obvious and expected part of being an elected official, but that is largely because Johnson's methods worked so well in strengthening Kleberg's incumbency. This electoral reality—that good constituent service translates to higher approval ratings from across the political spectrum—led the Johnson methods to become the model for constituent communications throughout Congress.[2] It remains so to this day, though the methods for communication have expanded.

Responding to a constituent concern or need requires a coordinated effort within a congressional office. As a concept, this is called constituent relationship management (CRM), a close analog to customer relationship management in the commercial world, and it is central to being an effective legislator. It is how elected officials learn what their constituents want, which allows them to enact positive legislation. It is also how they service those who sent them to Washington—constituent satisfaction is directly correlated to effective communication. Success in these tasks spells reelection, which is always a consideration for congressional offices.

Historically, the technology used on the Hill evolved slowly, with congressional offices relying on paper mail and phone calls to interact with constituents. Over time, elected officials established procedures and systems for tracking, ordering, and leveraging interactions with constituents. Through this, legislators not only listened to constituents but also communicated with them. Low-tech solutions were sufficient in years past, so long as constituent communications remained relatively small in volume.

With the rise of the Internet in the 1990s, communication from constituents has grown immensely. The Congressional Management Foundation reports that the quantity of messages received by Congress quadrupled between 1995 and 2004.[3] Responding to letters, phone calls, e-mails, and other digital communications requires multiple levels of approval and edits to ensure the content aligns with the member's views and strategy. While this process of tracking, sorting, and responding to voter input helps build valuable relationships with constituents, it also takes a lot of time and effort.

Elected officials are constantly innovating and adapting their strategy as new communication mediums arise, but though technology solves many problems, it also poses a significant challenge to congressional offices: with vast amounts of interactions, how can a small team with limited resources keep track and make sense of a near-endless amount of constituent communication?

The crux of the challenge is that as communications options for citizens increase and diversify, the technology on the legislator side must be consolidated to provide an integrated, strategic approach to constituent communication. CRM software systems make this possible, but there are only a handful of firms providing the innovative, new technologies that help over 500 U.S. Senate and House offices run better, faster and cheaper.

Understanding the challenges these firms are working to solve requires a closer look at how congressional offices communicate with constituents and how the technologies they use impact this process.

A PEEK BEHIND THE CONGRESSIONAL CURTAIN

The U.S. Congress is a complex legislative body. Each of the 435 congressmen, 100 senators, 4 delegates, and 1 resident commissioner has his or her own office with a dedicated staff. Members of Congress typically have offices in both Washington and their elected district or state. While member offices collaborate on policy and often socialize together, they make personnel and technological decisions independently and based on their unique priorities. The House and Senate do have central finance, IT, and other offices, but these groups have little authority over how individual legislators make decisions on day-to-day operations, such as the method and frequency of communication with constituents.

Each office is a self-organizing entity, and at the beginning of every session in Congress legislators vote to readopt rules for operation. These rules dictate budgets, which in turn determine which technologies an office uses and acquires. Unlike an election campaign, however, where a candidate's spending is restricted only by the amount of funds he or she is able to raise, congressional offices have greater resource restraints.

As students of U.S. politics know, the terms in office for the House and Senate are two and six years, respectively. In these short terms of service, members of Congress have three primary goals: to serve constituent needs and concerns, to enact beneficial legislation, and to be reelected. These are not competing goals but interconnected aspects of public service. Listening to constituents informs policy decisions, and engaging constituents builds valuable relationships, which in turn support reelection. Listening and responding to constituent correspondence is therefore an integral aspect of a legislator's duties on the Hill.

When it comes to directly serving constituents, the congressional staff works together to provide constituents with support and resolve their problems and concerns. The staff hierarchy within each office is fairly standard throughout Congress and shapes this correspondence system. At the bottom of the office hierarchy are staff assistants (SA) who answer the phones and assist in logistical tasks. The first promotion for an SA in Washington is typically to the position of legislative correspondent (LC), who is primarily engaged in responding to constituents about policy issues. Though an entry-level position, LCs are the pistons that drive the constituent-correspondence engine.

Above the LCs are legislative assistants (LA). LAs cover specific policy areas with duties focused on drafting and monitoring legislation and assisting the LC in responding to correspondence. Overseeing the LCs and LAs is the legislative director (LD), who advises the member on legislative issues and is generally responsible for managing the office's correspondence with constituents.

In a representative's district office, an SA would look to be promoted to either a caseworker or field representative. Both of these roles involve direct interaction with constituents. Both caseworkers and field reps report to a district director. Finally, the office will have a communications director, tasked with cultivating relationships with journalists, and in some cases has a dedicated staff. Above each of these positions is the chief of staff, who reports directly to the member of Congress. A typical House office is composed of about 15 to 20 staff members, whereas a Senate office varies from as few as 50 to as many as 75.

These staffers generally fall into one of three roles: constituent service, legislative policy, and communications. This office organization often creates internal fiefdoms, with staff holding in isolation their slice of the constituent engagement pie. These internal fiefdoms often operate with a surprising lack of coordination on strategy, best practices, and especially technology.

The staff makeup of a congressional office would ideally have constituent services on one hand, legislative on the other, with the communications staff straddling the two to best promote a legislator's message. Yet somehow the communications folks in each office often forge their own fiefdom, with a focus on "spinning" news and public opinion rather than staying up to date with legislative changes and efforts. The result is that few look for a way to approach constituent communication in a unified manner.

Well before my current occupation, which is running a company that provides software to Hill offices, I worked as an LC and LA on the Hill, and I observed this inefficiency firsthand. For example, I was once working on outreach and my congressman's Web site, positioning myself for the office's press secretary position. I brought some radical views to the table. Our member had been redistricted, meaning he had new voters in his home district who did not know him and were more left of center (while our office was right of center). I saw that we were not going to be able to win new areas without bypassing the media filter and interacting directly with our new constituents. I argued against putting all our eggs in the same media basket. Previously, Congress did not have the same opportunity to directly engage voters, but e-mail and Web sites were revolutionizing interaction (I am dating myself, but social media as we think of it today did not yet exist). I did not get the press secretary job, and soon I left the Hill to help change the way legislators communicate with constituents.

Both internal logistics and political pressure are the kinds of challenges congressional staff run into when driving constituent communications, and it is this kind of fragmented approach that leads to technological silos. A technology silo refers to how data on constituents, their preferences, interaction with them, and the tools used to collect this information reside in separate environments, or silos. The problem with technology silos is that they hinder effective communication, with constituent information housed in different locations and used in different ways, making it difficult to synthesize the data. In my more recent experience, I worked with an office that had different databases related to the e-mail newsletter, website, constituent mail, direct mail, and telephone town halls. Pulling and aggregating data from all of these sources just to have an updated e-mail list required a week of delays. By this method, offices are hard pressed to rapidly respond on important legislative initiatives, let alone know a constituent's true history of interaction. Without a single record showing how the office interacted with a constituent, it is difficult to conduct strategic, coordinated outreach.

Nevertheless, for many years, offices (and the vendors supplying Congress with communications technology) focused on building and improving individual digital tools and programs rather than approaching an office's communications efforts as a whole and using technology that harmonizes the different ways legislators track and respond to constituent information and interaction.

To better understand how Congress has gotten itself into this fix, let us step back and look at how congressional CRM has changed since the days when Lyndon B. Johnson first implemented his rigorous efforts on the Hill.

CRM BEFORE THE INTERNET

Communicating with voters and forging strong relationships is not unique to the twenty-first century United States. It is wrapped up in the U.S. political system and always has been, though the method for achieving it has changed over time. Traditionally, correspondence was exclusively composed of regular postal mail and phone calls, the bread and butter of congressional–constituent communications. In Lyndon B. Johnson's early days on the Hill, paper correspondence was the only cost-effective way of communicating over any real physical distance. Johnson used this medium to great success, responding to every constituent letter the day it arrived and, during slow periods, writing "unsolicited letters of praise, congratulations, and condolences to Texas constituents," all personalized to the recipient and signed by the congressman.[4] This letter-in, letter-out process became the model for modern legislators and their staff.

Representatives have long employed the privilege of the frank—mail sent to constituents about official congressional matters at taxpayer expense. It was from this practice that some of the first inefficiencies were introduced into the CRM process. Offices typically employed (and continue to employ) a vendor to manage the franked-mail database and design, which created a wealth of data that was held distinct from other constituent-interaction records. When the amount of constituent communication was relatively low, this practice of holding constituent data in different places did not have a major impact on other communication efforts. As we have seen, however, this changed.

As the nation's telecommunications capability developed, phone calls between constituents and congressional offices were of some use. Of late, tele–town halls have become increasingly popular. These are mass conference calls, where constituents—reached using a database of constituent phone numbers—can learn about their representative or senator's efforts and even provide input via "insta-polls" using touch-tone telephone keys. These uses of the telephone, however, are more recent innovations, and for many years long-distance phone calls were cost prohibitive, making paper correspondence all the more important.

Even when fax transmission was developed and came into vogue on the Hill, paper letters remained the primary method of communication. Pre-Internet computer technology developed and was adopted by congressional offices to manage databases of people and track messages. These were some of the very first uses of computers and databases for implementing business process improvements. Even with these advances, overall, Congress before 1995 was overwhelmingly a paper-based organization.

A BOOM IN ADVOCACY AND CITIZEN ENGAGEMENT

The Internet's growth in the 1990s presented constituents with new ways to interact with Congress. New digital tools offered fast and cheap ways to interact and gave voters an easier way to contact their representatives and take part in shaping public policy. This was a great benefit to citizens, giving them access to lawmakers like never before.

Legislators, however, were cautious about exploring the cyber terrain. In 1995, the late Senator Ted Kennedy (D-MA) became the first in Congress to build a Web site for his office, but it was not until a year later that others in the House and Senate followed suit.[5] There were other watershed moments in technology on the Hill, such as then-senator John Ashcroft's (R-MO) 1996 online petition, the first of its kind.[6] But because each office on the Hill operates independently, the congressional move to the Internet happened at different paces and with different technologies and vendors.

As a collective body, the House of Representatives acted to upgrade congressional IT facilities and its online presence in the 1990s.[7] Through the Library of Congress Web site and the House Web site, the public was given unprecedented access to congressional information, including some audio and video from hearings.

As new tools were brought online, however, representatives found a staggering increase in communications from constituents. This was the other side of the digital communications coin. As much as technology empowered citizens to take part in the legislative process and contact their elected officials, it also made it difficult for congressional offices to consolidate efforts and information.

In decades prior, Congress had experienced some surges in constituent communication, but they were short lived and infrequent. Constituent communications surged again during the Clinton impeachment, with offices receiving 1,000 to 10,000 e-mails a week.[8] After the trial, the numbers did not return to normal levels but continued to grow.

Others looking to influence Congress also took notice of these new methods of interacting with elected officials. In fact, an entire technology market was born composed of companies creating software tools to promote advocacy initiatives. These systems help organizations drive their activists to engage legislators by matching citizens to their elected officials and helping compose e-mail messages. The largest of these vendors, Capitol Advantage, was so successful with its e-mail advocacy platform that it was acquired by the Roll Call publishing group for $43 million in 2008. This rise in advocacy technology had a profound effect on the volume of messages sent to the Hill and today accounts for up to 75 percent of the peak e-mail volume received by elected officials.

While receiving and recording the growing volume of traditional and digital communications was possible, offices encountered the logistical hurdle of responding to so much constituent communication. Making sense of the data and fitting it into the process for developing responses to constituents was a significant challenge. Some offices used separate infrastructures for postal mail and e-mail. For example, some programs were implemented just to handle the bulk e-mail received from advocacy groups. Overall, basic correspondence was (and is) done in different ways depending on how the constituent communication is received. This reveals just how fragmented congressional offices are vis-à-vis constituent engagement.

In the new millennium, communications technology has developed at an even more rapid pace. Since 2000, the percentage of adults using the Internet for a variety of purposes skyrocketed to 80 percent.[9] For adults aged 34 to 64, about 7 in 10 use the Internet to visit a government website.[10]

The growth of Internet use among voters, coupled with the low-cost nature of operating online, means congressional offices are looking for the new tools and programs that help them better connect with constituents.

The volume of communications from the public to Capitol Hill continues to climb. In 2008, for example, the House of Representatives received 200 *million* e-mails, with an equal amount sent from House computers.[11] With each new or improved tool brought into a legislator's communications efforts, the amount of constituent information and interaction grows. As legislators acquired new technology, in many cases, exploring new tools or updating existing tools was a higher priority than integrating and harmonizing communications efforts. For this reason, managing constituent relationships has become increasingly difficult.

The problem rests in the way new communication tools—whether social media, tele–town halls, or the next generation of tools—have been added to an office's existing communications efforts and IT infrastructure. As new communications technology came to market, members of the House and Senate incorporated tools as needed. For example, the original providers of CRM databases failed to improve their systems, leading directly to the introduction of competing database platforms optimized for the bulk delivery of e-mail newsletters. While the new tools offered greater opportunities for representatives to interact with constituents, the underlying technology that supports it did not improve at the same pace. Nor did the ad hoc, build-as-you-go method of implementing new technological tactics support a coordinated outreach effort.

The tools were used in moderate isolation from each other, creating technology silos. Web site forms, e-mails, and, later, social media interaction all offer valuable communication with constituents, but unless the information gathered can be consolidated, synthesized, and, most importantly, responded to, offices miss opportunities to listen, engage, inform, and influence constituents.

The inefficiencies inherent in this approach became apparent as more voters contacted their representatives through increasingly diverse online methods. The rising volume of communication with constituents has overwhelmed many offices, which lack the staff, resources, and technology to effectively manage so much data.

ENTER THE VENDORS

Because congressional offices have fixed budgets and resources, they must rely on vendors to provide the CRM technology and support needed to manage the large volume of constituent communications. The software vendors who moved into this market offered some of the first database engines with workflow processes. For example, a UNIX-based system—Quorum—was offered in the early 1990s and quickly established itself as the leader in this new market.

The major firms working with Congress in these early days of CRM technology included Capitol Letters, Affiliated Computer Services (ACS), InterAmerica, and Monarch. None of these vendors remain today. Lockheed Martin, a major provider of government IT systems, acquired the government businesses of both Capitol Letters and ACS and is the leader in market share with its Internet Quorum product.

These early CRM systems were a bureaucratic approach to software implementation, more concerned with management than constituent engagement. The software provided some internal structure to the process, and while in practice these systems held true to a CRM philosophy, the focus was more on the process than the outcome. To be fair, the underlying computing power of these early CRM systems simply did not have the complexity and versatility that is available today.

For the vendors that worked on the Hill, progress toward a more modern CRM came slowly. Only subtle innovations were introduced to the marketplace and only after efficiency problems could no longer be tolerated. These systems, without significant enhancement, would become increasingly insufficient to meet the needs of elected officials.

As Internet capabilities and programs improved, representatives and senators brought new tools—such as social media and improved Web sites—into their communications repertoire. New vendors rushed to help legislators master the digital tools, but these new vendors did so without considering or integrating the other communications tools elected offices used. This fueled a fragmented marketplace, with communications technology providers and consultants supporting the development and best practices for new communication tools. Yet this approach failed to resolve the fundamental challenge: congressional offices need a faster, cheaper, and better way to manage the entirety of constituent communications in a coordinated, centralized manner.

The total number of vendors offering these much-needed CRM solutions is relatively small, given that there are hundreds of congressional offices. Lockheed Martin remains a major player, but other vendors have stepped into the congressional IT market as well. Some firms, such as General Dynamics and iConstituent (which acquired InterAmerica) have been working with Congress for years. There is also a group of newcomers driving innovation and integration in CRM software, including

Fireside21 and others. These companies are changing the way offices on the Hill approach CRM, moving away from segregated communications tools toward more integrated products.

OPENING, INTEGRATING, AND INTERACTING

On President Barack Obama's first day in office, he signed the Memorandum on Transparency and Open Government as part of the White House's Open Government Initiative. In addition to reforming the way special interests influence government and tracking how the federal government uses taxpayer money, the initiative focuses on openness and new technologies that help the public take part in and understand federal decisions.

While this initiative does not force Congress to change its practices, it does underscore a federal shift toward more transparent operations and new technologies. The Internet and Web technologies have significantly removed barriers to understanding government data. Elected officials are already being held more accountable for their decisions and votes. To be sure, some members of Congress are well on their way to more transparent practices and methods for voter input. As the Open Government Initiative moves forward, however, CRM systems that facilitate constituent interaction will allow legislators to reflect the kind of openness and engagement to which the public may become accustomed.

Every congressional office conducts outreach and constituent communications, but this outreach has not always been done in a technologically sophisticated way. Offices now have the opportunity to implement smarter systems and processes to extract the greatest benefit from their constituent communication efforts. Looking ahead, the systems and software that help Congress manage constituent communications will continue to evolve, ushering in a new, more transparent, and more engaging congressional approach.

Just as important, however, is that the CRM systems of tomorrow expand congressional offices' ability to integrate information and interact with constituents. While the specific products that will help Congress achieve this either are still in development or have yet to be invented, the CRM systems that will become dominant in the coming years and decades will be able to offer improvements in a variety of areas.

The primary area is improving the consolidation and integration of data, software, and media. Those running for office can raise large sums of money and need not worry as much about their return on investment.

In Congress, however, resources, funding, and staff are limited. The growth in voter communication is sure to continue, and offices will increasingly require tools that help them do more with less. This will be as important for effectiveness as it will be for running an efficient, low-cost operation.

Congressional offices are already beginning to use CRM systems that are more effective at aggregating information and making the response process more efficient. The next step will be to continue these innovations as they apply to social media interactions with constituents. The advent of social media impacted all industries that leverage public dialogue or interaction to promote and achieve their goals. In Congress (as well as in other fields), the future of CRM is in fully integrating social media data into the overall function of tracking and ordering constituent information. This includes assimilating these interactions with those gathered through a variety of media and helping to streamline constituent responses in social environments.

More meaningful engagement with constituents will also become increasingly important. Technology is changing the way people interact and communicate. Lyndon B. Johnson's approach to managing constituent relationships focused on responding to voters individually. This one-to-one interaction was and still is a standard CRM method in Congress, whether responses are given on paper, through e-mail, or over the phone.

Social media, however, is driving a different type of engagement. Services like Facebook and Twitter have changed the public debate into a multiparticipant conversation. Congressional offices have been challenged to interact with constituents in these new ways. The technologies and software that help offices make sense of these interactions will prove vital as more people use social media tools, either those currently on the market or those yet to be developed.

The perfect turnkey CRM does not yet exist, though the vendors working with Congress are making significant strides toward it. The best CRM tools in the future will tie into the social environment and make sense of it, allowing the user to bring constituent interactions and information garnered from social networking platforms into the CRM process. In short, it helps turn social media users into supporters and an impersonal "fan" or "follower" into a meaningful relationship. This is the very essence of managing constituent relationships. The vendor able to achieve this while also integrating all other communications tools and tracking constituent information will be one of the major stakeholders in the future of congressional CRM.

NEW IMPERATIVES

Technology is changing at a rapid pace. Only 15 years ago, many legislators questioned whether e-mail was a worthwhile tool and congressional use of Web sites was still in its formative stages. Today, every congressional office has a Web site, and the ability to correspond by e-mail is a given. The Internet and online capabilities have changed the way the world interacts and, as a governing body, the U.S. Congress has done well to move into the digital space as much as it has. A member of Congress is vested with the duty to represent his or her constituents and to put forward and support legislation that reflects the needs and aspirations of the people he or she serves. New technologies—particularly those used for communication—are vital for achieving these congressional responsibilities.

Yet there is still work to be done. While legislators use new tools to communicate with constituents, they continue to struggle with ways to effectively manage and respond to the huge volumes of communication from voters. Each letter, phone call, e-mail, tweet, or other communication from a constituent is an opportunity to forge, strengthen, and facilitate relationships. With the volume of communications sure to increase, Congress requires innovative CRM solutions that best track and harmonize constituent data and interaction.

Today, a new generation of vendors servicing the House and Senate offer more sophisticated software and technology that supports a representative's efforts in forging, managing, and recording constituent relationships. Yet the vendors driving this innovation are few because of the size of the market, because it is new, and in part because there are significant barriers to entry into the congressional software market.

Integrating new and better CRM technology is not only about resolving the immediate logistical challenges of responding to large volumes of constituent communications. It is also about helping elected officials become better legislators. Members of Congress will be increasingly held accountable for their decisions in Washington as voters continue to reach out to their representatives in large numbers. An improved CRM system will streamline interaction with constituents and allow members of Congress to be more fully aware of what voters want, which helps them make policy choices that best satisfy their constituents' needs.

If the volume of messages sent to legislators continues to grow and diversify at the current rate, elected officials may need to reexamine the foundational doctrine of responding to every constituent correspondence. As Congress puts new digital tools to use, and as the voting public becomes savvier in its online communication, offices will need to change and adopt more sophisticated and integrated approaches to their CRM philosophy and software. With the right CRM tools, elected officials will be better able to serve voters, interacting with constituents in a more collaborative way. This approach will surely lead to better policy and constituent satisfaction.

While firms working on the Hill today offer CRM technology that is vastly improved from years prior, a more social CRM software that captures all information and interactions from all mediums is still in development. However, when this social CRM is eventually brought to market, there will be new communication challenges and technologies, requiring still more innovation and flexibility to satisfy new and changing needs. In this way, the work of innovation never ends. But this does not dissuade those of us dedicated to helping Congress better connect with its constituents. We are operating in an age of opportunity, and it is the job of elected officials—and the vendors that support them—to seize that opportunity and serve the people.

CHAPTER 9
An Explosion of Innovation: The Voter-Data Revolution

Robert Blaemire

Political campaigns in the twenty-first century use computer-generated databases for all forms of voter contact. Whether calling voters by telephone, sending them direct mail, or walking door-to-door, it is virtually unheard of to do so without a computerized voter file. Whether the goals are fundraising, voter persuasion, attendance at rallies, or get-out-the-vote efforts, these tasks are made far easier and more efficient by having this capability. The existence of a voter file is almost an assumption in modern campaigns, and the competition among vendors isn't between those who have them and those who don't but in the amount of data appended and the flexibility that will be made available for accessing that data. It is far more an assessment of quality over quantity, and voter file usage has grown exponentially.

But this was not the case for very many years. I write this from a unique vantage point, having been at the forefront of the development of these modern tools, first as a longtime Senate staffer and campaign worker and later as the founder of one of the country's foremost communications companies specializing in voter files. Communicating with voters has always been the task of a campaign, but being able to harness computer techniques to process data faster and more efficiently created a business that didn't exist when I first ventured into politics. It's almost amusing to look back over these years and realize we were inventing new ways to accomplish ancient political tasks and creating a new business as a result.

This new style of campaigning began by recognizing the growing capabilities of computer technology and marrying those processes with the traditional demands of political campaigns. We would find that Democratic state parties would become the sensible vehicles for bringing these new techniques to the attention of campaigners. We adjusted our roles to adapt to the swiftly changing technological capabilities available to us. As a result, I found myself in the forefront of this new business—one that is now institutionalized—of bringing computerized voter files into modern campaigns everywhere. And now I am involved in maintaining a national voter file database overlaid with predictive models that are once again changing the campaign horizon and creating fabulous advantages to political practitioners.

FIRST FORAYS

I arrived in Washington, DC, in the fall of 1967, a freshman at George Washington University aspiring to a future in politics. On my first day in Washington after my parents dropped me off, I went to the U.S. Senate, hoping to meet my state's senator, Birch Bayh of Indiana. After all these years it feels fortuitous that I was able to meet him on that first day to volunteer my services and change my life.

I was offered a volunteer job on Saturdays, which entailed entering, by hand, vote totals onto computer forms so the 1968 reelection campaign could institute its first ever computer-targeting effort. Within the next few months, I was showing up more often in the office and taking on more tasks, usually those things other staffers didn't want to do. Eventually I made myself valuable enough to the necessary number of staffers that I was offered a part-time job, splitting the Senate's lowest salary rate with two other fellow volunteers.

Over the next months, I maneuvered my way deeper into office life and was offered a job in which I didn't have to share a salary. It was working for the office manager, both in the mailroom as well as stuffing envelopes and running errands. While running those errands around the Capitol I came to learn how the Senate worked, how constituent services were handled, how mass mailings were produced, and, most importantly, the services the Senate made available to Senate offices. One of those was computer services. I learned that senators were allowed to accumulate mailing lists for franked mail, but our office only had a list of 13,000 people and mailed to it only once a year.

Over the next 13 years, as I served in a variety of jobs with increasing importance, including traveling with the senator for five months during his successful 1974 reelection campaign, one mission was constant: to build a larger mailing list for a more aggressive franked mail program so we could have some possibility of generating news about Senator Bayh without depending on the Republican-leaning news media in Indiana. When we left office in 1981, we had 2.8 million names with over 250 identification codes on our mailing list and had been the Senate's largest mailer for three years running. With this experience, I gained valuable knowledge about databases, computer services, and what worked or didn't in the world of computer-generated direct mail.

We lost our 1980 reelection campaign in the Reagan landslide and, after 13 years on Bayh's staff, I found myself looking for work. After spending a year running an organization trying to fight the negative campaign tactics of the New Right, raising money with direct mail throughout that year, I was offered a job by a small company tasked with acquiring voter files for the AFL-CIO in order for them to perform matches and find out which members were registered to vote. We would be free to sell those voter files—computerized lists of registered voters—to campaigns. I knew nothing about the existence of voter files in the country, only that Indiana didn't have voter lists computerized, a painful lesson I came to know while overseeing our campaign's voter contact program.

While there was nowhere to go to learn about voter files or how to acquire them or how to process them on a computer to make them usable, there was also no one to tell me what I couldn't do. As a result, I made more money in 1982 than expected and left the company to go out on my own, changing directions shortly thereafter to join Below, Tobe & Associates, a Los Angeles firm that produced computer-generated mail for Democrats in southern California. They had just signed a contract with the Democratic National Committee to acquire voter lists for the DNC's direct-mail fundraising and needed to start a Washington office largely to assist in this effort. That's when I really got going in this area.

THE ERA BEGINS

In 1984, I sold my first statewide voter file project to a client, meaning we were to build a voter file from scratch, often keypunching paper lists to get them in computer form. The candidate was Congressman Al Gore, running for the U.S. Senate in Tennessee. When the list was built, we soon convinced the Tennessee Democratic State Party to take over ownership of the database. This made sense for three reasons.

First, it put the state party back in political campaigns, providing a real service to candidates. Second, it provided candidates access to high-quality data either for the first time or better than they might otherwise have. And third, it allowed a vendor like us to reach campaigns we would never otherwise reach. This made an enormous amount of sense to me.

Also in 1984, I persuaded the Indiana Democratic Party to build a voter file for the same reasons, which became our second state party voter file project. By 1986, the number of state parties hiring us for this task grew to six, a number that doubled two years later. Soon, the DNC began funding these projects, and an increasing number of state parties had their own voter files, extending data and computer services to a growing number of campaigns. The logic of this approach and the benefit to state parties became clear to those of us in the business as well as an increasing number of political operatives.

By 1990, state party work had become the centerpiece of our business. Because of it, we were far more engaged with the Dukakis campaign in 1988 than we otherwise would have been. More and more states were developing voter file projects, and our competitors began taking on these projects as well. By the end of 1990, I decided to leave Below, Tobe & Associates and start my own company, Blaemire Communications. Having become somewhat of a voter-file expert, working with state parties on my terms led me to venture out on my own.

In a very short period of time, I was accumulating state-party contracts, and my company became largely focused on building their voter files and providing computer-generated products for campaigns throughout those states. Those products included mailing labels, phone lists, walk lists, file matches, poll samples, and laser-generated direct mail. Not only were those of us in the business concentrating on state parties but the role of state parties within the Democratic community was expanding as a result. Political operatives were coming to expect a high-quality voter file at the outset of their campaigns, and the number of mail and phone vendors generating business because of the growth of computerized voter contact was increasing as well. Computerized voter contact using voter files had become completely institutionalized in the Democratic political community.

During the period of 1991 and 1992, we had an aggressive Democratic presidential nominating process, one in which every candidate made sure quality, computerized voter files were available in early primary states for their direct voter contact efforts. This was not only good for my business but recognition that this aspect of campaigning had really become accepted. I continued to add Democratic state parties to my company's portfolio and, when President Clinton was looking toward reelection in 1996, he had a whole new crew at the DNC focused on this aspect of the upcoming campaign.

We may not remember that, in 1995, the Clinton reelection was not considered a sure thing. The DNC wanted to be sure that all state parties had quality voter files available for the president's reelection. My company became one of two with whom the DNC contracted to build voter files for states where projects like this did not exist. By the beginning of 1996, virtually all state parties had a voter file they owned, managed by a reputable vendor.

Soon after 1996, my company experienced what I have come to know as one of the three major developments in this business that substantially changed our entire landscape. It had become possible to downsize the computer services business away from the mainframe to a less expensive PC-based network. This development not only lowered my costs but also allowed my company to move out of the mainframe facility it was in and into our own offices where we could manage our own network. While my overhead went up considerably, my job costs virtually disappeared.

We moved into our own facility in 1997 and produced all of our own work in house. I increasingly traveled to meetings with Democratic state chairs as the vendor who represented more of them than any other, often returning with new client prospects. Our state party work meant an even greater role in providing data during the Gore presidential campaign, with many of the orders placed by DNC staff for data and products in the states for which we were managing voter file projects. Ninety percent of our products were printed materials—lists, labels, and laser-generated mail. Then came the second of those three major developments, the Internet.

In the early part of this century, sending data via e-mail became the rule, where it previously had been the exception. Orders had always been placed by telephone or fax and now they were usually placed by e-mail. And my job costs went down as printed lists and labels became almost completely replaced by e-mailed phone files or mail files.

Now I was into my second decade in the business, a decade spent compiling data from many and varied sources, receiving it on paper to be keypunched as well as put on nine-track tapes, eight-track cartridges, or diskettes of varying sizes. Soon, diskettes would be replaced by CDs or data would be received via FTP or online download processes. Another effect of the Gore campaign had a much different impact on this business.

Because of the long recount in Florida and the revelations about "butterfly ballots" and the inconsistent methods of voting within the state, Congress passed the Help America Vote Act. Designed to standardize the voting process across the country, at least in federal elections, it also resulted in states creating statewide voter files. Instead of acquiring voter files county by county in order to compile a statewide file, single databases were now becoming available through the secretaries of state. No more would we have to build a file like Maine's, compiled from 517 different town files.

So the business was getting easier and less expensive, and everything could move faster. While FedEx had seemed like a miracle with overnight deliveries, it would soon seem prehistoric as data pulled for list production could be delivered mere minutes after the client's request.

My role had been pretty well defined by the political community. We were the experts who knew how to manipulate the data in order to get our campaigners the data they wanted. Even if they asked for something they really didn't want, we were in a position to keep them from making costly mistakes and make sure they got what they really wanted for voter contact. We stood between the customer and the computer to make sure the process was done right. I can't count the times a campaign in a Democratic primary would ask for a mail file of frequent primary voters, neglecting to include in that request a requirement that those primary voters be Democrats. Knowing the data better than the client put us in a position to help them use that knowledge to target accurately and effectively.

MORE CHANGES IN THE LANDSCAPE

But this gatekeeper role, too, would change. The widespread adoption of the Internet led to the creation of online tools that would extend to individual campaigners the ability to do for themselves what we were doing for them. I first heard about the Voter Activation Network (VAN) in 2002 and soon became convinced that we had to develop our own online system or we would be left behind. Soon, the competition for the online business also stiffened with the appearance of other online vendors. In the fall of 2003, Blaemire Communications released its version of an online voter file interface, known as Leverage.

Leverage placed the processes we would normally employ on behalf of the client in the client's hands. Now, selecting voters and producing data for voter contact were decisions totally governed by the user, no longer by the vendor. The business was beginning to look nothing like it had. Happily, our system soon became the second most popular among state parties. In 2004 our company managed more voter file projects than any other vendor, and only VAN had more state parties online. Many of our state party clients had us build and manage their voter files but hosted them online on the VAN. During the 2004 campaign, our client base was augmented by the DNC having us build a number of other states to put onto Leverage so the Kerry campaign would have online access. By the end of the election, we had over 1,100 users on Leverage.

Also during 2004, a coalition of progressive organizations came together to try and help a Democrat get elected president. The group—America Coming Together (ACT)—got involved in all manner of election-oriented projects in several states. It was organized by Harold Ickes, formerly deputy chief of staff for President Clinton; Ellen Malcolm from *Emily's List*, Steve Rosenthal of the AFL-CIO; Andy Stern from the Service Employees' International Union; Carl Pope of the Sierra Club; and others. ACT became a good client for me in the end but had a larger impact on my life than it first appeared it would.

Early in the cycle I was invited by Mark Sullivan, the head of VAN, to join him at the ACT headquarters for a meeting. Mark felt that if ACT did much of what they were planning, VAN could not handle all of it, and he would feel better if he were allied with our company. After the meeting, I followed up with the requested proposal for building a national voter file separate from state party ownership or involvement. Once that was submitted, I was no longer in touch with ACT. For reasons that did not become apparent until later, none of my phone calls or e-mails were returned, and I turned to more pressing business. While the silence was only caused by the unresponsiveness of one staff person, it convinced me that my services were not needed. Later, I learned that the person I referred to should not have been the one responsible for voter file planning and that my interests fell into a black hole only because ACT was a fledgling organization just getting started.

As ACT got going and I began fulfilling requests from various ACT staffers and field operatives, they reorganized in mid-2004, and I was asked once again to meet with them. At that meeting it was made clear that the new people in charge had no idea I had submitted a proposal and agonized over the copy I brought with me, saying their lives would have been so much easier had we won the contract. No one was building and managing their voter files who knew what they were doing. This rein-vention of the wheel was painful to them, as one might expect. I was encouraged once again but, as before, nothing happened with it, and we returned again to normal business, now getting busier with the coming presidential election. Soon, the DNC hired us to host a number of states on Leverage, and life got about as busy at our office as it had been before.

Around Labor Day, Sullivan called again to request I join him at another ACT meeting to help them fix severe issues that had developed in their overall voter file and voter contact projects. This ended up being

handled in a conference call. On this call, now with another new set of
ACT staff, we were asked to take over the entire ACT voter file operation.
The issues were not VAN issues—users throughout the ACT universe
seemed happy with VAN. But data issues seemed persistent—updates
weren't happening, state files had gaps in them, matches weren't being performed as expected. They had no one to handle the inevitable data questions that had long been part of my life. But there was no way we could
do that at that late date. We were simply too committed with our existing
clients to take on one that would not only be our biggest but in a period
when it would be too late to staff up in order to handle it. This was surely
the biggest piece of business I had ever turned down, but I really had no
choice. I felt that a juggler might be able to juggle 10 balls in the air at
once, but if you threw in an 11th, all might hit the ground. That could very
well happen to us.

We all know now that John Kerry was not elected president. I think it
is a fair assessment to conclude that the ACT project overreached and
failed to accomplish much of what it set out to do. As a result, Harold
Ickes brought together his partners in the ACT venture to figure out
where they should go from there. The conclusion: solve the database
piece. The progressive community involved with ACT felt that there
needed to be a national voter file available to all of the organizations they
could count on, one of high quality with substantial enhancements and
consistently kept up to date. Many of the 501(c)(3) tax-exempt organizations determined they could not use data owned by political parties,
something I had learned from them during the year. Therefore, my company could not solve their data needs using voter files that we managed
for state parties. The result of all of this was the creation, by Ickes, Laura
Quinn, Al Dwoskin, and others, of a limited liability company called Data
Warehouse. Laura had been the chief technology officer at the DNC
while Al, a successful businessman, was also a key player in DNC and
ACT fundraising. Later, the name would be changed to Catalist.

Throughout 2005 and into 2006, I continued working at Blaemire Communications with state parties and large progressive organizations. In 2004
our biggest client had been the DNC, but it was soon replaced by the
National Education Association. Our portfolio of state parties covered 26
states, 9 of which were on Leverage. Other clients included the Sierra
Club, NARAL, Planned Parenthood, and the League of Conservation
Voters plus a large number of Democratic pollsters and consultants. As
good as things were, I had a growing concern about Catalist. The existence
of a national competitor with capital raised by investors, not from revenue
it had to generate, made me uneasy. While uneasy, I also had a number of

friends who had gone to work there, mostly from the DNC, which had been so good to me.

As a result of those friendships and because I never viewed competitors as enemies, I cooperated with Catalist when they asked me to help them with data, handling certain projects for them. Eventually, after conversations with Catalist staff about forming a closer alliance between our firms, we were put on a monthly retainer to help answer voter file questions and to generally assist them in getting their business into shape. Many people may have felt I was cutting my own throat, but I felt it was sensible to work together with them rather than to stiffen the competition and eventually have my head bashed in. Direct competition simply did not make sense.

THE LANDSCAPE CHANGES, AGAIN

After the very successful Democratic election in 2006, the landscape changed again in a very major way. Howard Dean had been elected DNC chair and, after the 2006 election, changed the course of the DNC and as a result my business. At the postelection meeting of the Democratic Party in Jackson Hole, Wyoming, Dean announced that the DNC would provide voter files online to state parties for free. All data was to be compiled by DNC staff in house, and all state parties would be provided with VANs populated with the DNC voter files. The impact was something I immediately comprehended. Knowing the nature of the DNC technical staff and the relationship they had with VAN, I knew this would mean there would be no future state party business for Blaemire Communications. This was true for all other voter file vendors as well. And as much as the new policy was resisted by some of my clients, Dean stuck to his guns and forced the states to comply. No one in my business was asked for a minute of their time nor paid a dime to help the DNC do the project right. We were totally cut out.

This made 2007 a very tough year. Watching my clients disappear—free is very persuasive—I had to rethink the entire business. Similarly, many of the large organizations we depended on were gravitating to Catalist. Either they needed a national database—which we didn't have—or their officers were a part of Catalist, or both. Throughout this period, I continued doing work with Catalist and was being given an increasing number of friendly signs. I have likened the period to the DNC saying, "Go away kid, don't bother me," while Catalist was saying, "Why don't you come and join us?" It was not an easy decision, however. I had loyal employees I needed to worry about, but I also was growing weary. The year was difficult, like nothing I had ever gone through, and there were lots of aspects of running a business that I would not miss. So Laura Quinn, Catalist CEO, and I began a lengthy series of discussions that would eventually lead to merging my business with Catalist.

The possibility of changing this part of my life led to a great deal of reflection on the business. When I began, the business really didn't exist. In talks with individuals or groups, I always had to define what a voter file was and how we went about compiling one. Few campaigns had any understanding of how to use computers for real individual-level targeting and voter contact. But now the world had changed. Not only did all campaigns understand and require a voter-contact campaign, usually with a voter file, but the Internet had so democratized the business and wildly expanded the number of people processing voter data on personal computers that many people began to see the role I played almost as if I were a dinosaur. Maybe it was time for a change.

ENTER THE PREDICTIVE MODEL

The Catalist model is a unique one and something that made me feel comfortable quite quickly. I always built databases for clients paying me to do so. Building voter files is a costly process and, since I had never raised capital in any way, I could only build most state voter files when a client was paying for them. Catalist was building a national database to help progressives and Democrats, much of it paid for by investors, made available to organizations and campaigns through flat-rate subscriber fees. In other words, the more people bought from me in the past, the more they paid. Now, progressive and Democratic organizations and campaigns could pay flat costs for data everywhere in the country, removing the financial disincentive to using as much data as they might really need.

Also, by providing that access online with agreements from subscribers that would have their contact data plowed back into the online database, Catalist had a consistently growing database that provided a unique opportunity to go beyond what I was able to provide with Blaemire Communications by creating synthetics from the data. Whether these are called synthetics or models or microtargeting doesn't matter. The database could now be overlaid with this artificial intelligence, these predictive models, in a way that none of the old-guard voter-file vendors could compete with. Being at Catalist increasingly made sense to me.

The predictive modeling is what I would refer to as the third major development in this business. It is the ability to process a massive amount of information in a way that allows us to effectively predict behavior in many aspects of politics. No longer is it possible to be satisfied with simply having a long list of voter characteristics to choose from in the targeting and delivery of messages. Now, with enhanced databases that include hundreds of fields of commercial data, census data, specialty data, and individual-level response IDs, modeling techniques are employed to score the voter files with these synthetics. We were now presenting clients with the ability to target voters by partisanship in states that don't register by party. We could predict whether a voter would vote even though his or her vote history may be spotty. Other targeting was available that was completely unique—voters likely to own a gun, be a hunter, attend church weekly, and so forth.

The world of data is ever evolving, largely because we are in the midst of an explosion in technical innovation. The challenges to keep up with the developments in the online digital world are ever present and often daunting. It seemed to me then and now that Catalist is uniquely situated to remain on the cutting edge of those innovations, a posture that can serve the cause of progressive politics quite well. But Catalist is not the only place where Democrats or progressives go for data, regardless of what we might wish for. A large number of campaigns have access to data that is compiled by the DNC through the various Democratic state parties. There are also vendors who strive to compete in this space, most of which work for campaigns in both parties.

I am no expert on how this is done by Republicans and conservatives but have long been aware of the Republican Party's Voter Vault. This is a national voter file available to GOP campaigns that was once the standard others sought to match. I'm not sure that can be said any more, and I understand there are efforts among several conservative organizations to begin building a Catalist-like data infrastructure available to conservative campaigns and organizations.

Regardless of where campaigns go to get their data, there is a growing generation of campaigners who understand how important this aspect of campaigning is. While voter-contact campaigns neither create nor prevent landslides, they are important in closely contested races. I know of a number of experiences where it was clear that our efforts made the difference. In Mississippi several years ago, for instance, our voter file was used extensively by an aggressive and expensive phone and mail program in the governor's race. When the Democrat won by less than 1 percent, it was hard to ignore the importance of this effort.

In 2008, it became particularly clear that this form of campaigning was effective. The Catalist client base pulls data down from the Catalist on-line system for voter contact throughout the country. During the Obama campaign, our clients were pounding on our system as never before, using more data for mail, phones, and in-person contact than we had ever experienced. Also, the response data being obtained through the voter ID phase of the campaign was uploaded to the system, providing us with a large amount of individual data from which we could build models. All of this data, both coming out of the database and being added to it, allowed us to measure these efforts against controlled universes, comparing those who were contacted with those who were not. The results were startling. Voters contacted by at least one of the Catalist clients turned out in considerably greater numbers than those who were not. And among those who turned out, the Obama support measurement was even more gratifying in its effectiveness. In other words, the capabilities created by our models allowed more pinpoint targeting and, as the results have shown, a more effective brand of voter contact.

WHAT'S NEXT

Attention will now be turned to taking information like the data added to our database in 2008 to try and model communication channels, to discern whether a voter should be contacted by phone, by mail, by e-mail, or in person. Increasingly, we will be able to learn lessons important to political success because of the amount of data going into the system and coming out of it.

Computerized voter contact and sophisticated voter files are here to stay. Where they once satisfied the simple desire to make sure a campaign could send mail to a household or contact only those citizens who were registered to vote, it has arrived at a point where individualized and variable communication takes place consistent with what the predictive models tell us to do. For a campaign that in the past used voter-file data and always communicated with the four-of-four voter (someone voting in the last four elections), a turnout model will now take its place. The greater level of accuracy and possible cost savings will drive this on and into the future.

There have always been challenges in politics—challenges for campaigners to seek the best ways to target voters and communicate messages. That is more true today than ever before. How do we reach the 18- to 35-year-olds in the twenty-first century? They don't watch commercial television, listen to commercial radio, open their mail, or read newspapers or magazines. They can't be reached by traditional phone banking, and door-to-door efforts can never be assured. This directs all of us in the business of voter contact to increasingly rely on the digital space, to find ways to better target online communications, to communicate via the social networks, and to use those computers on our televisions known as cable boxes to communicate messages to targeted households. What is being attempted now may become commonplace within the decade. Those of us active in the 2008 presidential campaign are reminded that Facebook and YouTube didn't really exist in the previous presidential contest only four years earlier. Can we even imagine what might exist in 2012 or 2016 or 2020?

This part of politics has come a long way in a short period of time. While computer- generated voter contact hardly existed in the 1980 campaign that had such a major impact on my life, it was my profession only a few years later. While it is still my profession as I write this in 2011, it looks very little like it did when I started my own company 20 years ago. I won't even venture a guess as to what it might look like 20 years from now.

CHAPTER 10

Organizing Technology: The Marriage of Technology and the Field Campaign

Josh Hendler

Much has changed in the modern political campaign over the course of the last three presidential election cycles. The most dramatic change is the emergence of technology as a mechanism to engage volunteers and improve how campaigns are run and operated. Field organizing is now deeply connected to technology in many ways, and good field organizers are very familiar with data and social media.

Profound technological progress has been made in the field programs of Democratic campaigns. I've seen this up close and personal, first as a field operative and most recently as the technology director for the Democratic National Committee and Organizing for America. I would argue that some of the greatest potential to enhance field programs and structures with technology lies largely unfulfilled. Looking to the future, I believe that the best hope of moving the field forward involves a close partnership between engineers and organizers.

MANCHESTER, NEW HAMPSHIRE, 2004

My first foray into politics came during the 2004 presidential campaign. It was a major turning point for technology and politics, mostly because political campaigns could no longer afford to ignore the world that was changing around them. But it was also because an influx of politically charged technologists, angry over a frustrating situation, wanted to do something about it through their craft. I was one of the first engineers who decided to leave their corporate jobs and join the campaign life.

When I first arrived in Little Rock, Arkansas, to work for Wes Clark's fledgling presidential campaign, I was not entirely sure what to expect. I had worked a bit with the Draft Clark movement, a grassroots enter- prise with the aim of convincing the general to run for office. I knew more about Wes Clark than I did about working on a campaign. My first few weeks were an incredible learning experience. I had no idea what *GOTV* meant—a term (meaning get-out-the-vote) that was at the core of our (and every campaign's) field program.

Working in Little Rock at campaign headquarters allowed me to build critical campaign technology and roll out Web applications on the cam- paign's Web site. Work ranged from creating fundamentals—like the core Web database for the campaign—to helping the political team build databases of voter lists. These efforts allowed me to see the campaign from a national viewpoint, but I was missing an important perspective— what the local campaign office was like.

If I was inspired and excited during my first few days in Little Rock, I was at the other end of the spectrum when I was shipped off to New Hampshire for the last few days before the primary. The campaign was clearly not going to succeed, and while I was proud of what we had done, I was also more realistic about what technology was able to do. We could not change the media narrative, we could not stop organizational infight- ing, and we could not fundamentally change the outcome. I was not hopeful about New Hampshire and did not think I was going to be able to help very much. New Hampshire, however, turned out to be incredibly instructive.

Walking into a campaign office in the middle of a GOTV program looks like organized chaos. I met the relevant data people in the office, and after several hours I was genuinely surprised. The New Hampshire field operation was run out of a single Microsoft Access database. The data director for the office (who seemed quite competent) would cut lists and save them as spreadsheets, or he would print walk lists and they would be distributed through the office. The database held the voter file, the list of those registered to vote, which is the core of any field program. It allows campaigners to contact only people who are eligible to vote on Election Day rather than wasting time and energy speaking to people who cannot legally participate. Using a voter file, as opposed to the phone book, radically increases the efficiency of a field program.

I also spent some time in New Hampshire calling potential voters. I was frustrated when I dialed a disconnected phone number or when

I heard that the voter I was trying to reach had not lived there for years. There had to be a better way than cutting lists out of an Access database, calling voters who were not there, and e-mailing lists around on a buggy wireless connection. They couldn't even get the right voters on the phone. This was the moment that I realized that there was potential to fix a big problem.

WASHINGTON, DC, 2004

After Wes Clark's campaign, I returned to my corporate job. Weeks later, however, I submitted my resignation and joined John Kerry's campaign. I had found political campaigns intoxicating. They were fast paced and results driven, and they had a clear goal—winning 50 percent plus one additional vote on Election Day. The clarity of the mission and the clear role for a technologist was exciting, and it was something that I could not turn down.

I was assigned to work on the Internet team at Kerry headquarters in Washington, DC. The Internet team was the precursor to today's new media or digital shop. I also learned that the technology team at the DNC was playing a parallel significant and independent role in shaping technology for the campaign.

Most of my work on the Kerry campaign focused on two important but different areas. First, I worked to ensure that our donation technology systems could handle the large volume of transactions as we approached the 2004 Democratic Convention. Online fundraising had become a critical element of the overall campaign fundraising apparatus, and ensuring that the fundraising system could withstand the traffic was critical.

The second tool that I focused on was called PhoneCorps. That tool empowered volunteers in nontargeted states to call volunteers in targeted states and ask them to attend a canvass or phone bank. Both the Dean and Clark campaigns used variants of grassroots calling tools. These were systems where a user sitting at home in front of his or her computer could enter contact information, download a script and lists of phone numbers, and start making phone calls asking people to vote.

We were intrigued at the success of grassroots calling tools; the raw numbers of calls at both the Dean and Clark campaigns were impressive. However, we were not sure of the quality of calls made by volunteers sitting at home. We had no data about whether those calls were helpful or detrimental, and we would not know for sure until Election Day. Our solution to this problem was, in retrospect, somewhat obvious. Instead of having our volunteers making calls to ask people to vote, we would focus on another goal—ensuring that there was good turnout to phone banks and canvasses in swing states across the country. Our team of regional "desks" who spoke to campaigns across the country constantly heard from field offices that they needed help, and volunteers was something we could provide.

The major upside of recruiting volunteers via our tool was that it was countable. When a volunteer called another volunteer using the tool, they would enter whether or not the call recipient had RSVPed. Those results could then be tracked against the people who actually showed up for the event (though this proved harder than we had anticipated.) We could also measure the RSVP rate and the success rate by the state of the caller and the call recipient. These were hard numbers, and we could measure our impact on a day-to-day basis. We knew that our volunteers were doing something meaningful. This allowed us to direct nontargeted volunteers via e-mail to PhoneCorps and targeted volunteers directly to local events.

The Internet team considered PhoneCorps to be terrifically successful. We recruited thousands of volunteers across the country who we knew would make a difference making calls and knocking on doors. It was, however, an early lesson in the lack of coordination between field and technology. While there was a terrific team at the DNC managing field for the national campaign (headed by the wonderful Karen Hicks, a veteran field consultant), the Internet team was running its program largely independently. The field team sat on Capitol Hill at the DNC, while the Internet team sat at Kerry headquarters downtown. While we were certainly able to help the field program nationally, we knew that there was never deep enough integration between technology and field.

There were also frustrating moments that showed how much more opportunity there was for earlier engagement with technologists. Several days before the election, a field team official approached the Internet department's organizing team and asked if we could help. They needed to find a way to distribute lists to call centers around the country. Could they use PhoneCorps to distribute the call lists? The answer was maybe, and it would require quite a bit of last-minute rejiggering of the existing technology. The changes were made and pushed out in the hours before Election Day. And when Election Day came, the tool was barely utilized. I knew these problems were solvable but couldn't be adequately addressed with last-minute hacks. I was frustrated. In retrospect, it is yet another example of why technologists can't be an accessory to a political campaign but need to be critical actors engaged earlier rather than later.

WASHINGTON, DC, 2007

After the loss of the Kerry campaign and after a stint working with the Labour Party in the United Kingdom during their 2005 general election, I moved into Governor Howard Dean's DNC as the director of political data and analytics. Dean had started to shift the DNC's direction and was intent on making sure it had twenty-first century technology.

Focusing on data at the DNC allowed me to address some of the less sexy but incredibly important issues like the party's national voter file. This effort was as much political as it was technological and involved close collaboration with all 50 state Democratic parties to come up with a unified national data sharing agreement—one that would allow both the state parties and the national committee to use the data without having to constantly negotiate agreements or determine who owned a particular data point.

Early on, I was incredibly impressed and slightly surprised by the new DNC's commitment to investing both in data and the state parties. I sat at a senior meeting with Tom McMahon, the DNC's executive director, and Mark Brewer, the chair of the Association of State Chairs and, in conjunction with Ben Self, the DNC's then technology director, explained what was needed to develop a more unified national voter file. I expected to hear snoring; data wasn't sexy, and in my experience it was the last thing people wanted to invest in. Instead, the response was overwhelming, and the enthusiasm in the room was exhilarating, if unexpected. The DNC leadership got it.

One of my first moves at the DNC was hiring Katie Allen, a seasoned field organizer, within the technology department to help me keep grounded in the reality of an organizer's life. Over the next two years, our focus would remain almost entirely on the data: How could we ensure that we had the best possible phone number for a voter? How could we use consumer data to better predict whether or not someone would turn out to vote on Election Day? I was confident data would actually help win votes on the ground, but I also knew it was only the beginning of what was possible.

Technology use by the field campaign was also becoming a hot topic. A number of outside progressive organizations had banded together with investors to create a data technology company called Catalist. This was a very significant development in the progressive technology world. This also meant that we were presented with a critical question: should we build our voter file within the DNC or work with an outside group?

On the one hand, working with Catalist meant that we could outsource a very significant technology challenge. Our team would not need to be nearly as large, and we could spend time focusing on other projects. On the other hand, we could not control our own destiny. We would be putting an essential element of party infrastructure in the hands of an outside vendor. The decision was not an easy one and would surely make people unhappy either way. We also had to consider the will of the state democratic parties, who had become equal partners for the first time in managing the national voter file. After close consultations, the consensus within both the DNC and at state parties was a preference for owning our own infrastructure as well as our data. This was a pivotal moment for the Democratic Party and progressive groups. People were finally taking data seriously, and they were investing real money in solving these problems.

Perhaps the largest change I was able to enact was to ensure that no field office would ever have to use an Access database again for the voter file. As a result of the efforts of our team and the team at the Voter Activation Network (VAN) that had built the software, we were able to provide a national Web-based interface for access and distributing lists of voters. Put into place in early 2007, VoteBuilder allowed any field organizer to log in to a Web site, create a search based on any data points within the system, and generate reports. A field organizer could now search for voters in New Hampshire who had voted in 2004 and 2008 but not 2006, were male, and had registered to vote as a Democrat. They could then take that search and use a Google map to select voters for a walk list. That walk list could then be pushed to an iPhone, where a canvasser could log in and walk with it.

Choosing the VAN as the voter-file platform of choice was controversial at the time. The VAN already had many state parties as clients and was well on its way to getting more over the course of the year. But they also had competitors who had invested significantly in their platforms and client relationships. There were many internal conversations at the DNC about the prospect of choosing a "winner." Would we be better off just letting the market decide and letting state parties decide for themselves? How could we decide between a set of vendors, each of which had their own passionate defenders? On the other hand, we knew small state parties couldn't afford to pay for a platform. And we also knew that when field organizers traveled, a unified national voter file interface could yield huge benefits. Furthermore, with the DNC operating a national interface, we could effectively enable the collection of all Democratic political data in one place for the first time ever.

Although some of the competitors had good product offerings, after conducting a thorough review we concluded that VAN had the best feature set. We also realized that migration to the VAN would be the simplest, considering the number of states that had already adopted it as a platform. After a period of intense negotiations, we eventually signed with the VAN to host the voter-file interface in all 50 states plus the District of Columbia.

The other major project that occupied my time at the DNC was called Neighbor-to-Neighbor. Initially spearheaded by Keith Goodman of the DNC's political department, the goal of the project was to bring the lessons from distributed phone banking (largely from 2004) to canvassing. If volunteers could use a Web-based tool to make phone calls from home, then why couldn't they also use a Web-based tool to print a packet with a list of doors to knock on?

Neighbor-to-Neighbor's goal was to empower distributed walking, which means that any night, a user could log in, print a list of names and addresses, go canvassing, and enter their information. Printing out the walk packet would take minutes and would not involve a trip to the local field office. The project was built in coordination between the DNC's political department, its technology department, and Blue State Digital.

Neighbor-to-Neighbor was not a wonderful success from a programmatic perspective. Prior to the 2008 campaign, there were not that many people who printed out walk lists and went canvassing. Neighbor-to-Neighbor did, however, show a great deal of potential from a process perspective. It represented a close collaboration with organizers, and there was a new emphasis on iterating, or continually improving, the product and early user testing. I sat through an informal focus group in northern Virginia with committed volunteers who saw the product. Their feedback was not all positive, but it was an important connection between engineers and organizers that had not existed before. We were now having direct conversations with volunteers who had visited field offices frequently, made calls, and knocked on doors. They were not the vanguard of those using online organizing tools, but rather they were everyday volunteer organizers who understood more about persuading voters than using online systems. Even though the feedback did not dramatically change the product, I knew that this was exactly the sort of feedback loop that we needed.

CHICAGO, 2008

While I would not have guessed it in 2007 during the early days of Neighbor-to-Neighbor, I spent the last several months of 2008 focused on the Obama campaign. I did this as a consultant with an international software consultancy, ThoughtWorks, which had been hired to work in close collaboration with the Obama campaign, the DNC, and Blue State Digital to improve Neighbor-to-Neighbor and ensure that it worked smoothly on (and before) Election Day.

The product that I worked on in 2008 through ThoughtWorks differed from the product that we had originally built in 2007. Rather than being a canvassing tool it was now almost exclusively dedicated to allowing volunteers at home to make voter contact calls. One major change was that the new Neighbor-to-Neighbor was linked into the rest of the party's data infrastructure. When someone was contacted using the tool, the record that the person was contacted would be available through VoteBuilder (the DNC's national voter file interface.) This was a significant step forward for field and technology integration. Field organizers constantly complain about data from new online tools that do not flow back to the voter file or central constituent database. How could you have a complete snapshot of a voter if offline data lived in one database and online data lived somewhere else?

Much of my time had been spent shuttling back and forth between the campaign headquarters in Chicago and Boston, where most of the engineering work was being done. Unfortunately, the engineers were once again in a different room from the organizers. I focused on making connections, helping the developers understand what the campaign staff needed, and helping the campaign staff to understand what the developers needed. Coordination only went so far. Neighbor-to-Neighbor was being managed out of the terrific Obama new media shop, and while the organizing team was involved, it was largely focused on its important offline priorities.

Thankfully, the team at Obama headquarters that I worked with was full of stars. Keith Goodman worked out of Chicago, playing the role of product and project manager. Judith Freeman and Chris Hughes both played integral roles in ensuring that the project succeeded. Neighbor-to-Neighbor was responsible for over one million calls on Election Day 2008. The system also worked without any outage over the course of Election Day. I felt lucky to have had the privilege to work with both the campaign team and the talented development team, but I came away from the experience thinking that there remained potential for much better collaboration between engineers and organizers; the lack of a common language between them still reared its ugly head.

WASHINGTON, DC, NOVEMBER 2010

Almost seven years after moving to Little Rock to work for Wes Clark, a tremendous amount had changed in political technology. Soon after the

2008 election, I became director of technology at the DNC, which included Organizing for America, the successor organization to Obama for America.

This was my second time working within the DNC and another opportunity to make a lasting difference within the national Democratic Party. One of the biggest challenges that I had seen before was the lack of technological innovation coming out of the party. While private political technology companies often came up with exciting new products, technology *inside* the party was often more associated with fixing people's computers than rolling out field-organizing tools. To change this situation, I hired Nathan Woodhull, a technologist and organizer, to lead the DNC's innovation labs team. My idea was simple—create a team whose goal was to work closely with other labs, come up with new software ideas, and prototype them. Even if 9 out of 10 projects were considered failures, the one successful project could be a huge success.

As expected, the innovation lab had both successes and failures. We were able to spend a significant amount of time working closely with the DNC's terrific organizing team and talk to them about what mattered. Our team was prolific, and we produced a number of online political tools ranging from a successor to Neighbor-to-Neighbor to an iPhone-based canvassing application. We focused much of our time on fundamentals and continued working to ensure that we had great data for organizers and that the technological plumbing existed for allowing others to get access to that voter data. It was these fundamentals that were often forgotten in the past—and were just as critical as ever to get right.

Building the iPhone canvassing application was an incredibly instructive experience. From a user-interface and usability perspective, the app that got built was unparalleled. A user could pick up an iPhone, click a few buttons, and start canvassing within 30 seconds. Data entry was similarly streamlined, allowing users to easily enter feedback from users at the door and have data streamed back into the system either in real time or when the user was back within Wi-Fi or 3G service.

The app never quite lived up to its potential. The reasons, while hard to know for sure, were twofold. First, as was evidenced by various attempts at Neighbor-to-Neighbor, users are skeptical of canvassing by themselves. Canvassing can be a scary experience, and taking the initiative to start canvassing without working with a field office is difficult. Second, it wasn't possible for field organizers to transfer walk lists to iPhones. So if a field organizer spent time cutting a universe for a list, they could not give a volunteer with an iPhone at the field office that list. Intriguingly, the source of the problem turned out to be about humans, not technology. We had failed to anticipate the organizers' perspective properly, and as a result the technology wasn't as successful as it could have been.

In my capacity as DNC technology director, I was able to work hand in hand with many of the top progressive technology firms. New firms like NationalField popped up during the 2008 election cycle, born out of frustration of field organizers that there was no way to manage volunteer and staff reporting properly. More established firms like NGP and VAN (which merged while I was working at the DNC to become NGP VAN) continued to roll out new products. These firms all shared a common element; they were all founded by technologists and organizers who were frustrated with the status quo.

THE PROBLEM AFTER ALL THESE YEARS

Having now worked in political technology for more than seven years, I have observed one problem that continues to haunt many projects: the distance between offline organizers, online organizers, and technologists, while shrinking, still represents a significant barrier to deploying technology successfully in politics. It is not that these groups do not communicate; there are often long and extended dialogues about what should and should not be built. Rather it is more often a failure of process and a failure to see the venture as a partnership rather than work for hire.

As I have seen from playing a role in the birth of several grassroots voter-contact tools, the process has improved over time. Offline organizers have started to understand technology. The premise that it is okay to take a risk and to sometimes fail has started to become more acceptable. Technologists must now balance the demands of distinct offline and online organizing teams. These groups do not always see eye to eye and have different needs and responsibilities within the campaign organization. Until greater collaboration exists, and as long as there are partitions between engineers and organizers, the promise of political technology, especially in field, will not reach its full potential.

THE PATH FORWARD

If the story of field and technology is one of progress but unfulfilled hope, how do we move forward? Here are a few ideas:

Engineers Should Become Organizers, Too

The greatest success I have seen with organizers working in politics occurs when engineers who have actually participated in the process are the ones creating the tools. That means going out on a canvass and knocking on voters' doors, making get-out-the-vote calls from a campaign headquarters, or entering data after a team comes back from canvassing. It is hard to describe all of the details of the organizing domain's challenges, and there is absolutely nothing better than having engineers who understand the pain firsthand. That is, for example, exactly how VAN—progressive field technology's most successful company—was formed.

Iterate Quickly, Fail Fast

Fear of negative press is a constant specter on campaigns. This is paired with an instinct for political organizations to overplan projects and to write long specifications for an application that will be extinct by the time it is completed. Both of these instincts work against the likelihood of success of technology projects in politics. In order for projects to have a chance of succeeding, political organizations need to be willing to build tools incrementally and to learn from either their success or failure. Campaigns have a hard time acknowledging that failure can be just as valuable as success, but it is the only mechanism for determining what actually works.

There Is Nothing More Critical Than Feedback from Volunteers

Political technology often builds tools focused around the most important audience of all—volunteers. In some sense, it is this audience that is the most poorly served. They are often the guinea pigs for new tools that do not quite work the way they are intended. A frustrated volunteer translates to a volunteer who may not come back. The most important aspect of any project that is intended for use by volunteers is ensuring that there are frequent communications between the users of the application and the builders. This can be accomplished via informal focus groups, weekly conference calls, or individual calls.

Believe in Progress and Innovation

While there is clearly potential for further collaboration between engineers and organizers, the story of technology and politics has largely been a story of innovation. New tools haven't always made people's lives easier, and innovation hasn't come easy. But on the whole, innovation in political technology has resulted in more volunteer engagement, not less. It has lowered the bar to entry for people who never volunteered with a campaign before to take action. Data has improved, if incrementally, over the years, and there has been a general trend away from segmentation and toward integration.

2012 AND BEYOND

As the Obama campaign team in Chicago forms, there will be both new challenges and old problems. They will have to decide how much technology they want to build versus buy. How much time should they invest in building core infrastructure themselves? Weighing the interests of fundraising, field, and online organizing will only get harder in 2012, with greater technology needs on all three fronts. There are, however, several lessons from previous campaigns that the Obama campaign (and frankly, any smart presidential campaign) should keep in mind.

First, be pragmatists at heart. Political campaigns are over in a heartbeat, even when you start early. That means that every decision needs to be weighed against the clock, and that clocks runs out much more quickly than anyone would like. This means cutting projects that may take too long even if that project is near and dear to your heart.

Second, focus on the field-facing technology equally as much as consumer-facing technology. While not public-facing as much as consumer-facing technology, there still exist tremendous opportunities for fundamentally improving the lives of field organizers and volunteers with relatively simple technology. As stated before, this will require incredibly close collaboration between the technology and field arms of the campaign.

And finally, think broadly about technology's role in the campaign. While technology will be a services organization in some sense, it shouldn't solely exist to serve other departments. Technology should have an opinion as well as a seat at the table in major campaign decisions.

CHAPTER 11

A New Model: VAN and the Challenge of the Voter-File Interface

Mark L. Sullivan

1996

As the final weekend of the campaign approached, those of us who were privy to the daily tracking polls could hardly help but panic. In the waning days of October 1996, my boss and idol, Senator Tom Harkin of Iowa, was in a free fall. A huge summertime lead had vanished, leaving us in a dead tie with Jim Ross Lightfoot, our challenger with a hard-right record and plenty of aw-shucks rural charm.

With the media buys decided, the public debates behind us, and the last glossy brochures hitting the mailboxes, it was now down to the field program. In truly close races, the edge goes to the campaign that does the better job of cajoling its known supporters to get to the polls before time runs out.

But our field operation was suddenly struck by catastrophe. The normal logistical hurdles back then were daunting enough on their own. On top of that, an unexpected snafu in the ordering process meant that Election Day "walk decks"—thousands of stacks of note cards about voters supposedly arranged in walkable order and shipped to Iowa from a company in Virginia—weren't sorted correctly. Hundreds of thousands of note cards needed to be manually resorted into proper walking order, an urgency that required every human resource to be reassigned.

That weekend, every volunteer and staff member in sight dropped their other responsibilities and seated themselves among the endless piles of boxes, cards, and maps. As the campaign's research director, that included me, so I spent that last weekend getting a glimpse into the unknown and complicated work of the field operation.

Fortunately, that was Tom Harkin's last race of the twentieth century, both literally and metaphorically. By the time he ran again in 2002 we were set to take the world of field organizing from an era of 3″ × 5″ index cards and handwritten notes into the Internet age. The payoff would be impressive: success would create vast new efficiencies empowering state Democratic parties and the DNC and providing a technological advantage for Democrats for several election cycles (and counting).

But the revolution would not come easy. Competing visions would cause bumps, setbacks, and sometimes great conflict. And during the six years the revolution unfolded and spread, the answer to one central question would define success: how do you scale it? A true solution for the progressive movement would ultimately facilitate many thousands of users simultaneously entering and extracting vast amounts of data—and that test would separate winners from losers.

FIELD OPERATIONS AND THE VOTER FILE

The field operation is the part of the campaign that works to push supportive voters to the polls on Election Day as well as during early or absentee voting windows. Because it involves one-on-one communication—volunteers knocking on doors, phone banks dialing up supporters, and poll watchers monitoring polling locations to track who has already arrived to vote—the gains are marginal. Each successful iteration produces exactly one vote. In a blowout election, the field operation is largely irrelevant. But in close races, the candidate with the better field program is the one more likely to eke out that extra 2- or 4-point advantage needed to go over the top.

A good field operation requires enormous coordination of resources. Huge numbers of staff and volunteers must be deployed, their effectiveness overwhelmingly driven by the campaign's command over data. The advantage goes to the campaign that (1) knows the most about its voters and (2) manages to use its resources most effectively to act on that knowledge.

Part one of that equation involves long and costly efforts to "ID" the voting population. By knocking on doors and making phone calls, campaigns try to build up a knowledge base of their voters and get a handle on the following: Which of the two million Iowa voters are likely to support us? Who supports our opponent? Who is sitting on the fence, and what can we do to persuade them over to our side? Who is likely to vote on their own and who needs a push?

A new campaign manager's earliest responsibilities include a thorough analysis of the voting population to assess how much voter ID needs to occur and to budget accordingly for the early stages of the field operation. In the twentieth century, this could be an excruciating process. To begin with, the voter file was simply a complicated beast to deal with. Back then, few desktop computers could process a database of millions of records with any reasonable performance. No commercial software existed to facilitate easy access to the data. Campaign staff often relied on highly technical, and not always especially communicative, staff or volunteer computer geeks for this analysis.

In many cases, parties and campaigns contracted with voter file vendors who would house their data on mainframe computers and ship printed lists, mailing labels, walk decks, or data files to the campaign as needed. In the case of the 1996 Harkin campaign, the vendor had to begin preparing the walk decks weeks in advance of Election Day, meaning that any additional voter ID efforts wouldn't be accounted for. Then the decks needed to be shipped all over the state. The process was long and tedious at best and left little room for flexibility. Reflecting on the added stress of the ordering mistake, field director Lisa Sherman recalled, "You just couldn't pivot."

Worst of all were the extreme problems with storing data collected in the field. Even if you succeeded in scheduling lots of volunteers in just the right targeted neighborhoods, they would return at the end of the day with walking lists and calling lists covered in cryptic scribbles. Given a lack of efficient systems for data entry, those lists would notoriously pile up in boxes, often left to collect dust once the campaign was over.

Even if one campaign in a state was somehow good at data entry— meaning they were successfully capturing their IDs, cleaning up phone numbers, noting bad addresses, marking deceased voters, and so forth— that data would rarely get shared with other Democratic campaigns spending resources trying to communicate with the same voters. And it was even more unlikely that this data would migrate from one campaign cycle to the next.

2002: BUILDING A NEW MODEL

When Al Gore faced George Bush in the 2000 presidential election, his Iowa campaign poured last-minute field resources into efforts to encourage supporters to take advantage of Iowa's new no-excuses absentee voting law. The Iowa battle between Bush and Gore ended in a razor-thin margin tilted by the Gore absentee strategy. Of all the votes cast at the Iowa polls on Election Day, Bush led Gore by 7,000 votes. But at 4:00 a.m. when the absentee ballots had been counted, Gore's 11,000-vote lead pushed him over the top. Things in Florida may have gone awry for Al Gore that night, but the superior field strategy gave him a 4,000-vote margin of victory in Iowa.

By the time Senator Harkin would be up for reelection in 2002, he was determined to exploit that strategy on a vastly larger scale. Facing yet another fierce battle, this time against Greg Ganske, an affable and moderate congressman from Des Moines, Harkin was determined to build the most effective field operation ever seen, one tightly coordinated with Governor Tom Vilsack's own reelection race. The plans called for 100 paid organizers who would spend the summer knocking on doors, identifying supporters, and especially trying to get friendly voters to fill out those absentee request forms.

To pull this off effectively, two big changes had to take place. First, if the Iowa Democratic Party could put the voter file online and make it available to every Democratic campaign everywhere in the state, vast efficiencies would be gained. Never again would resources be spent twice calling the same bad phone number or mailing to the same dead voter. And if that database were permanently available, data could even persist from election cycle to election cycle.

Second, not only should the data be available to activists wherever they were, but so should the tools needed to solve the implacable problems associated with data entry. To squeeze as much efficiency as possible out of paid organizers, they would be armed with Palm Pilots instead of walk lists, making their data transfers almost totally electronic—no more indecipherable scribbles.

To accomplish these goals, the Iowa Democratic Party kicked off a formal process to move the voter file online. They issued a request for proposals in the summer of 2001, inviting firms to bid for a contract through 2002. These included Trimeros and Astro 2000, two companies starting to get actively involved in online voter file work, as well as some local technology companies with a more corporate bent.

The party appointed a review team to vet the proposals, choose a list of finalists, and then meet with those finalists for detailed presentations. As the trusted data consultant to both Senator Harkin and Governor Vilsack, I was asked to represent both leading office holders on that committee.

But something was lacking from every proposal. The nonpolitical firms bidding were unable to demonstrate any likelihood to grasp the central concepts of how campaigns work. Trimeros, a known entity that had entered the contest with a decided edge, turned the committee off with a lack of willingness to meet the party's ambitious development goals despite a steep price tag.

As I reported my frustrations back to the two campaigns I was representing, they both insisted on positing the same absurd question: in a world where Dick Cheney could pick himself to be vice president, why didn't I just do this work myself? The answer was easy—because I wasn't a Web programmer and I knew nothing about programming for Palm Pilots. Those answers met only with increasing pressure to "figure it out" so that the technology program could move forward under the direction of someone more trusted by the leading stakeholders.

Ultimately, that made sense. I had worked on campaigns for a dozen years, I adored both Tom Harkin and Tom Vilsack, and I was completely committed to the teams the Iowa Democratic Party and the two campaigns had in place. I had taught myself to build databases to solve campaign challenges that were not traditionally data driven and taught myself to program so that I could turn those databases into useful applications for myself and others. I was (and remain) obsessed with the kind of details that others find unimportant, resulting in an ability to create systems that were both powerful and intuitive.

What I needed was someone to help balance out my technical skills, and by chance I had recently met Steve Adler while we were both consulting for the Massachusetts AFL-CIO. Steve was likable and smart and understood Internet programming, so we decided to join forces to tackle my Iowa project. Suddenly I found myself joined at the hip with a new business partner, getting a crash course in Web programming, and working exhaustively to build something vastly more complex than either of us had ever taken on. I worked from my home in Cambridge while Steve worked out of his house in Rhode Island, spending countless hours on the phone together.

One day while Steve and I were programming together in his cramped home office, a graphic designer we had hired called to ask an unexpected question: what was this thing called? His design had to include the name of the product. I explained that the client was the Iowa Democratic Party and their name should be on the product. Sure, he said, it's the party's thing, but what is the name of the actual *thing*? The question had never crossed my mind, but under pressure I blurted out a description of what this thing was—a voter, um, activation, um, network.

Just like that, I had named our product and our fledgling new company. Since that name was now baked into our graphic design, I let the party know, uncertain what the reaction would be. Executive Director Jeani Murray immediately took a liking to the acronym VAN. At her request, we secured the URL drivethevan.com as its entry point, and a generation of vehicular puns and analogies rolled off the assembly line.

The Iowa Democratic Party started to distribute access to its new system in the early months of 2002, making it available not just to the marquee races for governor and senator but to legislative races as well. Meanwhile, we struggled to keep up with demands for core functionality and performance. By summer we had to take on the unique challenges of the Palm Pilot–based canvassing operations and the demands of the ambitious absentee ballot collection and tracking effort.

The Iowa Democratic Party had experimented with Palm Pilots the previous summer. In a world where smart phones were yet unknown, Palm Pilots represented cutting-edge technology and introduced enormous efficiency by wiping out most of the data entry needs. Canvassers would enter information collected at the door straight into their Palm Pilots. At the end of the night the Palm Pilots would be synced back to a program on a campaign computer. It took a few more clumsy steps to transfer that data back into the online voter file, but the impact on productivity was enormous.

Through the combination of an incredibly well-organized canvassing operation and sophisticated new technology to manage it, our campaigns enjoyed two advantages our Republican counterparts clearly lacked—a giant lead in absentee voting and reliable knowledge of just how big that lead was. As canvass leaders across the state acquired absentee voting data from county clerks and loaded it into the VAN, I would spit out summary reports each morning of that activity and e-mail them to top campaign staff. That report, nicknamed "the drug," showed an ever-increasing gap between the early voting performance of registered Democrats and Republicans.

We entered Election Day with the confident knowledge that we held a virtually unsurpassable lead of more than 60,000 Democratic voters over Republican voters among the votes already cast. Almost as satisfying was our ability to glean from Republican claims in the press that they had little knowledge of just how lopsided those numbers were.

Election Day 2002 was a rough one for Democrats across the United States. While we celebrated a carefully orchestrated field-driven victory in Iowa, Democrats were pummeled nearly everywhere else. While Tom Harkin was winning a comfortable victory over the fifth sitting member of Congress that he had defeated in his career, Democrats lost enough other races that we lost control of the Senate and Harkin lost his Agriculture Committee chair.

Looking ahead to the challenges of 2004, including President George Bush's reelection bid, many Democrats turned to Iowa for inspiration. Could the lessons from Iowa help erase the advantage Republicans supposedly had from their vaunted "72-hour program?" We hoped so, but scaling our voter file technology from Iowa to a national program would involve more pain than we could imagine.

LOOKING AHEAD TO 2004: ACT AND THE BATTLE OF PHILADELPHIA

As soon as the dust settled from 2002, unprecedented efforts to defeat George Bush began to take shape. Wealthy liberal donors like George Soros funded a new independent entity called America Coming Together (ACT) that promised to raise $100 million to fund a massive field operation in more than a dozen key battleground states.

I soon found myself at the ACT planning table with top political operatives of all stripes from across the country. Somehow this group of people faced the burden of managing a field operation in battleground states on an unprecedented scale, and technology like ours would be critical for its success. VAN's accomplishments quickly drew both heightened demand and heightened scrutiny. Our first chance to prove ourselves to ACT would come with a pilot project in Philadelphia, where Mayor John Street was up for a tough off-year 2003 reelection fight.

But even as ACT signed us up to build the database and Palm technology for the Philadelphia canvassing operation, they obsessed over the question of whether we could scale the technology. Supporting a successful field operation in Iowa was one thing, but could we do that in Philadelphia and then in states like Ohio and Pennsylvania in 2004? Steve Rosenthal, ACT's executive director, would repeatedly grill us about "capacity," not surprisingly since we were little more than two people who had thrown together a technology platform that managed to survive a general election in two states.

As we began to slowly hire more talent, the capacity questions would inevitably focus on how many people we had. But we would argue that the relevant question was not how many people we had but what kind of vision we had for scalability. However proud we were of the attention our Iowa program had drawn, we knew better than anyone the technical limitations of what we had built.

To scale from 20 team leaders with specially set up computers to thousands of canvassers scattered across the nation, it was clear that we needed to radically change the program. We laid out a four-part plan to drastically revamp the relationship between the Web application and the Palm Pilots.

This ambitious development agenda included (1) dynamic scripts that would control the content of the Palm Pilot application; (2) our own proprietary Palm Pilot application, fully generated by the Web application and scripts; (3) a Hot Sync client that would enable Palm Pilots to hot sync directly to our servers to eliminate reliance on any other local software or transfer procedures; and (4) technology to allow many Palm Pilots to hot sync simultaneously with a server, since thousands of Palms would need to sync each day, often during concentrated periods.

We arrived in Philadelphia with a clear mandate for scalability from ACT and an obsessive focus on our four-part plan for getting there. It would take every resource we could muster to pull it off in an evershrinking time frame. But we had barely arrived at Mayor Street's campaign headquarters before other competing agendas began to emerge.

It quickly became clear that we weren't in Iowa anymore, surrounded by allies who implicitly trusted me as their reliable adviser on matters technological. Instead we were in the domain of a tough, respected, and streetsmart lead campaign strategist named Tom Lindenfeld and plenty of his allies and protégés. Lindenfeld knew Philadelphia, he knew field, he knew data, and he knew what he needed to run his field operation. On top of that, he was extremely close to and trusted by ACT chief Steve Rosenthal.

We immediately ran into conflicts with the team in Philadelphia, who were demanding new features for the Palm Pilot application, such as tools to allow canvassers to track lunch breaks. We could not possibly focus on the features Philly wanted, whether useful or quirky, and meet the scalability mandate from ACT. The only path forward was to take a stable, useful, and proven core application and focus relentlessly on the scalability agenda.

Meetings and phone calls became ugly, laced with insinuations or outright claims that we weren't listening, or were lazy, or didn't care, or just didn't understand field operations. On a day-to-day basis we worked closely with some talented technical staff brought into the campaign by Lindenfeld. One day we learned that one of them, Howard Moseley, had been building his own alternative Palm application, one that had some of the features we were refusing to build. Now Lindenfeld had a great weapon against us—proof that his own team could build the features that we were too "stupid" or "lazy" or "stubborn" to make.

Thus began a complete schism, with Lindenfeld and his team abandoning parts of our technology and building and advocating for their own competing technology. They began a new company called Sirius Technology Solutions (which seemed to suggest that they, unlike us, were "serious") and began to aggressively show off their "better" technology.

Back at ACT, Rosenthal and others were caught in the middle, uncertain whom to believe—the kids at VAN with some success under their belts or the highly trusted Lindenfeld and his team. And as fall approached it was time to begin gearing up for field operations on the ground in Ohio and other states.

Finally, they came to a decision. ACT would contract with VAN to build the technology for Ohio and Missouri and with Sirius Solutions to build a statewide system for Pennsylvania. Following the launch of those systems, additional state contracts would be awarded based on success.

So we pulled out of Pennsylvania altogether, began building a multi-state ACT platform starting with Ohio and Missouri, and stayed laser focused on our scalability program for the Palm Pilots. In early 2004, ACT did indeed begin to award new state contracts. We won nine of those contracts based on our continuous success in scaling our program. Only one state contract went to another firm—Oregon went to Astro 2000, which was based in Portland and was too tightly tied into the political establishment there to get displaced.

Throughout the year we heard little more than rumors out of Pennsylvania, where the technology program apparently never came together with any success. Sirius Solutions did not win any more state contracts from ACT, and after the 2004 election we never heard of them again. Our stubborn focus on building a scalable program distributable to thousands of staff and volunteers had been the right call.

DNC AND THE PATH TOWARD VOTEBUILDER

While we were working with ACT in 11 states, expansion of voter file technology available directly to campaigns was largely left to the state parties, who engaged VAN and other companies in competitions for their business as they chose to go online. We repeatedly went up against Trimeros and Astro 2000, as well as another new entrant into the market, Blaemire Communications.

Bob Blaemire had worked with a big list of state parties as a voter file vendor. Rather than conceding the new Web-based voter file business to other firms, he entered the market with a new online voter file product called

Leverage. As a seasoned data firm rather than a software shop, Blaemire had the system designed by spec rather than build it himself. But those disadvantages were offset by deep penetration into the party market space, loads of personal relationships, and a well-earned reputation as a data expert.

By summer 2004, VAN emerged from these competitions with 11 state parties under contract, along with its 11 state ACT contracts. Leverage, Astro 2000, and Trimeros all had a few state party contracts as well, but a variety of state parties had still done nothing to go online. As summer approached, the DNC panicked over the half-dozen presidential battleground states, including electoral giants Florida and Ohio, that had done nothing to acquire an online voter file. They put out word that they were seeking bids to put those six states onto an online system through the 2004 election.

VAN and others bid to build these six key party voter files, though from our perspective the process seemed perfunctory from the start. When we went to the DNC to do a formal product demonstration in support of our bid, key decision makers, known for their cozy relationships with Blaemire Communications, didn't even show up. Blaemire was indeed awarded the contract for the untested Leverage product. And dreadfully that fall, the parties in Florida and Ohio both reported significant crashes under pressure. The DNC had to rush staff into those states to make up for the unreliability of voter file access.

Once the 2004 cycle was over, dramatic change was in store for the DNC. Following an exciting but failed primary campaign for president, Howard Dean took over as chairman, promising to ensure that the Democratic Party would become a *national* party. Gone were the days, he insisted, when Democrats could afford to focus on 15 states and try desperately to eke out a win in national elections. The Democrats were going to be a national party with resources in every state.

Dean's team quickly cleaned out the DNC technology department and empowered their new chief technology officer, Ben Self, to move the institution into the Internet age. Among other challenges, Self was determined to assemble a truly national voter file, a 50-state database that could be used for consistent modeling and targeting across the nation. (Ironically, a core group of the departed DNC technology staff started a competing effort, called Catalist, to build a national voter file. Both efforts met with considerable success, meaning the progressive community leapt from zero to two national voter files. This might be considered an embarrassment of riches or, more likely, a wasteful duplication of effort.)

While the DNC focused on data, the state parties continued to contract with VAN or other providers for their front-end interface to the voter file. By the end of 2006, 25 state parties worked with VAN, while the rest were scattered among competing solutions, including a new competitor from Boston called Sage Systems.

Sage was started by a pair of well-known political consultants in Boston. Friends of ours and thus keenly aware of VAN and its rapid growth, they took us on by claiming that their new product did everything: it was the software package that managed the voter file, volunteers, and donors all in one. We suddenly found Sage competing aggressively against us, and their claims were quite appealing. Why have a system focused on just field when you can have it all?

As the Ohio Democratic Party sought a replacement for their failed Leverage system from 2004, I travelled to Ohio to meet with executive director Mike Culp. When he explained that he really wanted his voter file system to handle his fundraising and compliance as well, I gave a painfully honest answer: VAN could deliver the best voter file tools available to Ohio Democrats, but for fundraising and compliance the party would be better off also working with NGP Software or Patton Technologies, two Democratic companies battle tested in the intricacies of those fields. If he tried to find a company that promised to do all those things, I was confident none would be done well. As I spoke these words, I knew I was kissing that contract goodbye because Sage would say, "No problem, we can do it all."

Six state parties hired Sage in 2006, including the fierce congressional battlegrounds of Ohio and Pennsylvania. And, once again, key field campaigns were plagued by catastrophic system failures as they reached autumn intensity. Under heavy usage, the generation of walking and calling lists became intolerably slow or impossible, and field operations were paralyzed.

As Ben Self and his team at the DNC watched yet another system failure unfold in Ohio, they vowed to pursue a national interface solution—a common national front end to the national voter file they had built. They were determined that the party's presidential nominee in 2008 would inherit a national voter file infrastructure certain to perform. So in the fall of 2006 the DNC put out a request for proposals for a national voter file interface.

With 25 state party clients and a history of reliable performance when others failed, VAN bid with confidence to be the vendor for the national party. After a rigorous selection process we were awarded the contract in February 2007 and immediately took on the challenge of turning 25 state party VAN systems into a single 50-state system to be dubbed VoteBuilder.

Six years after building the prototype in Iowa for managing voter contact programs, we were now able to take our accomplishments to their logical conclusion. No staffer on any Democratic campaign would ever again do without the best tools in the industry for efficiently managing their voter contact problem. Staff moving from campaign to campaign would always hit the ground running with familiar and reliable tools. Industry standard practices would make canvassing data highly likely to get into the right database. Data collected at every level would be preserved for future campaigns and would feed the best possible nationwide modeling and targeting programs.

2008 AND BEYOND: TECHNOLOGY CONVERGENCE

In the years preceding the DNC contract with VAN, our focus had already shifted fairly heavily toward challenges peripheral to the core needs of voter file management. We had developed increasingly sophisticated tools for managing volunteers, scheduling them for activities, and tracking their performance. We then built broadcast e-mail tools and automated telephone tools into the VAN platform. And we built tools for managing constituency casework and tracking membership programs.

We also began an intense focus on the biggest emerging technology gap—the disconnect between the staff-facing VAN voter file and public-facing Web sites. During the six years that VAN was revolutionizing the way Democratic campaigns managed voter file and volunteer data, equally profound changes were happening on the consumer-facing Internet side. Millions of activists were now being engaged online to write checks, sign petitions, buy merchandise, enter contests, and engage one another over issues and interests.

But these public-facing Web sites were entirely isolated from the VAN tools. They dropped data into their own databases—databases that behaved like afterthoughts, were not designed to facilitate powerful and user-friendly interaction with the data, and were disconnected from the voter contact technology. In 2004, on the day that John Kerry accepted the presidential nomination at the Democratic convention, a quarter of a million people signed up to volunteer on his Web site. But there were no tools in place to facilitate any kind of follow-up with those critical human resources, so all that valuable data went into a black hole.

How could we get the activists signing up to volunteer on the DNC's public Web site tied in with the serious voter contact work that needed to get done through the voter file? Under the guidance of Ben Self and DNC political director David Boundy, the first significant effort to bridge that gap took place in the summer of 2007 when the DNC commissioned an integration project called Neighbor-to-Neighbor from VAN and Blue State Digital. From the DNC Web site, any committed volunteer could sign up to talk to voters. The site would pull an appropriate targeted geographic list from VoteBuilder and then walk the volunteer through the steps of knocking on doors or making calls and entering the results of their work.

Meanwhile, as the battle between Barack Obama and Hillary Clinton wound to a finish, we eagerly awaited the end so that we could start taking direction from a nominee and focus our work for the general election on that campaign's organizing style. Only in early June 2008 did the dust finally settle. For everyone involved in building the Democratic Party's national voter file, it would be hard to imagine a presidential nominee more likely to exploit that work than Barack Obama, a one-time community organizer.

Within hours of Senator Clinton's concession, the Obama campaign, also a Blue State Digital client, took control of the DNC and presented specifications for much tighter integration between VAN and Blue State. Under absurdly tight timelines, the Neighbor-to-Neighbor program was rebuilt around the nominee's organizing style, and gaps between VAN and the Web site were quickly filled. Never again would someone sign up on the campaign Web site and not immediately be pushed into the core VAN volunteer management database.

Having built a truly national and hyperefficient voter file platform, the challenges ahead would center on integrating those tools with the other key aspects of campaign technology, especially social networking. The Neighbor-to-Neighbor program in 2008 only scratched the surface of the possibilities of a true marriage between friendly consumer-facing Web tools and the voter contact program.

In 2012, Barack Obama's reelection campaign will build sophisticated new tools for engaging activists online, plugging them into teams, and putting voter contact and other campaign work into the context of competition and social interaction. Anticipating tough competition in every battleground state, the campaign assumes the margin of victory could lie in squeezing every advantage from its most valuable asset: its human resources. The technology needs to exploit all the motivational forces that make humans productive—group identity, competition, sense of community, and so on.

Instead of remaining in silos, fundraising and field operations will also converge in the 2012 cycle. That effort that will be accelerated by the 2011 merger of VAN and NGP Software, two highly compatible companies drawn together by respect for each other's accomplishments on behalf of Democratic campaigns and widespread recognition that it's time for these major components to come together. That means all contact with voters and activists will be informed by more complete knowledge of all aspects of their participation in campaigns. Soon, the Mike Culps of the world will get the right—and correct—answer on whether a unified system can conquer field and finance together.

Like the voter file challenges that plagued campaigns a decade ago, the challenges of data and technology convergence today are highly complex yet promise another period of rapid change in how political campaigns function. Fixing the voter file through modern technology ironically brought back an era of door-to-door canvassing and more personalized campaigning.

Today's rapid convergence of media types, databases, means of communication, and hardware devices promises to make campaigns even more personal and meaningful. Voter contact is overwhelmingly more effective when it comes from a neighbor, a friend, or someone who shares your interests and speaks your language. The next edge will go to the campaign that exploits technology to make it all personal.

CHAPTER 12

Innovative Tactics: The GOP Goes Online

Michael Turk

In the early 1990s, the Internet was the realm of computer nerds and academics. Political organizations had yet to recognize the vast organizing potential of the Web. Direct mail and television ruled the political world. At the time, the Republican National Committee (RNC) was relying on regional lists for its voter contact efforts. Wanting to address the shortcomings of disparate voter lists, Chairman Haley Barbour decided to make a significant investment in a national database of voter information. At the time, he and the committee had no way of knowing that seed would grow into the core of the party's online offering.

In the almost 20 years since the invention of the browser and the development of the RNC's voter file, the era of data-driven politics has come to realization. Campaigns today have access to tools that were unheard of when I and others built the first campaign Web sites.

While campaigns have not fully realized the benefits these tools can create and have not yet made campaign communications as personal and relevant as the data will allow, they have made great strides. I am fortunate to have been a participant in the growth of the Internet in politics during this period—serving as an operative in a state party, the e-campaign director of the RNC, and for the reelection campaign of President George W. Bush, and a consultant in private practice.

In that time, Internet campaigns have gone from simple "brochure ware" Web sites, which consisted largely of pretty pictures and text, to sophisticated, data-driven operations. In the 17 years I have built and managed

Internet campaigns, the media has been writing the story that "this year" will be the year of the Internet. The elections of 2008 and 2010, however, came far closer to delivering on the full promise of the Internet by demonstrating the power of Web campaigns. Highly targeted data, paired with powerful applications for voter contact, communications, and fundraising, significantly shifted the bar for tomorrow's political campaigns.

An old adage says that political campaigns simply look to perfect the last campaign rather than innovate for the next one. The Internet, given its propensity for rapid change, makes that approach untenable. Understanding what's possible with the next campaign, however, requires an understanding of how political technology has evolved. The history of online campaigns can teach us much about the way campaigns may innovate in the future.

The Obama campaign's online operation has received much praise for its technical sophistication. The engine that drove the 2008 McCain campaign has received little attention, though it was equally if not more impressive in many respects. The capabilities of the McCain platform rivaled and may have even exceeded Obama's. Likewise, the Kerry campaign's fundraising in 2004 received great media attention, while the Bush campaign's online operation received less fanfare but ultimately set the stage for what Obama did in 2008.

Much of the coverage of political technology in recent years has stuck to a common theme—"the GOP is behind." That conventional wisdom has a kernel of truth but is largely incorrect. Republicans have, in fact, been the driving force behind many innovations in online politics. Democrats have focused a great deal of attention on the human aspects of campaigns, from Howard Dean's "people powered" campaign to Barack Obama's record-breaking small-dollar fundraising. Less attention has been paid to Republican campaigns despite the fact that their Democratic counterparts have often mimicked what the GOP was doing.

In fact, the RNC pioneered e-campaigning. The history of the RNC's online effort is the story of data and one party's almost obsessive pursuit of it. The RNC, over nearly 20 years, has made data the driver for its candidates and campaigns. The Republican Party's infrastructure reflects the role of data in connecting with voters, and the party's Internet efforts reflect the evolving nature of campaigns. But one constant has been the role of innovative online tactics.

THE GOP GOES ONLINE, 1994–1999

The Republican National Committee was faced with a dilemma. Despite its successes in 1994, the RNC often found, in the crunch of campaigns, that lists were incomplete, which caused problems with creation of direct mail. The vendors that serviced the party's data needs were balkanized and unreliable.

Following the 1994 elections, Chairman Barbour embarked on an ambitious program to create a national voter file. While the new list was meant to address challenges with the committee's direct mail program, the decision would create the core of a Web-based data operation nobody at the time could possibly have appreciated. Between 1994 and 2000, the RNC's 50-state voter file became critical to the party's effort to identify likely voters in the 2000 campaign and soft Republican voters who had failed to turn out in 1996 and 1998. Because the list extended to states that had never been competitive, like West Virginia, the knowledge the list provided began to create opportunities for the GOP.

At the same time, the RNC spent considerable effort getting state parties to gather information to append to the file. Meetings of the party executive directors often featured presentations on ways to identify and gather lists that would become part of the master file. The data collected gave the RNC and its parties an ability to target messaging to voters and make appeals personal. While the database was not yet connected to a Web site, the party and its candidates were making investments in this new communications platform. In early 1995, no more than a few state parties were investing time or resources building Web sites. The few that did built static sites with relatively limited options for voters to connect to the state parties. As an example, I built the New Mexico GOP's first Web site in 1995 with little more than a *Teach Yourself HTML* book to guide me. The inclusion of surveys and forms was about as extensive as user interaction got.

In 1996, the Republican field of candidates—including Bob Dole, Phil Gramm, Steve Forbes, Dick Lugar, Lamar Alexander, and Pat Buchanan—all took to the Internet to make their case. Even at that time, presidential campaigns had the best toys. The Republican field demonstrated early technical prowess, providing tools such as a Letter to the Editor tool, Interactive Flat Tax Calculator, forums for coordinating campaign activity, and streaming media. While that streaming media was limited to audio over a modem, it set the stage for the rise of video and interactive content to come. These initial forays into Internet communication were archaic by today's standards. The sites focused primarily on list building and distributing campaign messaging.

The 1996 campaign was the first in which presidential hopefuls used the Internet, but it was also the first in which campaigns learned the lessons of parodies, misuse of campaign Web sites, and security flaws.

In October 1996, a tool that let visitors send a campaign postcard to friends allowed opponents of Dole to insert messages antithetical to the campaign's own. Further, the tool could be manipulated by changing the postcard's ID number in the URL, allowing people to view cards created by others. The campaign was also criticized for not verifying e-mail subscribers before adding them to the campaign's list.[1]

List development was the principle focus of early Internet operations, with campaigns trying hard to grow their e-mail lists. Making online donations to campaigns was unheard of in 1996. However, as campaigns progressed and the presidential campaigns of 2000 began to heat up in the summer of 1999, an advisory opinion requested by Bill Bradley's campaign paved the way for Internet fundraising. The Federal Election Commission approved Bradley's plan to accept donations online[2] and allowed them to be counted toward matching funds. The donation rush this created was significant. Within a few months, most presidential campaigns were taking online donations, a cottage industry sprang up to provide donation processing, and the stage was set for the significant fundraising efforts we saw in the campaigns of 2000 and beyond.

MESSAGE, MONEY, AND MOBILIZATION, 2000–2003

Shortly after the FEC gave the green light to presidential campaigns to take donations online, the first instance of what would become known as a "money bomb" took place. In the days following the New Hampshire primary, John McCain raised more than $2 million dollars.[3] The money raised allowed him to continue his campaign into the spring.

The money bomb demonstrated the potential of the Internet to level the playing field. While Bush had raised more than $68 million, only about $300,000 had come in online. McCain, by comparison, had raised roughly $4 million online. With a flood of small-dollar donors, smaller campaigns could compete effectively. To garner attention but also to provide a greater deal of transparency, George W. Bush's campaign for president in 2000 made the decision to post all of its donors on the campaign Web site.

The year 2000 was a record year for fundraising but one that would be dwarfed by future contests. Ironically, it was only after the campaign finance reforms of 2003 that money in politics absolutely exploded. Despite predictions that campaign finance reform would remove the influence of money in politics, the inflow of cash actually exploded after the Bipartisan Campaign Reform Act (BCRA) was signed into law. One reason fundraising flourished was the ease with which the average donor could now give to the candidate of his or her choice.

While the rise of the individual donor was shaking campaign fundraising, perhaps more important were changes in campaign tactics that would come to shape the role citizens could play in identifying, communicating with, and turning out voters. Several major developments in "citizen-centered" politics—driven by Internet tools—began to drive a sea change in the way people interacted with campaigns.

During the 2000 primary, Republican campaigns began to involve voters and activists in the campaign in new ways. The Web sites of Republican challengers began to incorporate more opportunities to take direct action during the 2000 cycle. Steve Forbes' e-Precinct and George Bush's Team Leader programs allowed supporters to create their own activist profiles and provided tools for direct action on the campaign's behalf. These programs were further developed after the campaign as the RNC's Team Leader effort. These groundbreaking initiatives empowered activists to spread the campaign's message and established affinity programs that rewarded supporters for completing actions. The RNC's Team Leader program, for instance, allowed activists to earn points for taking action to help the party. Those points could be traded in for apparel and tools to aid in activist efforts. As an activist earned more points, the rewards he or she could get increased.

Around the same time, the RNC realized the potential for its voter file as a tool in the dawning age of new media. The committee had, up until this point, provided each state with their voter file as a flat database. The data gathered by the state parties had been aggregated, enhanced, and shipped back to the states on CDs containing the data for that state. The committee realized the value of Web-based services and decided to make its voter file available as hosted software, called Voter Vault. Giving state and candidate committees access to the voter file in a simple, easy-to-use way would invite legions of volunteers to begin adding and correcting data and set the stage for a massive ground operation. The Democrats during this period were having similar awakenings within their own party as a new wave of Internet-driven activism was taking hold.

To properly manage online activists, the Republican Party would need to provide opportunities for engagement as they had with the Team Leader program. However, those opportunities would need to be tied to metrics and goals by which the campaign could measure its success and further its objectives. The party had been acquiring commercial data and investing in new models of identifying voters. Known as microtargeting—using data models to gauge propensity to vote and the likelihood of voting Republican—the practice took hold during the 2004 campaign. This data, tied to a disciplined ground game, would make the 2004 campaign a watershed year and change the way campaigns were run.

The volume and type of information the RNC was gathering allowed the party to fine tune its message and provide tools that allowed a volunteer to self-identify issues or groups of importance to him or her—for instance, hunting and fishing or small-business issues—and get matched to similar voters in other areas. The goal wasn't telling your life story, as it seemed to be for many Dean supporters; it was taking your life story, matching it to data gathered by the party, and using it to connect with other voters on issues relevant to both the activists and the voter they were united with.

The Internet rush that took place between 2000 and 2003 had a number of significant failures in addition to its many successes. During this time, the RNC invested resources in a number of initiatives that didn't pan out, including GOPNet—the party's attempt to become an Internet Service Provider and Web portal—and GOPlanIt—a proposed master calendar of GOP activities. While those efforts may have fallen short, the drive to innovate was alive and well and would be on full display during the presidential election of 2004.

SUCCESS HAS MANY FATHERS

Following the implosion of Dean in Iowa, a number of articles began to make note of Dean's biggest failing—that he ran a campaign based on an echo chamber of supporters rather than a concerted effort to identify and turn out actual voters. A campaign's use of the right tools will never overcome the lack of a coherent message and a compelling candidate.

The Kerry campaign, coming out of the primary season, learned the lesson of Howard Dean's online fundraising success. In the three weeks after John Edwards' withdrawal, Kerry raised 50 percent of the total he had raised to date. Kerry's focus on online fundraising continued through the summer as he set record after record for fundraising by month. The Bush campaign, by comparison, had tremendous success utilizing tried-and-true tactics of direct mail and telemarketing. The campaign focused on contacting voters through their networks of friends, neighbors, and coworkers, raising nearly $260 million offline compared with $14 million raised via the Internet.

Tools on the Bush-Cheney Web site—dubbed "personal precincts" by those with the campaign—allowed supporters to become the campaign's messengers. Building on the RNC's Team Leader program, the Bush Volunteer program asked supporters to recruit new volunteers and open their homes to neighbors by holding Parties for the President, and it connected activists in safe states with voters in target states via calling and letter-writing tools. The investments in data and microtargeting also paid off as the campaign used highly targeted voter data, matched against subscriber roles from Yahoo and AOL, to deliver turnout messages in the closing days of the campaign.

The data that drove the Bush campaign was born of an intense review of the practices that had led to a narrow win in the 2000 election. Just as the review of direct mail tactics 10 years earlier had led the RNC to invest heavily in a centralized database, the review that followed Bush's narrow election drove new ways to use that data. Microtargeting uses massive amounts of data and analysis to identify voters—their buying patterns, the products they consume, and the television channels they watch all combine to form a portrait of the likely Republican voter.

The campaign had discovered that only 15 percent of its voters lived in solidly Republican districts. To reach the rest, the campaign would need to spend considerable resources identifying Republican voters in Democratic districts. Unfortunately, traditional campaign tactics of calling and going door to door to identify voters would be just as likely to contact, and thus potentially activate, Democratic supporters. By looking at the behavioral characteristics that indicate voting tendencies, the campaign could limit its interaction with hostile voters while maximizing the resources it used to motivate friendly audiences.

Through the use of the personal precinct tools, the microtargeting data was put to full effect. One such tool asked activists in nontargeted states to self-identify their interests—such as small-business ownership or military service—and matched them with voters with similar characteristics in target states. The tool suggested talking points based on those characteristics and allowed them to write letters, which connected on a personal level and allowed voters in states that might otherwise be ignored to play an active role in the campaign.

Campaign models indicated a pool of swing voters that totaled only 7 percent of potential voters, making the need for accurate targeting even greater. The campaign eschewed the traditional model of using television to reach a large group of undecided voters and instead focused a significant portion of the budget on mobilizing known supporters.

It was to the last group that most of the campaign's Internet operations were geared. As the Bush campaign marshaled its resources for the campaign, the RNC began building tools that would allow state party poll

watchers to report on Election Day activities, including turnout figures
on a precinct-by-precinct basis. As numbers flowed in throughout the
day, it was obvious that the campaign's model had worked.

FAILURE IS AN ORPHAN

The success of the 2004 campaign would unfortunately be matched by
the failure of the election cycles between 2005 and 2008. With the popularity of Republicans waning, the political environment for the GOP had
become toxic. At this obvious low point for the party, a storyline began to
emerge that the GOP was failing online. Despite the fact that the party
was having trouble attracting support offline, its failings were portrayed
as losing a battle of innovation online.

Following the election in 2004, the RNC again invested in a long-term
strategy to bring more data into the party and connect more supporters.
Federal election law allows the national committees to transfer unlimited
sums of money to the state parties. The RNC realized the law could also
allow unlimited in-kind contributions as well.

The RNC was expecting to spend millions to replace its now four-
year-old Web platform. The resources that would be developed could
easily be replicated across a network of sites, all tied to the same hardware, the same database, and sharing the same tools. In other words, the
RNC could develop tools once and then provide them to state parties to
use. In exchange for the platform the RNC provided, all of the data collected through volunteer efforts and e-mail sign-ups would become part
of the RNC's master database, but the state parties could manage their
piece as if it were hosted separately.

By consolidating its hosting in this way, the RNC could, in essence,
consolidate the party's data from across the country in a central location
and merge it with the information contained in Voter Vault and the collective information gleaned from the microtargeting work.

The party, in early 2005, also became the first to embrace a number of
emerging trends, including launching a podcast series of book reviews,
airing a video series featuring two future Internet stars (Facebook's Katie
Harbath and GOP consultant Mindy Finn), interviewing elected officials,
and driving Amazon sales on behalf of conservative authors.

While the party received kudos for the work it had done in 2004, its
success at raising money online was soon called into question. The party
had, in the wake of Bush's reelection, continued to focus on direct mail
and telemarketing fundraising. Democrats, by comparison, had launched

an experiment late in the 2004 cycle to apply the long-tail approach to campaign giving and demonstrated the success of those tools through the fundraising platform ActBlue, which raised half a million dollars for the candidacy of Paul Hackett in a special congressional election in 2005 in Ohio's Second District.

The narrative that the Republicans were not adapting to the new tactics of online organizing was developing due in no small part to the GOP's lack of focus on fundraising over the Internet. That narrative would be solidified during the 2006 campaign.

Democrats had used YouTube videos to show Senate candidate George Allen making an awkward comment about a young man of Indian descent who was trailing the campaign on behalf of Allen's opposition. The so-called "macaca moment" effectively ruined the political chances of a man many believed had presidential aspirations. The Democrats were making effective use of a new medium to tarnish their opponents.

Further complicating the party's efforts to counter the prevailing narrative about the GOP was its own insistence on message discipline. During the debate over social security reform, the RNC had launched a microsite called PreservingSocialSecurity.com. The site asked supporters to share comments about the president's plan to reform the retirement program. However, the Associated Press noted the disconnect between supporters' use of the word *privatization* and the RNC's approved talking point.[4] The AP article ran on a Friday afternoon; by Monday, the site was shuttered. The party was having trouble reconciling the desire to support the president, the urge to be risk averse, and the need to utilize these new, uncontrollable technologies.

OBAMA VERSUS McCAIN

The Republican Party's troubles continued into the 2008 election cycle as the Republicans' eventual nominee, John McCain, failed to display the Internet prowess for which his 2000 campaign had become synonymous. While the Obama campaign had clearly studied the campaigns of Dean, Kerry, and Bush and had moved the ball forward, the McCain campaign's Web site appeared to some to actually move backward.

The reality, to some extent, was dramatically different. McCain's Web site was actually incredibly sophisticated. The platform McCain's team had assembled was one of the most powerful election platforms ever created, with an intricate array of tools that allowed almost the complete management of the campaign through the system. Beginning in 2006, the McCain team had been busy assembling a Web site that integrated an incredible amount of voter and consumer data. The campaign understood the value of connecting that data to its online operation but also to its field team.

Michael Palmer, McCain's e-campaign director, had helped develop the extranet the Bush campaign used to coordinate its field staff in 2004. The Bush campaign team built a robust platform for field staff to e-mail supporters at the local, county, state, and regional levels. The McCain team assembled a platform that would build on the Bush model and provide a platform to manage a national campaign, providing field organizers access not just to the list of e-mail subscribers but to the entire national voter file. Field operatives were able to create their own lists of voters and generate messages to them or direct volunteers to connect with them. The platform was a significant leap forward from the engine that drove the Bush campaign in 2004. The technology that drove the campaign was as sophisticated as any campaign that came before it.

Unfortunately for McCain, the greatest challenge the campaign faced was not with its technology but with its approach to the use of it. The campaign technologists focused so intently on the technology that they neglected the human aspect. They were so busy building the platform that they failed to use the social tools to attract an audience. For example, when the McCain campaign first launched its organizing tools in 2008, the tools that would allow you to create your own group had to be vetted by campaign staff. The campaign, however, was desperately low on resources and didn't have sufficient manpower to approve all the requests. Repeated attempts to get pages created went unanswered. Groups created on Barack Obama's page, by contrast, were approved instantly.

This difference in managing people, and guarding against misuse, allowed the perfect to become the enemy of the good. What may have been the most impressive political tool ever created was largely ignored as praise was heaped on the Obama campaign's online effort. The net effect of the 2005–2008 campaign cycle was to paint the GOP as solidly behind the technological curve.

REGAINING OUR MOJO, 2009–2010

The Grand Old Party faced a number of challenges coming out of the 2008 campaign. The newly elected Democratic president was popular, for one. In 2009, however, the tides began to turn. During the height of the president's push for health care legislation, the vaunted e-mail list of the 13 million people who had supported Obama for president was called upon to sign a petition of support. Just over 1 million did—a response rate of only 7 percent. For a list of the president's most active supporters, on the party's flagship issue, the response was underwhelming.

The GOP, on the other hand, was beginning to see signs of resurgence as Republican congressmen were making effective use of social media like Twitter to organize. In August of 2008, a handful of GOP House members had derailed the Democrats' plans for recess town halls by using Twitter to call attention to the majority party's abdication of its responsibility for dealing with high gas prices.

It wasn't until the fall of 2009 that the GOP came roaring back. An energized Tea Party movement had been building for much of the year. Conservatives had begun to assemble and were using online tools to do it. In November of 2009, the GOP swept the off-year gubernatorial races in Virginia and New Jersey. In early 2010, the GOP continued its winning streak, picking up the Senate seat held by Ted Kennedy until his death. In all three wins, the Internet played a significant role. Virginia Governor Robert McDonnell had invested significant resources in his online operation from a significant online ad buy to a mobile program and concerted efforts to reach bloggers. As we had seen with the 2005 special election in Ohio's Second District, the lack of any other race allowed donors to focus their giving. The Brown campaign raised millions in the coming weeks and eventually succeeded in winning the race.

WHERE WE ARE, AND WHERE WE'RE GOING

During the 2010 elections, the Democrats and the Republicans showed signs of rough parity. Were the GOP's troubles in 2006 and 2008 a reflection of technological ineptitude or simply the result of a bad cycle? What of the Democrats' ills in 2009 and 2010? The technologies available to both parties in 2012, so far as I can see, present no clear advantage. Both the DNC and RNC, and their respective candidates, have access to similar tools, so the party that puts them to the best use will likely determine the outcome. Based on the evolution we've seen with campaigns, I think these are the likely advances we'll see:

- *More personal relevance.* Continued improvements in microtargeting and ad networks that match voters to Internet users will make ads more effective and more meaningful. Expect presidential campaigns to spend more money on online ads and for those ads to be more relevant to the receiver.

- *More persuasion ads.* Campaigns have used online ads to drive fund-raising or traffic but rarely to change minds. That's likely to change as video preroll tied to specific keywords allows campaigns to target voters by interests and issues.

- *Social networks as a landing page.* Corporations are increasingly using Facebook as the landing pages for their ads. Campaigns generally direct advertising to the campaign Web site or a microsite. That trend will change as campaigns reach people on sites they already use.

- *Facebook data scraping.* Commercial data vendors are scraping user data and appending it to voter files. That data will become part of the ad targeting mix.

- *Empowering activists.* Like the Bush and McCain field tools and the Obama campaign's field organizing, the Web sites of 2012 will pair campaign voter data with online tools to make supporters part of their direct response marketing. That will include desktop and mobile apps for calling and walking, with the resulting data fed into the campaign's database.

- *Integration of campaign tactics, traditional media, and online tools.* Imagine a piece of campaign direct mail personalized with name, address, images, and copy all targeted to the interests and behavior of one voter. The mail piece contains the URL of a landing page personalized to the recipient. On the landing page is video, imagery, and messaging specific to the voter's issue preferences. Online ads seen by that voter mirror the same messages.

The ability of campaigns to make every message relevant and consistent across all platforms is within reach. In the near future, cable and Internet-delivered television will allow advertisers to target different messages to different televisions within a household—even while they watch the same programming. That capability will complete the campaign's ability to provide highly targeted, personally meaningful ads that resonate and connect rather than ads that get skipped or ignored.

'When we discuss the full realization of data-driven politics, this is the vision: for every message to be relevant to the voter and for campaigns to use multicast media to deliver individualized appeals. Will one of the 2012 campaigns put an end to the distinction between old and new media? Will they eschew the tendency to focus 90 percent of their budget on television while paying lip service to other avenues for reaching voters?

Technology available today should make possible just about anything the campaigns would like to do. Which party is ahead or behind online may well be determined by who is willing to invest in a transformative online campaign in 2012.

CHAPTER 13

Making It Personal: The Rise of Microtargeting

Alexander Lundry

Michael Meyers had a problem: he couldn't count to two million. It was 2002 and Meyers, as the new executive director of Michigan's Republican Party, was tasked with finding two million conservative voters, the vote goal set by the party for that year's statewide elections. But no matter what Meyers did, he could not get the numbers to add up. Michigan did not register voters by party, and the party's database of previously identified Republicans, party activists, and conservative coalition lists only tallied up to 900,000. Even when Meyers added in voters from heavily Republican precincts, he could only get to around 1.6 million voters. If he wanted to win on Election Day, he had to find 400,000 more Republicans.

Meanwhile, in deeply liberal Massachusetts, a successful businessman named Mitt Romney faced steep odds in his race for governor. Finding Republicans was not a problem for Romney in this party-registration state; the problem was that there were not anywhere near enough of them. Instead, the campaign needed to find a massive number of independents who could be persuaded to support Romney.

Meyers and the Romney campaign each ultimately landed in front of Alex Gage, a Michigan-based political pollster who had been working in Republican politics since Gerald Ford's presidency. For years, Gage had been trying to adapt the marketing techniques of the business world to politics, convinced that the manner in which corporate America found and attracted its customers held lessons for his political clients. Gage believed that the advanced marketing techniques used by some of the most innovative companies on the planet—LL Bean, American Express, and Capital One, to name just a few—could solve these campaigns' problems. Ultimately, the idea Gage took to Lansing and Boston was an entirely new and revolutionary product for political campaigns: microtargeting. When Gage finished pitching his idea to the Romney campaign's roomful of former business consultants, they replied, "You mean they *don't* do this in politics?"

WHAT IS MICROTARGETING?

Employing the same marketing methods corporate America uses to sell credit cards and coffee machines, political microtargeting collects and studies the enormous amount of data that is available about individual voters in order to answer a campaign's most fundamental questions: Who supports my candidate? Where do I find them? How do I persuade others to support my candidate? Answers to these questions in turn allow campaigns to build their direct voter-contact programs, a communications plan that relies upon contact methods that can be addressed to a specific individual—typically mail, phones, door knocks, or e-mail.

Traditionally, these voter-targeting questions were answered by using the most easily available data—things like geography, party registration information, voter turnout levels, and simple demographics. Precincts that voted more than 65 percent Republican would be blanketed with door knocks; registered Democrats would get mail about the candidate's education program; get-out-the-vote efforts would be focused on voters who only show up in presidential years; and anyone older than 55 would get a call about the candidate's stance on Social Security.

Unfortunately, these techniques can leave a campaign's best voters stranded and untouched. A blue-collar independent who sat out the last election and lives in an overwhelmingly Democratic precinct would be completely untouched by a traditional GOP targeting program. But microtargeting serves as a campaign's search and rescue mission, looking at the same voter and seeing that he also drives a truck, owns a gun, has three kids, and is very angry about illegal immigration. Not only is the campaign now communicating with that voter, but they can also talk to him about the issues he cares most about, increasing the effectiveness of the contact. Microtargeting means the difference between shouting to a group and speaking intimately with each individual voter.

And it works. Consider this example from President Bush's microtargeted reelection campaign: in New Mexico, 6,000 middle-aged, lower- and middle-class Hispanic women with children in public schools who were absolutely certain to vote received contacts highlighting No Child Left Behind and the president's push for education testing and standards. Bush won New Mexico by 5,998 votes.[1]

It's not just electoral campaigns that are using microtargeting to improve their political odds; this tool has also become a staple of interest-group issue-advocacy campaigns and membership organizations' recruitment of and communication with members. The "ask" of the individual could be to call their member of Congress, send a postcard, sign up to receive action alerts, become a member, or donate money. Regardless, if there is some call to action, microtargeting can be used to increase the efficiency and effectiveness of an organization's appeal. In fact, it is important to emphasize here that the only reason for a campaign or organization to do microtargeting is if there is a robust direct-contact plan with a correspondingly meaningful budget. Microtargeting is not an end in itself but rather a way to make smarter direct-contact decisions.

THE CURRENT STATE OF MICROTARGETING

In the 2012 campaign cycle, microtargeting will celebrate its 10-year anniversary, remaining a relatively new campaign innovation. In many ways, it is much younger; it only entered the political mainstream in 2008 when its practice extended well beyond the presidential race and the most expensive campaigns for the U.S. Senate and into nearly every race for federal or statewide office. Indeed, we are only at the very beginning of a true revolution in how campaigns are run.

There are, of course, barriers to its expansion throughout the campaign ecosystem, including issues of cost and access to data, a misunderstanding of the product, and a lack of experience with data-driven campaigns. In terms of cost and access, obtaining, assembling, and maintaining enormous databases is equally formidable from both a technical and financial perspective, but these are obstacles that will ultimately be overcome either by sheer time or through falling costs. So while these are legitimate encumbrances to microtargeting's expansion, they are only temporary ones.

More problematic are the misconceptions surrounding microtargeting. Some think that it is done at the expense of a broad, unifying campaign theme, but it is foolish to think that microtargeting precludes a campaign from broadcast messaging. Good campaigns will have one unifying style, slogan, theme, and feel, but this should not stop campaigns from customizing their messages to critical groups of individuals. Others think that microtargeting is only helpful at turning out a candidate's base supporters. If a campaign chooses to run a base-mobilization campaign, it can use microtargeting to do so, but it can also use this same tool if it prefers to run a persuasion campaign. Microtargeting helps to identify the voters you are most interested in talking to—those could be base voters, swing voters, or any other type of voter the campaign deems important enough to contact.

Campaign culture will also prove difficult to overcome. Convincing an industry that is dominated by gurus and gut calls that there is a better way to run a campaign and that there are smarter, more effective answers to campaign issues than simply going up with another television spot will be tricky. Data-driven decision making does not obviate the need for good instincts and the weathered campaign consultant, but it does make those calls easier to make, with evidence to back up your decision.

This new generation of campaigning has brought with it a new type of campaign consultant. The current crop of microtargeters includes consultants with a wide variety of backgrounds: polling, grassroots organizing, mapping, direct mail, public affairs, statistics, and political science, to name just a few. Microtargeting firms have mostly grown out of polling firms; in the political world these number crunchers have the most experience handling data and running statistical analyses, two critical components of microtargeting.

On the left, Strategic Telemetry is perhaps the most well-known microtargeting firm, having worked on President Obama's campaign in 2008. The biggest firm on the right is TargetPoint Consulting, the firm founded by microtargeting pioneer Alex Gage. Though it is hard to tell precisely, as both sides are very guarded about their methods, there does not appear to be any marked distinction between the two sides' microtargeting methodologies.

HOW MICROTARGETING WORKS

Consider a simple example: You are a volunteer for a Democratic campaign collecting signatures at a grocery store. A Toyota Prius parks near you, and the driver approaches. Do you make the ask? And if so, what issue do you lead with? Relying on your previous knowledge of and observed behavior of Prius drivers, would you predict this person to be an Obama supporter? If you were quantitatively minded, you might ask yourself how many Priuses you've ever seen with Obama bumper stickers and how many with McCain ones. Let's say you've seen four Obama Priuses and one McCain Prius. You could then back these numbers out to an 80 percent probability that this particular Prius owner is an Obama supporter.

You then decide to ask the driver for his or her signature, but on what issue? Given the Prius's record as the dominant hybrid car of choice and the fact that hybrid owners presumably have some interest in the environment, you decide to lead with a message about President Obama's support for cap and trade legislation. Congratulations! You've just microtargeted your first voter.

We are all microtargeters, whether we realize it or not. Maybe we are meeting someone new or we're sizing someone up at the grocery store; either way, we are collecting the data we have about someone, comparing that data to our previous experiences and knowledge, synthesizing it into some prediction about who that person is, and then customizing our interaction with him or her appropriately.

Microtargeting formalizes this process with advanced statistical algorithms and massive data sets comprised of millions of voters and thousands of variables. It is an analytical process that holistically looks at each voter's unique data footprint to reveal patterns in the data that allow campaigns to determine—with a stunning degree of accuracy—how likely a person is to vote, who they'll vote for, and what issues are important to them. Then, with all of this information, campaigns can craft direct voter-contact campaigns that send the right messages to the right people using the right medium at the right time.

The net effect is that direct voter-contact programs get more efficient and more effective. They're doing a better job sorting the most "profitable" contacts from the least, minimizing the number of thrown-out mail pieces, hung-up phone calls, and slammed doors from their opponent's supporters. And they're making the message itself more powerful and persuasive through customization, talking to their targets about the issues they are most interested in.

THE DEVIL'S IN THE DETAILS

While the processes and procedures of microtargeting vary from campaign to campaign and depend to some extent upon the preferred methods of the particular consultant or company, there are enough commonalities to outline a typical process from start to finish.

The process always begins with a customer file, which, in the case of political campaigns, is the registered voter file of a particular state or locale. From there, microtargeters try to append the voter file to as many other data sources as possible, using complicated match and merge database technologies. Commercial data from companies like Experian, Acxiom, and Equifax is merged with all the information from the voter file, which is then in turn combined with other publicly available data sets like census block group information or housing data. From there, a number of other applicable data sources are added as needed; these could include things like hunting or fishing licenses, social networking data, or proprietary data from the client.

Ultimately, for any given individual there could be more than 1,000 data points included in the final compiled database. The voter file alone contains name, address, and vote history, and then frequently includes partisan registration, gender, and even race in many Southern states. The census data provides insight into the type of community you live in, its ethnic composition, the number of students or military veterans living there, even the number of people on government assistance. The consumer data can reveal individuals' interests and habits such as whether they are baseball or football fans, what computer operating system they use, or the types of magazines they subscribe to. If the file came from one of the national political parties or one of their affiliated groups, then the proprietary data likely includes things like donor information, voter ID variables from previous campaigns, or "affiliation" flags that have been collected by previous candidates.

The compiled data file is enormous, but it is missing one key component: there is no information on individuals' current attitudes and behaviors relevant to the campaign's objectives. We do not know who they are going to vote for, how likely they are to vote in this particular election, or what their key issues are. Those unknowns are precisely what microtargeting is intended to answer. In order to answer those questions, the campaign conducts a microtargeting survey, which is very similar to a typical political poll except that it has a very large sample size in order to accommodate the algorithms used later in the model-building process. The surveys ask only very basic questions: turnout, a ballot question, some messaging, and maybe a handful of other questions customized to the unique circumstances of the campaign.

Once the survey data is collected, the analytical process truly begins. Remember that for some subsample of the electorate we have obtained "the answers"—we know exactly how 10,000 voters are going to vote, how likely they are to vote, and what their issues are. Analysis uses those answers as the variable we want to predict, frequently referred to as the dependent variable. The variables we use to predict the dependent variable are those 1,000-plus data points added to the file in the data-appending process. Inside of that 10,000-person sample file we look for patterns that are particularly helpful in identifying the people we are looking for. Once we've settled on a promising pattern, we apply that principle to the entire voting population.

Remember the Prius example from earlier: we are combining the data we have on some new person with our knowledge of other people who have the same characteristics in order to make a highly educated guess as to their political leanings. So, if 100 people in our survey matched a particular data profile, and 90 of them told us they were Democratic voters, we would then be able to reasonably infer that 90,000 of the 100,000 that fit that same data profile in the statewide voter database would also be Democratic voters.

When campaigns first began microtargeting, much of the modeling used tree-based methods such as the CHAID, CART, and C5 algorithms, meaning that voters were iteratively bucketed into increasingly sophisticated if/then statements. So, for example, the algorithm might find that if you were male and you were white and you were 50 or older and you drove an SUV and you did not have an interest in fashion, then your probability of being a Republican was 0.8. These segmentation schemes make a lot of intuitive sense and are fairly straightforward to build.

However, microtargeting models and methods have changed dramatically over the last few cycles, becoming much more complex and, correspondingly, much more powerful. Nonlinear models like support vector machines, black-box methods like neural networks, and more traditional tree-based segmentations are all used together in order to boost model accuracy. In the end, each model produces one very important number that is added to the voter file: a propensity score of how likely a voter is to be whatever it is that was modeled. The propensity scores can range from 0 to 1 and most typically are calculated for partisanship, candidate support, likelihood to vote, and support for an array of key campaign issues and messages.

Campaign contact universes are built by combining the various models and their propensity scores to build highly specialized universes. For example, a piece of direct mail about Second Amendment rights may go out to voters with high gun-rights propensity scores, high likelihood to vote scores, and only mediocre propensity scores on support for our candidate. Layering various microtargeting models on top of one another allows campaigns to build highly customized appeals to those groups of voters they are most interested in communicating with.

The creation of contact universes using microtargeting codes is a collaborative process between the microtargeting analysts, the campaign, and anyone else involved in the direct-contact program. Due to the high level of integration with the campaign's direct voter-contact program, the microtargeting analyst's campaign role is at the highest strategic levels, and this integration will likely become much deeper as the data management and analysis process becomes a more central part of campaigning.

THE BIG DATA REVOLUTION

It's not just campaigns where we are seeing data play a central organizing role. While the lion's share of coverage of the last decade's technological revolution has focused on blogs, social networking, and online video, a quieter, yet more profound, change has also occurred around the world of data.

These days, companies are generating, capturing, and analyzing massive amounts of data each and every day thanks to technological improvements in sensors, storage, and processing power. Every e-mail you send, each Web page you visit, and every item in your virtual shopping cart means another row or column added onto a database somewhere. We volunteer intimate details about ourselves to social networks. Even everyday devices like our phones, cars, and televisions have become data hubs.

Every two days, humans create as much information as they did from the dawn of civilization up until 2003.[2] This is the world of "big data," a term that has come to be used as shorthand for the proliferation of enormous databases that hold the promise of meaningful and actionable knowledge. Thankfully, Moore's Law[3]—the axiom that the number of transistors that can be placed inexpensively on a computer chip doubles every two years—has meant steadily larger storage arrays along with faster processors that allow the data to be analyzed quickly. The ability to do powerful, interesting, and useful things with data increases exponentially as we are able to collect more of it and access it more quickly.

Without organization, classification, and analysis, data collection is simple hoarding. Data, after all, is dumb. It takes heavy lifting to transform raw data into meaningful insights, knowledge, information, and action. So the growth of data sets has corresponded with a forced associated growth in statistical theory and methods, ultimately leading to the outgrowth of two related disciplines that lie at the heart of the microtargeting process: data mining and predictive analytics.

Strictly speaking, data mining is the process of searching for and identifying meaningful patterns in very large data sets. Unlike simple database queries in which an analyst must work forward from some hypothesis, data mining begins simply with a basic question: what type of voter is more likely to be interested in our candidate's educational stance? From there, the analyst looks for patterns and associations within the data it has on the item of interest. Data mining's limitation, however, is that it is backward looking and can only offer retrospective insights. Over the last decade or so, the field has evolved its algorithms and methodologies to allow it to be forward looking, shifting its practitioners from data mining to what is now called predictive analytics.

Predictive analytics is the exploitation of patterns and correlations in large data sets to make informed guesses about who an unknown person is and how likely they are to do or be something of interest to your business problem. Of course, this is the fundamental strategy of microtargeting. Indeed, a more technical definition of microtargeting would be the application of predictive analytics to direct voter-contact universe creation.

Together, the broader set of skills necessary to succeed in the world of big data is commonly referred to as data science: a combination, in varying degrees, of the roles of statistician, programmer, database administrator, and storyteller necessary to extract meaning from big data. To that list, the political world would add campaign operative, as microtargeting does demand a sufficiently large helping of domain expertise in the form of good political instincts. Big data and the data scientists who can understand it are changing the way campaigns are run, and it is only just beginning.

WHAT'S NEXT

Microtargeting will look amazingly different only 10 short years from now. The big-data revolution and the data science industry are still only in their infancy, and thus the pace of change is correspondingly aggressive. As more of our everyday activity either moves online or has some technological component, the nature of the data collected becomes increasingly diverse and powerful. Considering that, here's a quick look at where political microtargeting is heading over the next decade.

Text Mining

One basic but incredibly beguiling data type is simple text, often referred to as unstructured data since words, sentences, and paragraphs have no mathematical properties that can be analyzed or fit neatly into relational databases. It has been estimated that nearly 80 percent of actionable business information is collected as unstructured text,[4] not to mention the massive amount of text generated each day on Twitter, Face-book, blog posts, and Web site comments.

Both the business and political community are looking at text-mining tools that can automate the process of collecting, mining, and analyzing these data in meaningful ways. For example, social media tools will mon-itor keywords, tracking the frequency and volume of their occurrence while also coding the data for sentiment: did that tweet ultimately say something positive or negative about Barack Obama? Already, analysis of unstructured Twitter data has been used to accurately predict a movie's box office receipts,[5] the Dow Jones Industrial Average,[6] and even President Obama's approval rating.[7]

Location Data

The explosion in the use of GPS and corresponding location data also has great potential for political campaigns. Location-based services like Foursquare and Facebook Places encourage users to "check in" to a loca-tion, and it is not that hard to believe that the places someone goes to can reveal something about their partisan preferences. Voters at an opera house probably look a lot different than voters at a draught house. With the proper type of analysis, campaign strategists could deliver customized political appeals to online mobile users targeted to the known political inclinations of a destination's patrons.

Linking Online and Offline Data

As we increasingly live our lives online, it is still very difficult to link those online interactions back to a voter file with a name, terrestrial address, and phone number. The data volunteered on Twitter, Web site comments, and the like have incredible predictive potential, but most times this data is veiled by anonymity.

While there are some ways to solve this, they are either complex, expensive, or both, not to mention the sometimes murky privacy waters these services swim in. The most promising solution is the growth of Facebook and its goal of becoming the de facto standard for individuals' primary online identity via services such as Facebook Connect, the pro-lific "Like" button, and more fundamentally the Social Graph API. As it becomes trivial to attach an online record to a voter file, the predictive accuracy and power of microtargeting models will inevitably increase.

Online Display Ads

Linking online and offline data would also mean great changes for online advertising. Online display ads are typically bought in two different ways. Most commonly, advertising is displayed to all Web site visitors because it is thought the site has an abundance of campaign targets, for instance Republican primary candidates purchasing ads on NationalReview.com. Increasingly though, ads can be displayed to a very specific *type* of visitor to a site, identified by either cookies or pixel tracking, so a Democratic primary candidate might purchase ads on the *Daily Kos* that are displayed only to women between the ages of 18 and 35.

Ultimately, however, as it becomes easier to link online and offline identities, these display ads will be targeted not to Web sites or to specific demographic groups but rather to specific named individuals designated by a campaign. A Web site might be given a list of 150,000 individuals targeted for persuasion by a campaign, of which through some matching procedure they identify 50,000 of them as visitors to their Web site, and the next time they visit, they are served their customized advertisement.

Data Visualization

With the growth of these massive databases, there is a growing demand from nonanalysts for easier ways to interact with and make sense of all this data. For that, there is no better tool than data visualization—the use of charts, graphs, diagrams, and dashboards to summarize and display raw data.

As any spreadsheet user will tell you, rows and columns of data can quickly get unwieldy and out of hand, making it increasingly difficult to extract any meaning or information out of it. The visual display of quantitative information can reveal patterns, trends, and insights that may have previously been obscured in either tabular format or even with descriptive statistics. One famous example of the revelatory power of data visualization is Anscombe's Quartet,[8] four separate data sets that have identical statistical properties—mean, median, mode, and even their regression line—though they ultimately contain wildly different data points. The data sets' stark differences are only apparent when mapped onto a graph called a scatterplot.

Static visualizations can be very helpful to campaign analysts dealing with massive data sets, but the technological improvements of the last decade have also brought a high level of interactivity to data displays that enable users to discover even more as they manipulate and play with their data. Allowing campaigns to "see" their data in new and meaningful ways will correspond with increases in the power of that data. The rise of the data-driven campaign will likely also see the proliferation of data "dashboards" containing visualizations of key campaign metrics, making it easier for decision-makers to adjust strategies, tactics, and resources accordingly.

Targeted Television

Perhaps the most promising development on the horizon of microtargeting is the inevitability of household-level targeting of television commercials, commonly referred to as "set-top addressable advertising." This holy grail of microtargeters would radically shift television advertising from a purely broadcast medium to one with the supercharged capabilities of individually targeted communications.

Television, the most expensive line item in a campaign's budget, is the least targetable and the least measurable (in terms of impact and effectiveness); microtargeting would change that. Currently, TV ad buys can be targeted by things like channel, program, and time of day, but set-top addressable advertising would put an incredibly fine point on this practice, allowing advertisements to be delivered to a very specific household. Campaigns would be able to run a base-mobilization ad to a universe of households targeted for turnout and persuasive appeals to households deemed to be on the fence.

Data Harmonization

Ultimately, all of these impending developments point toward a new type of race for office: the data-driven campaign. Political consultants, realizing the power of data and analytics, are joining together previously disparate elements of the campaign. Formerly walled data gardens— finance, political, digital, and field—are increasingly interoperable, with common data standards, and in some especially advanced campaigns there is one database to rule them all.

This goal, alternatively known as data harmonization or master data management, means that campaign data flows in, out, and around each component of an organization. Fundraising data is used to inform digital's contacts, field data feeds into fundraising solicitations, Web site behavior informs political outreach, and so on. This sort of data sharing can lead to greater campaign efficiencies, especially when it comes to voter ID, fundraising, coalition building, and direct voter contact.

A campaign that effectively manages its data will be doing all of these things and more: data mining, predictive analytics, microtargeting, text mining, linking online and offline data, using location data, data visualization, and targeted digital and television advertising. Data flows steadily and easily through the organization, providing decision makers with a truly holistic, 360-degree view of each individual voter. It is the future of campaigning.

THE AGE OF MICROTARGETING

Microtargeting could not have come at a better time. The world of communication has changed radically, and political campaigns are struggling to change along with it. Broadcast messaging is not what it used to be decades ago when three television networks reached 80 percent of Americans. Instead, the media landscape has been completely shattered by the proliferation of niche cable channels and alternative satellite and digital delivery systems. What was three networks is now hundreds of channels, thousands of radio stations, millions of blogs, tens of millions of Web sites, and hundreds of millions of individual social network profiles. This fragmentation has only elevated the importance of direct, meaningful, and customized contacts with individuals. Personalized appeals are more likely to stand out in a cacophonous and competitive fight for a person's attention. Electoral campaigns, which at the end of the last century had grown to focus so much on television advertising, are now returning to their roots of direct voter contact through mail, phones, e-mails, and door knocks to deliver their message.

Microtargeting has changed the face of political campaigning, and as data-driven campaigning becomes the norm it will continue to be a disruptively innovative campaign tool. But despite all this, it is important to remember that it is not a turnkey, computer-generated miracle solution for a campaign. It's not a solution—it's a tool. Simply microtargeting will not magically turn a 10-point race into a 1-point race, but in a tight election, it could be just the thing needed to give a smart campaign its margin of victory.

CHAPTER 14

Acting Intelligently: A Brief History of Political Analytics

Aaron Strauss

"What's your zip code?" That's the question the clerk at Williams-Sonoma asks me every time I add an item to my kitchen collection.[1] Often I hesitate before answering because I know that my zip code will be matched to the name on my credit card and—as I'm likely to be the only Aaron Strauss in my neighborhood—Williams-Sonoma will start sending me paper catalogs through the "snail mail."

So the clerk's seemingly innocent question triggers an internal debate for me. Are the store's mailings going to be so interesting and helpful that their utility will outweigh the environmental damage caused by sending dead trees across the country to me? If the ecofriendly side of the internal debate wins out, I'll fib and reply to the clerk with my favorite, patriotic zip code, 01776 (Sudbury, MA—no, I don't live there).

Once Williams-Sonoma has my name and zip code, they'll do more than send catalogs. The company will take two steps to target me. First, they'll match my record to a huge database that has information about all Americans and about several aspects of my life. This information is not always accurate—often the data are educated guesses. For instance, one of these nationwide databases correctly assessed my partisanship, marital status, and early adoption of technology, but was wrong about my finances, interest in travel, and religion.

The second action Williams-Sonoma will take is to track my purchases. Nearly every major retailer—from bricks-and-mortar stores with discount cards (e.g., grocery chains) to Internet companies (e.g., Amazon, eBay) that require log-ins—tracks purchases. By matching sales to people, stores learn about their customers' needs and assess the effect of their advertising. Imagine, for example, that Williams-Sonoma starts an advertising campaign in Store A but not in Store B. The company will want to know if total sales in Store A outpace those in Store B (relative to past performance). But in addition to that overall sales figure, Williams-Sonoma will use zip codes and database records to identify specific types of customers (e.g., parents, young people, and urbanites) who respond to the new advertising tactic.

People who advise campaigns from an analytical perspective, as I do, love to perform these sorts of calculations, which identify the most compelling messages and target the most persuadable voters. However, a major roadblock to this research is the dearth of good data. While many corporations can track sales—their primary metric of interest—every minute of every day, campaigns' primary metric of interest—votes—are registered exactly once, at the very end of the election and via secret ballot. So votes cannot be linked to a specific individual and are cast after all tactical campaign decisions have been made.

POLITICAL DATA IS GETTING CHEAPER

Political practitioners don't throw up their hands for lack of perfect data—too much is at stake in these election outcomes, from local zoning laws that determine whether you can build a house to national issues such as the Supreme Court's next ruling on abortion rights. Campaign consultants take the phrase "Don't let the perfect be the enemy of the good" (usually used in reference to policy compromises) to heart when seeking political data. We settle for second-rate but still very useful information on voters' opinions.

Primarily, we acquire these second-best data by directly asking voters before the election which candidate they support (as well as a whole host of other questions). The potential problems with this approach abound: Voters might lie about whether they'll actually vote.[2] The person on the line might not be the person we think they are (e.g., a father who has the same name as his son). Voters might lie about which candidate they support, or they may simply refuse to answer.[3] One class of voters is too busy to ever take a 30-minute political survey, while another segment of the population is home all day by a phone with not much better to do.

With years of practice, pollsters have learned how to address many of these issues. The most effective approach is to hire an experienced polling team that can contact a representative sample of voters in an electoral district, along with professional interviewers to talk to these voters, but that can be expensive, especially for cash-strapped campaigns. There are alternatives, and twenty-first century technology is a major help.

A critical insight in the search for cheaper political data is that campaigns don't always need representative samples of voters. In the Williams-Sonoma Store A versus Store B example, the analysis compares store performance *before* the advertising campaign with store performance *after* the campaign. This example translates to politics if the analysis compares media markets rather than stores and asks voters their political opinions rather than tracks sales.[4] If a campaign starts running a new commercial in Media Market A and sees its standing among voters jump relative to the opinions of voters in Media Market B (who have not seen the commercial), then that's reasonably good evidence that the commercial is working. The campaign doesn't need a perfect representation of the electorate to estimate the effect of the new commercial: if the numbers say that the ad works with a sample that's 58 percent female, that conclusion probably won't change if the sample is actually 52 percent female. For practical purposes, the result is the same.

Options for good-enough and inexpensive public opinion data abound. Rather than have a professional interviewer call voters, campaigns can record a person asking questions, have a machine automatically call voters, and play the recording. Respondents key in their answers on their phones, and the results of this "robo-survey" go straight to the campaign.

If a campaign prefers live interviewers but can't afford them, one option is volunteer phone banking. In years past, phone banking meant organizing a time and place for campaign volunteers to show up; call sheets would be handed out, and campaign staff would supervise the effort. These days, volunteers can log on to a campaign Web site and register to call other voters from their cell phone. This technology obviates the need for a centralized location and, with the advent of smart phones, both the Web site interactivity and calling functionality reside in the same handheld device. You can make campaign calls from the beach, for instance. I've even seen a photo of people getting together and making calls from a hot tub.

An exciting, if not yet mature, aspect of political data is tracking voter interactions over the Internet. Early in the election cycle, a campaign's primary goals are to get recognized and to raise funds. The former can be passively tracked by looking at Web site hits, and the latter by viewing online fundraising databases. Both of these tracking methods reuse existing data (i.e., they are virtually free) and are excellent sources of data.

Successful campaigns in tough districts, however, need to persuade swing voters to come over to their side. If a campaign could passively measure its success online, it would have a fantastic ability to hone its tactics. One potential proxy for measuring persuaded voters is Google searches. Often when a person is curious about a candidate, they will search online for more information. If your Google searches are outpacing your opponent's (absent some scandal that has people racing to the Web for prurient photos), that's a positive indicator. If search engines started providing this data in real time with customizable geographic queries, campaigns could rely on this information more.

As Election Day draws near, campaigns decide which registered voters to target for get-out-the-vote (GOTV) efforts. Campaigns have the luxury of individualized, accurate, and cheap data to help with these endeavors. Voter files indicate which people voted in which elections, and political companies and parties now track this data over time, so if voters move across the county, their vote history moves with them.[5] For example, a Republican congressional campaign knows exactly which voters are (1) registered Republican, and (2) voted in only half of the recent congressional elections; these voters are prime GOTV targets.

These options are not a panacea for campaigns, however, as there are several instances in which a representative sample is necessary. When examining the horserace—whether a candidate is winning or losing—campaigns absolutely need a good pollster because certain segments of the electorate vote in wildly different ways. Often, over 90 percent of African Americans will vote for the Democratic candidate and perhaps up to 80 percent of white evangelical Christians will vote for the Republican candidate. In close races, a campaign's survey had better have the proportion of those two segments of the electorate (and many others) correct, or the poll may show the wrong candidate leading the race.

LATE TWENTIETH-CENTURY CAMPAIGNING

Before the advent of the Internet and servers that could handle massive databases, campaigns had to assess their efforts and target voters with either more expensive or less exact methods. The expensive avenue is to hire a pollster to call hundreds of voters every night, which provides an extremely rich data set. In campaign parlance, this procedure is called "nightly tracking." The inexpensive route is to analyze precinct results over the course of several elections.

In the early 1980s, Republican pollster Dick Wirthlin pioneered nightly tracking.[6] Wirthlin set up a sophisticated system called the Political Information System, or PINS, for the 1980 Reagan campaign. Nightly tracking not only captured the ebb and flow of the electorate's opinions but it allowed the campaign management to understand the impact of various decisions they might make. Wirthlin's partner in this endeavor, Richard Beal, explained that PINS was designed "not just to satisfy the information needs of the campaign, but to help the campaign decision-makers with their strategic judgments."[7]

In 1980, the "strategic judgment" Wirthlin and Beal focused on was how to allocate resources among the various battleground states. Presidential campaigns are unique because the structure of the Electoral College leads to some votes being worth more than others. Persuading a voter in the swing state of Ohio is much more valuable than convincing a voter in a reliably Republican state such as Utah. Thus, presidential campaigns face state-level resource allocation decisions in addition to figuring out which messages work best for which voters.

By tracking 20 battleground states and simulating the results of the election, Wirthlin and Beal focused on ensuring that Reagan garnered the 270 electoral votes needed for victory. Because Reagan crushed Carter by 10 percentage points, this level of precision was unnecessary, but if Carter had been able to close the gap in the final month, the PINS simulations would have been crucial.

After the 1980 presidential election, consultants figured out how to apply tracking polls to nonpresidential campaigns. Wirthlin protégé Vince Breglio used nightly tracking to monitor the ups and downs of the John Danforth senatorial campaign in Missouri. By correlating the numbers they were seeing in the polls with the actions the campaign was taking, Breglio was able to figure out if the messages they were broadcasting to Missouri voters were working. Danforth's opponent's campaign manager was quoted after the election as saying, "If we had that information we might have won." No campaign manager wants to say those words after a loss, so nightly tracking polls became staples of well-funded campaigns.

RESOURCE ALLOCATION IN RECENT PRESIDENTIAL CAMPAIGNS

In more recent presidential elections, the successors to Wirthlin and Beal have been able to mix historical trends with current polling data via

Bayesian statistics, which are actually quite intuitive. I personally worked on presidential resource allocation for the Democrats in the 2000 and 2004 elections, both of which were extremely close.

The 2000 election included an extremely tough map to game out. Because of hanging chads, most people remember Florida, but five states had margins of victory within one-half of 1 percentage point. Gore won all of them – New Mexico, Wisconsin, Iowa, and Oregon— except Florida.[8] Balancing those states, along with the seven others that were decided by fewer than 5 percentage points, was no easy task. We correctly sent Gore and Lieberman to Florida (Miami and Tampa) for their last campaign rallies; Gore had coffee at 4:30 a.m. on Election Day with Tampa nurses. On Election Day more Florida voters tried to cast ballots for Gore than for Bush, but sometimes luck is not on your side. Knowing that we would have won all five of the closest states if the ballots had been designed correctly is small consolation for the loss of the presidency.

In 2004, the map was easier to figure out: Ohio was the key state. The Kerry campaign, along with outside groups, poured a disproportionate amount of resources into the Buckeye State, which proved to be pivotal. Political science models showed that Kerry faced an uphill battle, which turned out to be too steep even with our extra efforts.[9]

The 2008 electoral map was closer to that of 1980, but with the colors flipped and the Democratic nominee, Obama, winning enough states to comfortably exceed the 270 electoral vote threshold. The novel occurrence of the 2008 cycle was Nate Silver publicizing these usually internal techniques to the world and introducing a sophisticated model with many bells and whistles.

PRECINCT-LEVEL ANALYSES

The vast majority of campaigns in the United States occur at levels below presidential, senatorial, or gubernatorial. These "down-ballot" races can rely on cheaper analyses. In the late twentieth century, that meant precinct-level analyses. These models are somewhat helpful for GOTV efforts but less so for identifying persuadable voters.

For GOTV, a campaign wants to know where its voters are and, more specifically, which voters can be induced to turn out via campaign activity. Geographical vote patterns in states and districts are fairly stable from election to election, which makes it easier to direct field resources to areas that include your partisans. As an example of this consistency, political practitioners label each congressional district with a partisan vote index

(PVI), which is calculated by averaging presidential votes in the district from the last two campaigns (as compared with the national result). For example, the district I was born and raised in, Virginia Eleven, has a PVI of D+2, which means a typical Democratic presidential candidate can expect to earn 52 percent of the vote (50 percent +2). In contrast, Kansas's First Congressional District has a PVI of R+23, meaning that it's a lock to vote Republican. Nonetheless, a statewide Republican campaign in Kansas would focus GOTV efforts in the First District in an attempt to run up the vote there.

The same analysis can be applied to precincts, which is especially helpful for campaigns that have small constituencies, like congressional or mayoral races. For GOTV, campaigns often assume that the percentage of potential voters who would be moved by a GOTV message is fairly constant across the precincts. PVIs demonstrate that vote patterns are anything but constant, so campaigns focus their efforts on precincts with high PVIs; they assume that in these districts the extra vote they pull out will tilt toward them.

Finding persuadable voters via precinct-level vote numbers is much more difficult. Often campaigns will look for precincts that voted for one party's candidate in one year and the other party's candidate in another year (or perhaps flipped parties between two races in the same year). There are a few issues with this approach. First, a precinct that moves from 49 percent Democratic in one race to 51 percent Republican in another race might only have 2 percent of swing voters (assuming constant turnout). Another precinct that shifts from 10 percent Democratic to 25 percent Democratic might have many more persuadable voters even if, at first blush, it looks like a lost cause for the Democratic nominee. When targeting voters, it's crucial to remember that (except in presidential races) each vote is equal.

A second issue with precinct-level persuasion targeting is that individual-level votes are not available under the U.S. system of secret balloting. Imagine a precinct that has 1,000 voters. One year, 600 of them vote for the Republican. The next year, again 600 vote for the Republican. Possibly, no voters changed their minds. However, up to 400 voters—40 percent of the district—could have changed their minds. The fact is that we don't know *which* 600 voters voted Republican each year. This hypothetical precinct might have more persuadable voters than a precinct whose Republican vote shifted by 200 people from one year to the next. Academics call this issue the "ecological fallacy."

The ecological fallacy is a serious issue and a major impetus for the switch to individual-level targeting. I have run or examined dozens of individual-level persuasion models over the past seven years, and it's rare to find that persuadability correlates with precinct-level vote shifts. Unfortunately, even though the political consulting world has relied on these data for decades, they just aren't accurate.

MICROTARGETING

In the early 2000s, Democrats and Republicans raced to set up microtargeting systems. The Republicans got a head start by testing their systems in 2003 before the presidential election. Media reports of the Republican's early efforts sent the Democratic Party into high gear, and we learned on the fly in the summer of 2004.[10]

In 2004, I got a crash course in microtargeting from our newly hired expert, Ben Yuhas. We brought in Yuhas from the big leagues of microtargeting—credit card companies, which have to solicit to the sweet spot of the marketplace: consumers who are financially strapped to the point that they need another credit card but are still going to be able to make payments. Microtargeting has two basic ingredients: (1) the quantity of interest that you want to predict (e.g., vote choice), and (2) as many potential predictors of that variable as possible. The end product of the microtargeting process is an estimated value (or "score") of the quantity of interest for *every* voter in your database.

The quantity of interest selected depends on the goal of the project. If a campaign wants to mail to every likely voter in a sleepy local election, the campaign's quantity of interest should be whether the registered voters cast ballots in previous low-turnout local elections. If a campaign wants to target undecided voters, the campaign should survey voters (through volunteer phone banks or robo-surveys, perhaps), ask who they are voting for in the election, and note which respondents are undecided. An advocacy organization might conduct a similar survey but examine a policy question and focus on whether or not voters support the policy. The more voters in your database for whom you know the quantity of interest's value, the better.

Voter files, which comprise records for every registered voter in a jurisdiction, can be obtained from political parties or election officials, usually for a fee. These databases include information on gender, age, address, party registration (where applicable), and race (where required by the Voting Rights Act). Access to commercial databases is relatively expensive but will provide a bounty of information such as magazine subscriptions, cable TV and landline phone plans, estimated income, and guesses of hobbies.

The statistical procedures used to microtarget find the correlations (i.e., the connections) between the dozens (or sometimes hundreds) of pieces of information you have about voters (e.g., age) and the variable of interest. Some procedures assume a linear relationship (e.g., liberalism declines as age increases), some assume a more complex relationship (e.g., liberalism declines as voters begin to reach middle age, but then increases as voters retire), and some home in on specific ranges of values (e.g., liberalism is highest for voters aged 18 to 24). Several of these interactions are combined to form a final score that can be applied to the entire voter file, including those voters for whom the value of the variable of interest is unknown.

With so many characteristics included in databases, a trait may well be correlated with the variable of interest purely by accident. Statisticians call this spurious correlation "overfitting" and employ two defenses. First, practitioners increase the number of voters with values for the variable of interest (e.g., the number of voters surveyed) as their database includes more voter characteristics. Second, and more importantly, models must be tested on a random "hold-out sample" that is not included in the analysis. This test helps ensure that models are not affected by the data used to develop the model (known as the "training set").

An important caveat is that the resulting microtargeting score is an *estimate*. No one will claim to know—with certainty—your vote in the next Senate election on the basis of your neighborhood, (approximated) income, and the type of car you own. But political practitioners will be able to make a good guess, especially if you live in a homogeneous neighborhood, belong to an ethnic group that generally votes one way, or live in a state with party registration (and you have registered with a party).

A classic mistake is to take a good guess and ignore the uncertainty surrounding it. For example, perhaps a microtargeting model predicts with 75 percent certainty that Joe Smith will vote Republican in the upcoming presidential election. The model shouldn't declare Joe a Republican and leave it at that. Rather, a good modeler would note that the model is somewhat uncertain about Joe, place him on a hierarchy appropriately (with the lowest probabilities of voting Republican on one side and the highest on another). This mistake is most often observed when microtargeters place people into "clusters." For instance, perhaps Joe is placed in the "evangelical Christian Republican" cluster; the microtargeter forgets that the model is uncertain about that placement and that Joe might in fact belong to the "moderate business Republican" cluster. (There's only so much a person's level of cable subscription can tell you.)

EXPERIMENT-INFORMED PROGRAMS

Developing microtargeting scores for all the citizens in a voter file is key to understanding the characteristics of the constituency, but this process is less helpful in determining how to influence voter behavior. To identify the most effective course of action to persuade or mobilize voters, the best practice is to conduct a randomized experiment. With the results of the experiment in hand, campaigns and organizations can spend the bulk of their resources (usually money) on a tactic that is known to be effective. This strategy is known as an experiment-informed program.

A randomized experiment compares the opinions or behaviors of two groups of people (the control group and a treatment group) for which the only systematic difference is that the treatment group received a campaign communication (e.g., a flyer in the mail). Thus, if the opinions (e.g., candidate support) or actions (e.g., propensity to cast a ballot) are different between the groups, the only two possibilities are that: (1) the treatment had an effect on voters, or (2) randomness affected the results. If the experiment includes enough people, the probability that chance caused the observed differences is statistically very small. Thus, an experimental approach is useful for comparing the effectiveness of various tactics.

Randomized experiments are not the only way to decide which tactics to use, but they are considered the gold standard. Campaigns and organizations might rely on the experience of consultants, anecdotal evidence, focus groups, or voters' self-reported responses in surveys (e.g., "I find that argument very convincing"). While all these methods are potentially useful, they are not scientific.

A return to rigorous methods in the political community began in 2000, when Yale scholars Alan Green and Don Gerber published a seminal paper on the effects of door-to-door canvassing, phone calls, and mail pieces on voter turnout.[11] This academic article started an avalanche of research on the various types of tactics campaigns might pursue. On the Democratic side, at least, an entire organization, the Analyst Institute, was created to promote rigorous decision making in the progressive community.

Randomized experiments are especially useful for proving that innovative approaches to voter contact work. For instance, experiments have shown that e-mail reminders to vote have a negligible impact (if that) on turnout. But is the same true of text messaging? During the 2006 election, a colleague and I conducted an experiment on newly registered and reregistered voters. We found that receiving a text message increased the probability of casting a ballot by 4 percentage points for this group.[12]

This result indicated that text messages were far more effective than other potential approaches.

Perhaps the most intriguing turnout experiment to date was performed by Green and Gerber (with help from fellow academic Christopher Larimer and consultant Mark Grebner), who tested the effect of social pressure on the probability of turning out. They mailed over 100,000 people in four groups (leaving unmailed an even larger number of registered voters). The first group received a generic "do your civic duty" flyer in the mail using language that community organizations typically use. The second group's mailing informed them that they were being studied and that whether or not they voted would be recorded by academics. The third group was told that who voted was a matter of public record (which it is) and was provided a list of their prior voting history. And, finally, the fourth group's mailing listed the voting records of their neighbors.

The results were groundbreaking. The civic duty message boosted turnout by 2 percentage points, which was about what organizations that mobilize voters thought was possible on a large scale. The "you are being studied" mailings increased turnout by 2-1/2 percentage points. The third mailing, which listed the recipient's own voting history, mobilized these voters by an additional 5 percentage points, very impressive for a flyer. The final group, who saw whether or not their neighbors voted, cast ballots at a rate that was 8 percentage points higher than the control group. At the time, such a significant difference in turnout was completely unheard of and, really, not thought possible for a large-scale mailing.

The beauty of experiments is that if they are scientific and rigorously performed, counterintuitive results are easier to accept. Perhaps an organization has a tried-and-true method of interacting with voters, but at a staff meeting an employee has an out-of-the-box idea. An experiment can test this idea; if the idea is a success, it can change the way the organization functions.

PERSUASION MICROTARGETING

The basic experimental setup is great for figuring out if a new tactic works or for identifying the best tactic among a finite set of options. In the last few years, a new branch of research has arisen in the field of experiment-informed programs: finding the voters that a campaign's messaging works best on.

Standard microtargeting tells a campaign which people are undecided or soft supporters, but it does not identify the voters who will be affected by the campaign's messaging. Experiments allow campaigns to locate these crucial targets. Complex statistical procedures can compare the characteristics of the control and treatment groups and find the traits for which the treatment group's actions (or quantity of interest) are most different from the control group's actions. This technique is so new that there isn't an agreed-upon name for it, but I prefer "persuasion microtargeting" because the process homes in on people who are actually persuaded by the campaign's treatment.[13]

The statistical methods that identify these persuadable voters are complex because the problem is inherently tricky. In standard microtargeting, every voter in the training set has a known value for the quantity of interest (e.g., "I support the Republican," "I'm undecided"). But in persuasion microtargeting, not a single person is known with certainty to be persuadable since each person belongs to either the control group or the treatment group, but not both. (A persuadable individual, by definition, would act one way in the control group and another way in the treatment group.) Through hard work, statistical tricks, and some ignoring of naysayers, this issue has been at least partially resolved.[14] Though our efforts as statisticians and evangelists are not complete by any stretch, current progress is encouraging.

The preliminary findings from persuasion microtargeting can be surprising. In a campaign environment, it is often assumed that people who are modeled as swing voters (or independents) comprise the persuadable population. However, while these middle-of-the-road voters are on average more persuadable, they are only somewhat more persuadable than partisans. As we conduct more experiments and apply persuasion scores in more campaign situations, the progressive community is crafting general theories that specify scenarios in which partisans play an outsized role in persuasion universes.

Because these results are often counterintuitive, statistically minded practitioners such as Todd Rogers, former head of the Analyst Institute, and I have become evangelists for this approach. Campaigns and organizations absolutely should test their assumptions about their target audiences. These tests are even more important when candidate and ballot initiative elections involve unique circumstances that may not fit into the new and evolving general guidelines. The entire procedure—an experiment plus persuasion microtargeting—can be executed in as little as two weeks, which gives organizations plenty of time to implement their large-scale voter contact programs.

CAMPAIGNS EVOLVE INTO WILLIAMS-SONOMA

Currently, only a small percentage of campaigns base decisions on the results of randomized experiments or analyses of natural campaign variations matched to voter data. Because of the electoral calendar and fundraising constraints, campaigns grow very quickly and are short lived. They often lack the time, resources, and amount of data required to conduct advanced analytics.[15] Institutionalizing these processes in long-lasting organizations and consulting firms is critical to their continued adoption.

As political data become cheaper and the analytics is mechanized, decision making in political campaigns and ideological organizations will become more data driven. Microtargeting and experiments are transforming the culture of campaigns so that all forms of voter contact, from Internet banner ads to television commercials, are tested, measured, and targeted. Given secret-ballot rules, the methods employed by political practitioners will never be as efficient as those employed by the private sector, which has access to real-time sales data, but we are catching up.

The campaigns that stand to benefit the most from these advances in analytics are not presidential and highly publicized Senate campaigns. In those races, the vast majority of voters have made up their minds, and those who do change their minds will do so on the basis of macro events such as an economic downtown. Rather, a well-targeted piece of mail or cable TV commercial will have the most impact in local elections and ballot initiatives, which many voters know nothing about. As the national parties, political technology companies, and consultants make statistical methods available to everyone, local campaigns will be able to act as intelligently as the local Williams-Sonoma. And, thanks to voter files, they won't even have to ask for your zip code.

CHAPTER 15

Bootstrapping an Enterprise: NGP and the Evolution of Campaign Software

Nathaniel G. Pearlman

For the past 25 years, I have been immersed, and sometimes mired, in the muddy world of political technology. Early in my career, a single individual could build a credible and competitive software application to manage all of a political campaign's relevant data. I myself performed this task three times in the pre-Internet era—in 1988, 1991, and 1997—when this niche market was smaller and less visible, expectations were lower, and technological times were simpler. Now things are different. The company that grew out of my third attempt to construct such software swelled from a one-man operation into a substantial firm, now called NGP VAN, Inc., that employs more than 130 people and is a significant player in the Democratic hemisphere of the political technology world. During those two and a half decades in which I grew from young programmer to the founder—and for many years chief executive—of a thriving political software company, the backwater business of political technology percolated, trickled, and then burst into a stream of national significance.

My story is about how the company I created came to flourish and how it both responded to and participated in the creation of the new world of political technology. I also say a few words about my own history and about the development of the broader political software market. I hope that this chapter provides a useful vehicle to understand some of the developments in political technology that have taken place as both I and the market matured.

At its core, today's NGP VAN creates and supports Web-based software-as-a-service applications for Democrats and their allies. Our applications manage massive amounts of data for the simultaneous use of thousands of campaign committees and their numerous staff. Those committees include Obama 2012, most of the Democrats in the Senate and House, numerous Democratic statewide or state-level campaigns, the Democratic national and state party committees, some political action committees, and many other organizations at different levels both here and abroad. The efforts of NGP VAN constitute a significant part of the fundraising, compliance, new media, and field campaign technology base of the Democratic Party. NGP VAN also builds political Web sites that deliver their data in real time into our applications. Our programs provide contact management, blast e-mail and online contribution processing, connections via application programmer interfaces (APIs) with other databases and software, and communications with externally designed Web sites and mobile devices. Our software is constantly being upgraded with an eye to keeping it swift, accurate, up to date, secure, and affordable.

This comparatively sophisticated operation did not come into being overnight. In 1997, when I started NGP Software, Inc., I had no experience running a business. Incorporation, the first bank account, and the first customers were all very exciting novelties. I had my own skills as a computer programmer, and I was a very interested observer of U.S. elections and politics. I also knew something about the existing political software industry. I had worked in the field for a few years and had first-hand reasons to hold some of the firms of the day in low regard. In early company statements I said that, "Democratic candidates and fundraisers are poorly served in the current political software market. Most current products are over-priced, aging, incomplete, or poorly supported." My goal when I started was simple—to change the industry by producing an affordable software product that was responsive to client needs and by treating my customers as friends and allies. In contrast with the then-current nonpartisan technology template, I elected to establish a partisan Democratic firm.

I learned to program in the early 1980s, working on the now paleolithic Apple II with its 64k of memory and 5¼" floppy disks, writing in Applesoft BASIC and 6502 assembler. Computer programming captivated me. My first passionate commitment to electoral politics was to Senator Gary Hart of my home state of Colorado, who ran for the Democratic nomination for president in 1984 and again in 1987. I earned a degree in computer science at Yale where I studied with Professor Alan Perlis, one of the early giants in the field. Perlis had a notion that a computer program is nearly alive. He called it an "organithm" (which is *organism* spoken with a LISP). I kept Perlis's metaphor in mind and have always tried to treat software products with due respect. I first started thinking about the nexus of my two interests in a paper I wrote for a political science course taught by Professor David Mayhew called "Computers and Political Campaigns." I uncovered examples of technology at work as far back as 1966, when Winthrop Rockefeller used punch cards and electronic data processing in his second run for governor of Arkansas.

My entrance into the political software field came in 1988 when, in my first job after graduating from college, I designed and programmed a campaign software program. I worked on a Macintosh IIcx in a programmable database system called 4th Dimension. One of my software constructs—the "current selection" (the result set of the last search, on which any other function or report can then be run)—is related to a concept in that early database. Along with contact and list management functions, the Mac software that I wrote allowed clients to file Federal Election Commission (FEC) reports and in some cases their state-level analogues.

In 1990, I learned about large political databases and geographical information systems as a programmer at the redistricting consulting firm Election Data Services. While there, I wrote an article for the March 1991 issue of the long-defunct *Campaign Industry News* titled "Campaigns May Wield Redistricting Tools." In that article, I conjured up an image of "a modern campaign headquarters" that could look "like a mini-Pentagon," with "huge video screens showing maps of territory to be conquered." I concluded that, "geographically organized data may be campaign software's wave of the future." I explained how, using electronic maps, "information from the campaign database, from donor lists to results of past races and demographic information could all be available." I was already invested in the concept of an integrated political campaign database operable through a single, understandable, coherent interface. My vision, science fiction then, is closer to reality now but far from fully achieved.

Later in 1991, working as an independent consultant, I used FoxPro, then the fastest programmable database, to create my second campaign software program. The program was marketed under the names Landslide and Hannibal to the two major parties and was widely used for list management, compliance, and fundraising. (Remarkably, 20 years later, there are campaigns that still use it.) Those were the days of Novell networks and client-server applications, the era in political software of many desktop applications with names like Bandwagon, Election Machine, and Campaign Manager.

Still in doubt about my career path, and supported by modest royalties, I passed the next four years in the graduate program in political science at the Massachusetts Institute of Technology. At MIT, I periodically updated my campaign software, deepened my knowledge of statistics and U.S. political history, met my wife-to-be, finished my coursework, passed my exams, and came to the conclusion that the life of a professor of political science was not for me. I left MIT a dissertation short of a doctorate and moved to Washington, DC, to start NGP.

In the beginning of 1997, after I decided to hang out my own shingle, I sought counsel from people in the field. I consulted with Matt Angle, who was then the executive director of the Democratic Congressional Campaign Committee (DCCC). Matt was not only an effective executive but one of the few people in politics who understood the potential of technology. Matt sketched for me the hierarchy of political consulting. The top dogs, in his view, were the media consultants, who were the most persuasive and best rewarded, followed by the pollsters, who also had a significant role in the strategic side of campaigning. Ranking lower was the hodgepodge of consultants who handled direct mail, telephone campaigns, and other goods and services required by political campaigns. Below them were the fundraising and compliance consultants. Inasmuch as there did not appear to be a place, even at the very bottom, for technologists, I decided to see whether I could gain a foothold by helping the fundraisers.

Matt's wife, Dolly Angle, was kind enough to introduce me to a few of whom she termed the "adults" among the fundraising consultants. I set out to make friends and to be helpful. I discovered that, although I was prepared to offer graduate school–level statistical analyses of fundraising data, the help that fundraisers genuinely required was far more down-to-earth. In some cases I merely upgraded the memory in their old computers or fixed—or established—networks in their offices. When I discovered that these fundraising firms were managing their data in mail-merge files, or with antique databases, or with numerous overlapping spreadsheets, I saw an opportunity. Since Microsoft Office's Access database was widely used, I learned the Visual BASIC language which is used to customize interaction with the database. The move from disparate lists and sheets to a single relational source was a key ingredient to the application I constructed for the Democratic fundraising community. I called that first product NGP Fundraiser Office to highlight that it integrated with other Microsoft Office applications like Word and Excel.

Putting to one side my ambition to build "real" applications in a more macho computer language and database application, I set out to solve the many intricacies of specialized political contact management: how to manage fundraising across multiple clients out of one database, how to track national and local contacts for political action committees, how to attribute a donation to a particular event for a particular client, how to credit an intermediary, how to manage numerous fundraising codes and household information, and how to merge duplicate entries in the fundraisers' own lists.

I set up the software so that it was easy to operate and would quickly produce customized fundraising call sheets for the exacting requirements of members of Congress and other candidates. I was aware that there were mature fundraising software products for nonprofits and other organizations, but nothing else was affordable and specifically customized for political needs. I allowed my software to evolve to fit the niche by responding to almost daily feedback. I delivered the changes and oversaw technical support myself by modem, using the application pcAnywhere, which allowed me to view my clients' screens in real time.

Over time, the software that I developed began to greatly increase the efficiency and sophistication of my clients' database management. I was committed to immediate response to my clients' needs and handled a wide range of technical problems for them. Because my software and services were affordable and solved their data problems, I succeeded in building a loyal and appreciative client base. The business model was sound: I was creating a financial layer cake of yearly support fees that enabled me to scale up the business and handle more clients. Though I had many sleepless nights worrying about whether the business would survive, I think that this slow bootstrapping of an enterprise (and the building of real relationships that it entailed) turned out to be a better path than if I had attempted to raise money, hire staff, and produce something fancier (such as the geographically integrated campaign system I had envisioned in my 1991 article).

My next step was to adapt the software to work directly for the clients of the fundraising firms—the political campaigns themselves. Campaigns must deal with what is called compliance, the process that results in the delivery of accurate reports, similar to tax returns, which federal, state, or local election commissions require of campaigns to account for the money they raise and spend. Fortunately, I had 10 years of experience with the arcane FEC and state rules and was in a position to meld compliance into fundraising. I knew that I was entering a weird, high-pressure, rules-based, support-intensive world in which there were numerous opportunities for pain and trouble and failure but where no glory whatsoever attaches to success. (Compliance continues to be one of the pillars of NGP VAN today, and we have a sizable and devoted team to support our effort.) With these features added, the product became NGP Campaign Office. Compliance today is still a moving target, full of intricacies and replete with sudden and sometimes irrational rule changes, creating an intellectual challenge that adds a layer of complexity to the writing of software and an additional headache to its support.

By the end of the 1998 political cycle, working alone, I had a substantial number of campaigns happily using my software. Customer service was taking a great deal of my time. I remember speaking that year with the head of Gnossos, a successful software company in the PAC (political action committee) market. Their CEO had calculated that technical support calls cost his company $50 apiece, and he talked to me about how to minimize those costs. I took all of NGP's calls myself, and each one required patience and took effort to handle well. It was not easy; after a while, when I was tired, I started to flinch when I heard the phone ring. But I believed that every support call was an opportunity to advertise our service and demonstrate how different we were from other firms. I believed that, working as we did for a small community of like-minded people, service should be thought of more as an opportunity than as an expense.

Gradually, my political software company and the field in general moved forward. One marker for us came in late December of 1999. Shelly Moskwa, who managed the books for Hillary Clinton for Senate, contacted me. Moskwa reported that the Clinton campaign was having major problems with their software, which was made by a competitor of ours. It was crashing regularly, and a succession of their technicians had failed to put it right. Shelly told me that they had an FEC report due the next month and that they were panicked about filing it properly. Could we possibly convert their data to our system in time for the filing? At the time, Hillary was making her first run for New York's open Senate seat (Daniel Patrick Moynihan had retired and Bill Clinton's second term in the White House was coming to an end. Rudolph Giuliani was the expected opponent; he did not drop out until May 2000.) It was understood that the Senate race would be extremely high profile, close, expensive, and visible.

At the time of Shelly's call, NGP Software had recently doubled in size from one to two people. Because technical support had become so time consuming, I had hired Louis Levine, a recent Claremont McKenna College graduate with a no-nonsense way about him. He and I worked out of the refurbished attic of my house. By most measures, we were exceptionally lucky to be considered by the Clinton campaign. But I had been around for a while, and NGP had finished the 1998 cycle with a good reputation. We were growing and had more than 50 federal Democratic campaign clients willing to testify to our good software and service. Louis and I discussed the situation; clearly, it was a great opportunity. The month before, we had converted Senator Mary Landrieu away from the same competing software firm. We had moved the Landrieu data painstakingly, creating a program that would translate the cryptic coding of financial transactions. We had also made some modifications in our own software to handle the loan and debt-tracking schedules that were necessary for that campaign. So we had that recent success with the Landrieu conversion under our belts.

I was cautious about taking on the Clinton for Senate campaign, as I was about all big opportunities. I foresaw that it would draw time away from our bread-and-butter work. I recognized that it could be disastrous to fail on a nationally prominent project. I also knew that the more than $30 million and numerous names and addresses that would have to be keyed into the database and accounted for exactly would test our software's ease of use and ability to scale. Despite these misgivings, we took the job. We had to rewrite some aspects of our software when we discovered that our FEC report calculations ran too slowly on reports as huge as Clinton's, and we spent some late nights at the Clinton campaign office. Our efforts and attention (which we accomplished while continuing to take care of many other campaigns) made a difference. Hillary for Senate had so many donors that the stack of paper from the report was over a foot high. As the deadline neared, we printed the report at our office while the campaign printed it at theirs, just in case there was a problem with either printer. Hillary's 2000 Senate race was an important milestone and proved that we could play in the big leagues. In a scene to be repeated often in presidential and large statewide campaigns, the Clinton campaign dramatically completed the report just minutes before the filing deadline.

A year later, after Hillary won her election, NGP had grown in size and client base. In the 2000 cycle, we added new senators-elect Debbie Stabenow in Michigan, Tom Carper in Delaware, and Mark Dayton in Minnesota and many members of the House. We were beating the existing competition in our niche. Louis proved to be a fortunate first hire, and more than 12 years later is still with us as senior vice president. In the two years we worked together in the attic we sometimes drove each other crazy. He held down the fort alone when I abandoned him to get married in Colorado or for other projects. Louis always had a knack with our customers, and over time he learned to program and became an expert in compliance. Louis served as a foil to me and helped make NGP's identity more colorful. Working together, I could see that we were on a path to sustained growth, and I set aside time to consider the enterprise culture I wanted to create, which in my mind at the time was fun, quirky, competitive, anticorporate, hard working, low on hierarchy, support focused, and mission oriented.

Meanwhile, I kept a watchful eye on the market, paying attention both to new entrants and old players and to adjacent technology spaces. There were many new developments. Several firms had received tens of millions of dollars of venture capital for online applications in the political space. A rival company confusingly launched a tool for political campaign Web sites with the same name as our flagship product. The Democratic National Committee initiated a technology infrastructure improvement project. Patton Technologies, a small enterprise with a base in compliance and accounting for Democratic state parties, reworked its software and sought to extend its reach. Other competitors ramped up their marketing efforts. Through all this, tiny NGP moved forward steadily, helping our campaigns by facilitating the efficiency of their fundraising operations and assuring that they had the tools to file accurate reports. New clients came faster and faster so that data conversions and support took more and more of our time. It was exciting each time we enrolled another notable politician. By 2001, we were able to hire a third person, the reliable Tim Kovacs, to help with these tasks. Mainly, we were just plugging away, building a client base one by one, by good service and word-of-mouth advertising, in a technology area that was still the middle of nowhere.

NGP continued to grow rapidly through the 2002 elections. We moved to a commercial condo near my house and hired our fourth employee, a capable and energetic database administrator named Danielle Costa, late in 2001, and our fifth, a hardworking programmer named Erin Butler, in 2002. I kept a close eye on the books and hired only when I unequivocally needed help and we could clearly afford it. Anyone who has been at the helm of an enterprise when it was taking off knows the roller coaster of stress and excitement that enlivened our days.

The next big hurdle was the transition away from client-server applications to Web-based software, which took place during the run-up to the presidential race in 2004. I had watched the development of Web-based software for a number of years. I had long recognized that the Web was the future, but I found considerable resistance among my own clients to allowing any of their data to reside at a remote host, and I was puzzled about how to navigate the coming transition. Finally, after a few false starts, I assembled a very small and very hardy group of young programmers, almost all in their first job out of college. Using the resources that were coming in from our existing product, and with the help of a few independent consultants, we took the plunge and rebuilt our software as a Web-based system, copying the interface as much as we could to minimize customer pain on migration. We stayed on a Microsoft platform, moving to Visual Basic.NET. The engineering team crowded into the rooms of our new location on Connecticut Avenue in northwest Washington, DC, some of us retreating occasionally for an attic foosball game. We were operating in a start-up environment in which engineers were still taking support calls, but morale and camaraderie were high.

We endured growing pains as we staffed up to 15 employees. But even with the new software development in full gear, we were doing a terrific job keeping the existing software application moving and supporting it among an ever-growing and more prominent client base. Many of the star employees of that period, like Eric Hamano, Craig Lebowitz, and Sandy Gani, are still with us today, and their presence continues to connect us to our roots as a hardworking upstart firm. Our business was booming, we were being helpful to Democrats, and the vast majority of our clients loved us, as our surveys (and our conversations with them) demonstrated.

In the 2004 cycle, though most of our business was federal or down ballot, NGP Software entered the presidential market. We were ultimately chosen for fundraising, compliance, or both by Gephardt, Dean, Kerry, Graham, Lieberman, and Clark. Our Web-based system was in an early phase of development and quite green, but because it was based in SQL Server it was capable of reliably managing many more records than our desktop software. The Dean campaign, which started out on our desktop product, soon clamored for the new software. We nervously delivered them the beta version of NGP Campaign Office Online, which they hosted on their own servers. Large political operations benefited most from the scalability and accessibility of the Web application. (Another beta client was Senate Majority Leader Thomas Daschle.)

The Kerry campaign, on the other hand, employed our desktop system. I visited Kerry headquarters in Washington, DC, reasonably often, working hard to support their need to scale that database and integrate it with other systems that they employed. Their technical leadership tried to make sense of the variety of database systems required to support a national campaign, and I had a great opportunity to track the boatload of innovations in technology that came about in the 2004 campaign. It was fun being trusted by many competing presidential campaigns.

We continued to work like demons throughout the 2004 election cycle, tending also to our burgeoning base of federal, state, and other organization clients and putting our resources back into improvements in the new Web-based software. We added the ability to process online donations, which we did on a different model than most of our competitors, electing not to take a percentage of each contribution we processed. Clients on our Web-based system could now easily operate the same database across offices in different states without installing software. We moved to a monthly rental model for our software, improving our revenues and allowing us to afford more programmers. By moving online, we leapfrogged several competitors and kept pace with the few that were already there.

As I learned, a growing business faces an array of challenges as it passes through different phases of growth. Building internal systems and processes is important and ongoing. Hiring and retaining good people is crucial, and overall we did exceptionally well in that regard. For a software business, keeping the application up with the times was also imperative. I struggled with this, but there were simply more directions to go and opportunities than we could manage. Whether to deploy programming resources to the urgent requirements of our largest customers or to long-term strategic product goals was a daily challenge.

Around this time, we started to track time internally and to build up a sales operation. We moved from our homegrown internal client-tracking database to a professional customer-relationship management tool. I also decided that I needed to make some investments in myself. I felt it necessary to work not just *in* the business but *on* it, and I found a number of forums and venues to step outside the daily operations and find ways to think broadly about the needs of the market. I also sought ways to grow as a manager, leader, and businessman. I was consciously transitioning myself from technician to entrepreneur.

The 2004 presidential campaigns spawned more successful startups in political technology, with the side effect that our customers now expected more of us. Among these new companies were Blue State Digital (which built a toolset for online campaigning and a consulting practice around them), EchoDitto, Mayfield Strategies (now part of Trilogy), and others. NGP generally worked congenially with these companies and, as a product firm, had no designs on a digital political strategy practice. I made an effort to build our offerings into a broader suite of products in an effort to beat what some of our online software competitors, such as Complete Campaigns, were doing. At this time I hired Chris Casey, a pioneer in the Democratic Web world, to bootstrap a campaign Web site practice.

We also added the wily Dodd Guevara, who I had noted for his inventiveness in managing the information technology for the Lieberman presidential campaign, as our first IT director. Another step forward was the hiring of Chris Massicotte, a former political fundraiser, to head our sales team. In 2005, we bought a small field-software campaign company called WinCampaign and acquired its strong salesman, Sam Osborne. We were growing quickly as an enterprise, but the requirements for campaign technology were growing as well and now extended to e-mail, Web sites, volunteer management, and more.

One of our other rivals, a nonpartisan political technology firm that had been around a lot longer and was at the time much larger had lost many of its prominent Democratic clients to us. In the summer of 2005, that company added a dose of the bizarre to the adventure of running NGP. It filed suit against us in federal court, with a laundry list of allegations including unjust enrichment and misleading advertising. The costs of defending such a suit appeared to be designed to be damaging or fatal; we were then a very frugal 15-person firm, and our antagonist had in-house counsel and a history of aggressive anticompetitive lawsuits. I was quite surprised at the creativity that they brought to their suit. For six years, they prosecuted the lawsuit as if it were a negative political campaign, creating attack Web sites, direct-mail pieces, advertisements in trade publications, press releases, and e-mail swipes at me and my firm. We did not respond in kind, preferring to stay on the high road. We received steady and moderating counsel from our lawyers Eric Yaffe and Iris Rosario. Over time, the opposing company abandoned several of their claims but took their false advertising claim to trial. In the end, Federal District Court Judge Thomas F. Hogan dismissed all the claims. The written decision dismantled their arguments and vindicated our strategies. I enjoyed our victory. I also came to the conclusion that if one company can deliberately cause another to waste time and money over such nonsense, then our legal system desperately requires reform.

Another significant development was the formation of an enterprise in an adjacent market, a voter-file data warehouse and center of data analytics for progressives called Catalist. I was glad to see our side invested seriously in data. I worked with Vijay Ravindran, their very capable chief technology officer, to hire a technology director for the Clinton for Senate and HillPAC operations in 2006. Many months later, when the Hillary Clinton for President campaign was in its planning stages, the prospective campaign manager, Patti Solis Doyle, told me that the person Vijay and I had recommended to the campaign had not been successful. She asked me to assume the role of chief technology officer myself. I debated the opportunity at length. There were many considerations, including whether I could find anyone to run NGP in my place and the fact that my company was also serving almost every other Democratic presidential contender. But after so many years in the parochial world of campaign software, I wanted change and new learning. I also believed that Hillary Clinton would make a good president and thought I could help her operation. I took the position, recusing myself from contact with the other presidential campaigns after having ascertained that I could provide a range of NGP services, not just my own time, to the campaign.

By 2007, "familiarity with NGP" was a standard line in the resumes of would-be Democratic staffers, and our software was nearly ubiquitous. I decided to celebrate NGP's 10th anniversary at the National Press Club. It was an important moment for me personally. At that time, I was spending a great deal of time at the Clinton campaign headquarters in Ballston, Virginia. I was consciously trying to put some distance between myself and my painfully close identification with the company that bore my initials and that had obsessed and stressed me for more than a decade. Fortuitously, I met Stuart Trevelyan, one of the founders of a progressive nonprofit technology firm called CTSG that he had helped grow to about 70 employees and then sold to a public corporation. I thought that Trevelyan had the right experience to help run NGP during my intermittent absences and hired him as president. Stu turned out to be a great match for the company, with a political background and commitment that went back to Bill Clinton's 1992 campaign war room, stronger day-to-day management skills than my own, and a sense of cool competitiveness that blended perfectly with the NGP vibe.

For that 10th anniversary party, as a labor of love, I compiled an eight-foot-long comprehensive visual display poster of NGP's history. It detailed the company's development and included timelines of everyone who had worked with us, their photographs, dates that we added key clients, and many other noteworthy events. I was proud and happy to be among friends, clients, employees, and family. I knew that the company was very likely on a path of continued growth and success and that we would play an increasingly important role in the Democratic political technology ecosystem. I should have been on top of the world, and in many respects I was. But the truth is that I found the day-to-day management of a software company deeply taxing, and I was profoundly ambivalent about what I wanted to set my sights on next.

By the 2008 presidential cycle, NGP had grown a great deal more. We had watched many other campaign software companies disappear or stagnate. We achieved by far the leading position in fundraising and compliance among Democrats. Meanwhile, in the adjacent world of software tools for managing the field component of an election campaign, the Voter Activation Network (VAN) followed a similar ascendancy. I had watched that market for several years closely and knew that the VAN had a formidable future in the Democratic political technology world. Fortunately, I found it easy to make friends and to cooperate with them whenever possible. VAN ultimately obtained a 50-state contract with the Democratic National Committee to serve as the voter-file software for the whole party, a landmark event.

After Hillary Clinton's withdrawal from the race in summer 2008, I returned full time to NGP. As always, things were busy and interesting. It felt like being among family, especially compared to the tensions and pressures of a presidential campaign. The political technology market was, as usual, in flux. New entrants to the market, Civio and National-Field and a number of others, arrived out of the ferment of 2008. Salsa/ Wired for Change sought to bring its nonprofit e-mail tools into the political market. Many political digital strategy consultancies were building their own online tools. VAN made some new forays, partnering with a voter data company called TargetSmart to create SmartVAN and adding Web site tools and automated telephone calling to its software platform. Stu and I wondered if NGP and VAN were destined for a head-on competitive collision.

With something like 60 employees and a client base that now included the national party committees, many labor unions, and numerous other organizations, NGP was long past being a lifestyle company for me. I felt the weight of responsibility to my clients, my party, and to our employees. Trevelyan and I made some moves. In January 2009, I sold some stock and Trevelyan became CEO of NGP. I kept in mind what I had read about the so-called "founder syndrome," where those in positions such as mine have difficulty surrendering the reins of the organization that they had started. (Planning for the future, I started other projects, including a small company called Timeplots that tells complex stories in visual form. Timeplots has already created some intricate political posters that have met with good reviews, including visual histories of the Supreme Court and the U.S. presidency.) I also invited Mark Sullivan and Jim St. George, the VAN owners, to hike with me and my siblings on the Inca trail so that there would be time for us to become more familiar with each other.

Meanwhile, the pace of change did not slow. I was delighted when we were able to acquire our long-time state party compliance software competitor, Patton Technologies, and bring the formidable Chris Patton to NGP. NGP also worked away at a project that we called Oberon, an ambitious overhaul of our main software platform. Following a market trend, we built a module called personal fundraising pages that facilitated distributed fundraising. And we finally added the DNC as a client, replacing their homegrown Demzilla application with our technology and, at their request, adding joint fundraising tools. The most significant change came at the beginning of 2011, when our ongoing efforts to merge with VAN came to fruition. I was completely persuaded that our combination was the right move for both companies and for the Democratic political technology world.

NGP VAN is working hard to help the Democratic Party and its candidates in 2012 with the core campaigning tasks that produce victory in tight races. At this moment, NGP VAN is a small jewel, a proud part of the development of the political technology industry in the United States. Many challenges lie in front of us, but we are well served by a company culture that is notably healthy and rooted in years of responsiveness to our clients. We have navigated tremendous technological and political changes—changes that created an equal mix of business opportunities and perils as the stakes grew higher. Our success means that we have great responsibilities. We are well positioned to help our party and our stakeholders into the future. However, if we do not continue to make the right decisions, serve our clients well, adapt to the changing environment, and continue to earn our place, we will quickly be upstaged by better products coming out of a rival firm, an adjacent industry, a presidential campaign, or someone else's attic.

NGP grew from a one-person endeavor into an institution that is now very much independent of me. The story of my company's evolution paralleled my own growth. I became less naïve, and for this I give a lot of credit to my staff, my wife, and to the entrepreneurs with whom I interacted in various forums. I ultimately came to the conclusion that my skills and aptitudes as an entrepreneur are best suited to the start-up and early growth stage of new enterprises and to the senior statesman role at NGP VAN that I now occupy. My campaign technology vision remains generally the same as the one I put forward in my article in 1991: an investigative and unified view of campaign data that facilitates political communication and campaigning. For us, this holy grail of campaign technology will probably always remain over the horizon. Innovation will continue to spring from campaigns and party organizations, from new start-ups and current players. In my considered view, we are still early in the history of the development of political campaign software.

CHAPTER 16

Actionable Data: Using Social Technology to Change Organizations

Edward Saatchi

Social technology has changed the way we interact with our friends, and it has already started changing the way we work, the way we campaign, and the way we collaborate as individuals and teams. I am someone who got very lucky in that I and two great people I met on the Obama campaign—Aharon Wasserman and Justin Lewis—built NationalField, the private social network for the Obama campaign. We decided to devote our lives to using social technology to change organizations. We stumbled into it, really. We created something people just *wanted* to use. We discovered that nobody else had done it before, and we turned it into a company. In the process we learned some valuable lessons about political data.

I am going to begin by telling you a story, the story of political data in the United States, which brings us to the present day with the power of social technology to change campaigns.

GOTV IN THE EARLY YEARS

The process of get-out-the-vote (GOTV) is a never-ending one of building, refining, and refreshing a giant Rolodex of every potential voter in the United States. Your job in a presidential campaign is to take an old Rolodex from the last election and get it as up to date as quickly as possible. That way, come Election Day when you only have 12 hours, you know exactly who to mobilize, who to call, and who to ignore.

There are two core teams that work on GOTV: the data team and the field team. Data provides the first list of voters for field to canvass. The recipe for the list is:

- Consumer data (do you prefer *Us Weekly* or *Vanity Fair*?)
- Old field data (in the previous election, did you tell a volunteer that you were interested in the economy or animal rights?)
- Fundraising data (when, how much, and to whom did you donate?)
- Electoral data (have you ever voted in a Democratic primary or registered to vote for a special election or a proposition?)

The field team prints out the list of voters compiled by the data team. Armed with addresses and phone numbers, they knock on doors and make phone calls to get 1 of 10 responses that range from "strong Democrat" (a 1), to "strong Republican" (a 5), not home, moved, deceased, and so forth.

Field gives the updated list back to data. Data puts the 1's in a potential volunteer list, throws out the 5's, and cleans the list of the deceased, moved, refused, and bad addresses and phone numbers. This cycle of data to field to data continues over and over until Election Day. The objective is that by Election Day you have enough volunteers to remind enough voters to vote to secure victory for your campaign. Analytics shows that field campaigns can move 2 to 5 percent, so people still do it.

The first voter file was the human brain—a politician heading back into a town he or she visited in the last election, struggling to remember first names, lost spouses, and what was important to the voter. This became a primitive customer relationship management (CRM) tool with which he was able to astound voters with his memory—remembering to ask about Sally, the German shepherd, little Christopher, and how the crops had come in after last year's terrible output. As he began campaigning this practice would become the first voter file, a comprehensive list of people that he met, talked to, and remembered. In politics, the data goes beyond what the human brain can hold pretty quickly; you either forget the data, or you start recording.

The next innovation for presidential campaigns centered on a national effort to get out the vote. Presidents had attempted national campaigns in the past, but the fear was that an actual nationwide GOTV effort directed from Washington, DC, with reports coming back to headquarters, would be too complex. The benefits were obvious—if you could find out where turnout was low, the president or a surrogate could make a call and help drive turnout up.

Lyndon B. Johnson was the person who made it happen first—not for a presidential election, but for the midterm—introducing the concept of real-time GOTV. Where possible he would make calls and divert resources before the polling day was up. National GOTV was born, and so too was the need to have real-time information. The telephone allowed data to flow instantly up the chain to the president so that before the day was out, GOTV efforts could be shifted to where they were needed. Resting at home after a long campaign and waiting for the results had come to an end. Mr. Gallup was to come, but here was the moment that political data on a mass scale was born and the potential to influence election results was introduced.

ENTER LEE ATWATER

Let us jump forward several decades to the first President Bush. It was the beginning of the 1990s, the President was riding high, and Lee Atwater was part of the team that must help the president win reelection. With Saddam Hussein defeated and the economy doing well, this should have been no problem, right? But as Atwater looked deeper he found that the Republican National Committee did not control the data vital to a national campaign; the state parties did. Even worse, the data was sitting in dusty cardboard boxes in the backs of campaign offices. In many states, it hadn't been touched since the midterms in 1990 (meaning that many voters had died, moved, changed their allegiance, and so forth), while in other states it hadn't been touched since 1988, as there had been no field effort in the midterms. Atwater was faced with old data—data that he didn't even control and couldn't target around on a national basis.

The campaign needed to build a national database, and Atwater made it a priority to do so. His objective was that 1992 would be the most innovative campaign of all time. The process of organizing and consolidating voter files began with Lee and gave the Republicans an advantage for the following 14 years. The power of field data was finally recognized at the national level. Now, instead of regional fiefdoms relying on the brain of the candidate, reliable campaign workers, or cue cards, data would now be analyzed and accessible on a national basis.

Several RNC chairs later, the Voter Vault—a single, unified voter file—emerged, allowing Republicans to trumpet microtargeting and assist them in beating Democrats. On the field side, Karl Rove used it to popularize his "72-hour strategy," a highly disciplined blitz in the three days before an election. Instead of building links with the community, the focus was on an enormous blitz of local and out-of-state volunteers who would drive the base, the sporadic voters, and churches out to the polls in the last 72 hours. The objective of field was to clean the list, recruit volunteers for the final 72 hours, and drive out voters at the end. This made sense for a few reasons but especially because Republicans historically had an edge in early voting; their voters did not require as much pushing to post their ballots, and so the final 72 hours was the time when they could really drive home their advantage. Voter Vault and the 72-hour strategy helped Republicans win several terms of Congress and two presidential elections—advantage, Republicans.

DEAN ROARS BACK

The pendulum began to swing back in 2004 with Howard Dean's failed presidential campaign. In fact, the roots of Obama-style field and data strategies can be traced back to Dean's campaign. Joe Trippi, Dean's campaign manager, pushed forward with the community-organizing methods from acolytes of Marshall Ganz, like Jeremy Bird and Karen Hicks, to capture field data and organize a community well before Election Day. Organizers now were not simply expected to clean lists in preparation for a GOTV blitz on Election Day but also to organize communities and build relationships through one-on-one communications with volunteers *months* before the election. Instead of relying on the party apparatus to control volunteers on Election Day—impossible because of Dean's insurgent background—they built a new apparatus of young people, online fundraisers, and others interested in politics that could use the Web to connect with organizers and each other.

It did not work perfectly. On caucus day many voters still did not turn out. Dean's campaign was bottom-up in the extreme and didn't have the technology or the discipline to get people out. The campaign crashed and burned, but Dean eventually became head of the DNC. Just as it was his campaign that innovated above and beyond Republican tactics, it was his DNC that finally leveled the playing field with Republicans on the voter file.

With the template created during Dean's campaign in place, the stage was set for continued innovation. It was the key players in Dean's New Hampshire operation who would go on to large influences in the 2008 election cycle in the Democratic Party. On the data side, the Internet was shown to be a force to be reckoned with, allowing far-flung voters with an interest in the candidate to *self*-organize volunteer meetings and *self*-organize fundraisers through the forward-facing site and through sites like Meetup.com.

Over 14 years, the Democrats had realized that field data was valuable and that they should have a voter file to capture and control information on a database. There was only one problem: it was the Wild West in the Democratic Party. Rather than no voter file software there were many small firms to choose from, and all were competing for contracts with the state parties. In 2006 the DNC under Howard Dean signed a contract with the Voter Activation Network (VAN) to provide a voter file for *all* the states. The playing field was leveled with the Republicans just before the 2008 elections.

ENTER OBAMA

And so we arrive at 2008, when the Obama team capitalized on a lot of the successes hinted at in the Dean campaign. Joe Rospars, who had worked with Joe Trippi on Dean's campaign, became the new media director for the Obama campaign and was now tasked with creating MyBarackObama.com, taking the successes of Meetup.com for the Dean campaign and online fundraising and applying it to a new kind of candidate Web site. Rospars brought in the software from the firm he had cofounded, Blue State Digital, which had already contracted with the DNC to build a Democratic social network. Those tools became the base of the Obama Web infrastructure.

The Obama campaign was the first to benefit from the new unified Democratic national voter file and used it relentlessly. David Plouffe put field data at the center of the campaign. Plouffe believed fiercely in the power of field data—that it was often more accurate, more timely, and more useful than polling. In Iowa, it was the field data that told us we were in a strong position before the polls picked it up. The Obama campaign united the data and field teams with more clarity of purpose and discipline than any previous campaign. The connection between an organizer in the field and a volunteer signing up on the Internet was instantaneous.

On the purely field side, the campaign saw the reversal of the Republican advantage in field and data. The 72-hour strategy was discredited along with the use of the Web to win. Rove had pioneered the idea that elections were won in the last 72 hours and that by recruiting for that period the candidate would always have an edge. The Obama campaign instead invested in relationships and community organizing, long-term strategies that played out over months of meetings, trainings, and one-to-one communications, all of which required huge coordination and manpower. The outmaneuvering was, "You think elections are won 72 hours before? Try organizing *four months* before, when we're in coffee-house meetings, living rooms, and organizing people in the community."

There was one small thing by the start of the Obama campaign that the market had not produced: an internal social network for the movement that would grow with President Obama and serve as a management tool for staff and volunteers. As presidential campaigns grew to the level of large corporations with the revenue of small countries, the reliance on spreadsheets and phone calls to manage the workforce had to end. The corporate world had created enterprise resource planning (ERP) systems to manage staff, improve productivity, and keep track of all the workflows with hundreds and then thousands of staff. These tools are the core businesses for big companies like Oracle and SAP.

In business terms, we had a CRM, a way to track voters and fundraisers (VAN and NGP), and a forward-facing site for people to come, learn about the campaign, and immediately start organizing (MyBarackObama.com), but no ERP. We had no system outside of spreadsheets to track productivity and workflow. On the Obama campaign, reporting was a central concern. Jeremy Bird, the field guru behind the South Carolina win, considered daily reporting a necessity. David Plouffe, for one, recognized that the field data was always more accurate than the old-fashioned poll data commissioned by newspapers. But we lacked the right system to pull it all together.

I'M NOT IN PARIS ANYMORE

I joined the Obama campaign in 2007, and my story is like the story of many of the people who I know from the campaign. There was a little more of a roadblock in my case in that I am a British citizen, I had never lived in the United States, and I had just left Oxford and started two concurrent master's degrees in Paris. But I was determined to help. For months before I arrived in Iowa, I had been slipping out of the *bibliotheque de la Sorbonne*, standing in the corridor trying to look inconspicuous, while calling Obama headquarters in Chicago to say, "I must help. How can I help?" Each time the response was, "DO NOT COME to the United States. Foreign citizens cannot be employed by a political campaign. You would be volunteering for 15 months."

Finally I got fed up with the rejections, hopped on a plane to Des Moines, presented myself at the volunteer office, and said that I would like to help. I was given a sign, a street corner, and told to stand there holding the sign. First lesson: there's always something to do on a campaign.

After several months I found myself in southern Georgia with Aharon, where we would meet our third cofounder, Justin. On his first day with us, Justin proved awful at registering voters. Sweetly shy, he couldn't get the hang of approaching strangers and getting them to register. But that evening when we finished working for the day, Aharon, Justin, and I started brainstorming about a way to connect all the volunteer teams we were building, an online place for them to write a blog about their team, post upcoming events, and share photographs from canvasses—a social network. That discussion led us to cobble together GAObama.com, a rudimentary Web site built that same night using Google Sites. By the following morning we presented the site to our volunteers.

The next night, we decided we had to have something better than the spreadsheets we were using to collect reports from volunteers. The current systems and long conference calls were tedious, imprecise, and wasted a lot of time. Aharon started talking about building a three-dimensional spread-sheet. He spent the night talking to his cousin, Dan Ordille, who said, "Yeah, that's a database, buddy." From there Aharon and Justin sat down and planned out how it should work, and we started talking about how it should be social and be able to aggregate data on the back end all the way up to field leadership without any difficulty. The focus wouldn't just be on sharing qualitative information instantly up the chain but also on the numbers and real-time data. To hell with the uneventful phone calls and the endless meetings where each person would stare into space waiting for their turn to read out an endless stream of metrics!

The first version launched the same night we had the idea. It was mod-eled explicitly on Facebook, but combined with the numbers we needed to know what was going on, the leader boards, and the tables. The second the data was made social—the second it was transparent, articulate, and visualized in a meaningful way—it unlocked an innate accountability within and competition among the volunteers. The numbers went up, and people drove themselves harder.

Immediately the nightly meetings that every regional head had with their staff changed from a mind-numbing recitation of figures to an analysis of and coaching based on the day's data. The conversation turned to, "Why do you think you got the highest numbers? What did you do that we could learn from? The flake rates are really high here; how many confirmation calls are we doing?" The bread and butter of the workplace, the actual work that was being produced, was front and center, and it was social and fun. We combined the microblogging with the microreporting for everyone. The microreporting meant limited but relevant metrics, quick reports showing up in real time for *everybody* and not just your boss. That complete transparency around numbers was a testament to Alex Lofton. Many people didn't feel comfortable with openness around the numbers on the basis that those who were blinkered were more focused.

We decided that as well as reporting numbers, people would put their pluses and deltas—things that are working and things that need to change—into GAObama.com to be sent up the chain to field leadership in Atlanta. As we read them the first morning—they were e-mailed to BlackBerries after everyone had reported—the reaction was an immediate, "Oh. My. God." Instead of one or two nuggets, almost everyone was reporting useful and actionable data. All those shy people who wouldn't raise their hand in a meeting to say they hadn't understood something were willing to be completely open and transparent so long as they knew it was going up the chain of command.

THE GAME CHANGES, AGAIN

The use of pluses and deltas on the campaign was a game changer. There is a weird relationship between people and the keyboard and screen at reporting hour. In short bursts of pure honesty, everyone transmitted via the pluses and deltas the things they wouldn't say in meetings or wouldn't say to managers, like, "We love you but we need more direction. We're not really aligned." Now we had a way of knowing that everything that Lofton said as a leader could be reviewed for its effectiveness, and course corrections could be made when someone on the ground (those closest to the reality of the voter/consumer) said, "Hey, HQ guys. Great idea but it just didn't actually work on the doors."

This extraordinary change lasted for four or five days before there were inklings of pushback. The pluses and deltas bypassed people in the middle; they went straight from the ground to the leadership in Atlanta. Middle management felt it was undermining their leadership and ownership—and they were right. Lofton, obsessive about people having ownership of their turf, immediately wanted a technical change to the way information flowed. We thought, "What about all this great data we're collecting? Will people be as honest about what's going on in their region if their direct manager can see it?" It felt like we were shutting off a tap that was making Lofton an incredibly responsive state leader, able to adjust in real time as feedback came in. We made the change, dreaded the next day's pluses and deltas, and went to sleep, waiting for the e-mail, and—nothing. No change. Still pure honesty and the actionable data Lofton had found so useful. The relationship between the person and the computer, and the guarantee that their report was private between them and their managers (yes, even including the one they were in the office with every day and who might get upset!) overwhelmed people's natural shyness. The default behavior of people on Facebook—to be open and honest— transferred to GAObama.com, and people felt safe being honest and sharing more than the campaign had been able to previously learn from the people on the ground.

By the end of the week we had built a social reporting tool with a uniquely transparent culture, all because of the power of social media. Retooled for the workplace, it focused us on making us feel smart and great about what we were producing. People started seeing how successful the program was, and we were asked to start implementing the concept nationwide, especially in Ohio and Florida. We would have to change the name from GAObama.com. We chose NationalField, from "National Field Program of the Obama Campaign."

The proudest moment for us was seeing people everywhere in the state clicking the refresh button on NationalField to see where they had come on the leader board and to see where their region had come on the state leader board. If they weren't satisfied they'd shout, "Region Eleven is shooting up! We have to go back out and keep canvassing. Get the car!" That innate competitive instinct was unlocked, and people were motivated to do better. People used the NationalField leader board to egg each other on and encourage everybody to do better. We were able to see the actual numbers shift before the election and the polls. For the first time, we were able to see how we were doing in real time.

After the campaign, people went to work at other companies, other campaigns, and the administration, and they all said, "My God, the intranet we use is terrible, clunky, nonsocial, and nobody logs in except to look at the staff directory" or "We tried a private social network like Yammer and it doesn't do anything. It's just chatter—we need NationalField." The feedback was clear: "Why don't you become a company, and we'll be your clients?"

So we took their advice and turned NationalField into a company. Right after the campaign we started building NationalField 2.0. We went to Aharon's house in the small town of Bridgeton, New Jersey, where his very forgiving and understanding parents allowed us to commandeer their dining room table for three months. Their lovely home became a mess of wires, eating on the couch, and kids (myself, Justin, Aharon, his cousin Dan, and our friend Brendan Farmer) screaming at each other,

"No! The top bar can't be blue! Are you insane? This is just like when you said the spark lines should be 18 pixels across. You're destroying this site!" Physical fights ensued over the font, whether we should invest time in Vadim Tropashko's theories of nested sets (we did), and whether we should focus just on fundraising (we didn't).

AND NOW, 2012

As we approach the 2012 election, NationalField has begun working with the Obama campaign to continue building on the work Justin, Aharon, and I started in 2008. The campaign and the software have evolved tremendously since our days in Georgia, and our mission has grown as well. We have recently taken in over $1 million in private investment to enable us to innovate and continue focusing on the thousands of staff and volunteers throughout the country on whom we remain focused, ensuring they're getting the data most critical to their jobs in real time.

Whether it's seeing the percent to goal or quickly analyzing best practices from someone 3,000 miles away, everything NationalField does reflects its singular purpose: break down barriers for communication to make you more informed. It's no longer just about aggregating the numbers from the bottom up so HQ knows where to commit resources. That approach proved immensely powerful, but what's equally exciting is facilitating the lateral communication between the thousands of teams and individuals working toward one goal: four more years.

So what's next? There a lot of Holy Grails that anyone at the higher levels of political technology will grab your arm and enthusiastically tell you about into the late hours. Two that you will probably hear a lot about are voter file and Facebook integration, and a single tool that can act as the ERP, forward-facing site, voter file, and fundraising.

As I see it, the market for political campaign technology is flawed in three ways, and someone needs to change it. First, the barriers to entry are too high for enterprise vendors. There are so many laws around campaigning that many vendors, like Salesforce on the CRM side, find it too difficult to penetrate the market. Second, political data is a market that, in the past, was controlled by a small group of friends. But the client (i.e., the candidate) doesn't control the data; it's in the hands of the state parties.

Third, the cyclical nature of the market creates disincentives to large investments in technology because political parties genuinely have money to invest once every four years. Even worse, individual campaigns can only invest in the final three months. The temptation has been to reinvent the wheel every two years and every four years. Before the rise of cloud computing it made no sense to invest in durable ERP or CRM systems that could take years to implement. It was actually *more* logical to reinvent the wheel. With the cloud, that approach no longer makes sense.

Why is all this going to change? In the political market, reinventing the wheel is going to become too expensive. The flexibility of enterprise software is going to increase, the barriers to entry will be worked around, and eventually someone is going to take the data and open the market to the light of day. NationalField is already a company that plays for both sides—politics and enterprise. We deploy over the cloud, we operate out of Silicon Valley, and we integrate with enterprise CRMs and ERPs. Someone, somewhere, is coming to change the market, and, I'm sorry to say, when they do, everything here will be out of date. There'll be no such thing as political data. There will be CRMs, ERPs, and social business software. Politics will become professionalized.

A final, very important word for anyone trying to build a political technology system: what we found with NationalField is that technology changes *behavior* but not the underlying *psychology* that drives behavior. Figure out what people really want and make sure your technology fulfills that psychological need. Think back for a moment. What is now our generation's iconic image of user and computer? It's no longer the hackers of the 1990s. The image we have in our collective mind is the Facebook mastermind Mark Zuckerberg, played by Jesse Eisenberg in the movie *The Social Network*. He's staring at the Facebook profile of his ex, waiting for her to confirm his friend request; he's obsessively refreshing to see if she'll accept.

The psychology of that final scene is, "I want to be accepted. I want to be liked by people I like." It's human nature, and we can't change it. By having Facebook, shy people are able to be social in ways that they otherwise wouldn't. Take that psychology and apply it to the workplace and you'll see the power that social technology can have on the way we work. Not silly things like sharing news articles but genuinely getting people excited about the community they're in. They are clicking the leader board, they are seeing how they are doing on the feed, they are getting the number one achievement on NationalField, and they feel great, respected, empowered, and included. They feel respected because their opinions are heard, empowered because they actually can see the numbers and understand their situation on the map or against their goals, and included in every relevant decision that's being taken.

It's not just social technology; it's technology that capitalizes on human nature. The smart innovators and game changers will continue to utilize this as they drive politics and campaigns forward in 2012 and beyond.

CHAPTER 17

Impasse: The Voting Technology Challenge

Stephen Ansolabehere

Before the 2000 election, voting technology was an afterthought. People knew the technologies on which they voted, but most were unaware that there were other ways to cast and count ballots or that some methods might be decidedly less accurate or less secure than others. There had been local foul-ups, such as the primary election for the Massachusetts 10th Congressional District, and there were some technical experts, such as Roy Saltman at the National Institute of Standards and Technology (NIST), who warned about the problems with voting technology.[1] For most of us, however, voting just happened. There was little research on voting technology, little innovation in the U.S. industry, and little government attention to election machinery.

The controversial count, recount, and legal battle over the presidential vote in Florida exploded the United States' complacency about voting technology. State governments quickly put in place new voting technology standards and clarified laws concerning what constitutes a vote. The federal government, which had never appropriated any funds to conduct elections, spent $5 billion on technology upgrades for voting machines and registration systems. Congress also established the first agency devoted expressly to the conduct of elections, the Election Assistance Commission (EAC). Academic research in political science, law, and technology set out to determine what technologies work and how best to implement them. While there were already firms in this niche market, industrial interest in voting technology, and especially in electronic and Internet voting, blossomed.

The 2000 election also sent shockwaves through the campaign world. The voting equipment failed; it undid the carefully planned get-out-the-vote and targeting campaigns of Bush and Gore in Florida and in other states, and it drove home the possibility that the "wrong candidate" might win by accident. Candidates, groups, and parties suddenly found that they needed to rethink their organizations in the event of a recount. The problems did not cease in 2000. Since then, we have had dozens of recounts, most prominently in the Florida 13th Congressional District, in the Minnesota U.S. Senate election, and in the Washington gubernatorial election. All resulted from continued problems with election equipment, and each recount underscored the unhappy lesson of 2000 that political campaigns and parties must now devote resources not only to the contest before Election Day but to the contest afterward as well.

Party organizations and political campaigns have had to adapt to this new reality. The presidential campaigns in 2004 and 2008 retained teams of election lawyers and poll watchers in advance of the election so that they could ready for potential legal battles like the ones that started the decade. This forced the campaigns to make difficult choices between activities geared to win votes and activities needed to prepare for lawsuits. For some, however, new modes of voting create new opportunities. Absentee, early voting, and vote centers—made feasible by electronic equipment—allow campaigns to target voters more effectively and improve their get-out-the-vote (GOTV) activities. And lurking just over the horizon is the promise and, some say, threat of Internet voting.

My own perspective on voting technology is of someone caught in the wake of the 2000 election. Like everyone else, the extent of the problems encountered in the Florida election came as a complete surprise. Yet two weeks after the election, MIT president Charles Vest asked me to lead a joint initiative with Caltech to develop a new voting machine. Our team, the Caltech/MIT Voting Technology Project, quickly learned that some even more basic resources were lacking in the election system, such as reliable information about vote totals and equipment performance. Simple questions about voting technology lacked ready answers at that time: Who uses what technology? What technology works best? How badly did the election system fail? How many people voted, and how many votes were counted?

The viewpoint of a researcher differs from the vantage of others involved in the development and maintenance of voting technology. We work with those in industry and government to improve implementation, but we do not ultimately manufacture the machines or run the elections. Our team provides information that can help election offices make better decisions, and we develop technologies and ideas that can improve the process in the future. Studies performed by our research team, for example, showed that the completeness of the vote counts varied systematically with voting technology and that eliminating punch cards could cut much of the error in voting tabulation. Computer science research by our project led to the development of the Internet voting system Helios (by Ben Adida) and audio voting systems for blind people (by Ted Selker). The spirit of such inquiry is to generate ideas and empirical findings that will help others conduct elections better.

TECHNOLOGY CIRCA 2000

After the courts had settled the election dispute and the lawyers had scattered, Florida still had a problem. Its voting technology had failed: equipment had broken down; ballots were formatted incorrectly; ballot readers did not produce consistent counts; absentee votes were handled improperly; and the law offered no clear path to follow toward a resolution. The state had become synonymous with poor election practice.

Before the recount was over, Governor Jeb Bush had formed a bipartisan task force to address the problems. The Governor's Taskforce on Election Reform was charged with recommending new technology for the state, improvements in polling place operations, a new registration system, and a revised election statute. At the time, Florida counties used four different voting systems: hand-counted paper ballots, electronically scannable paper ballots, punch cards, and mechanical lever machines. And in the wake of the election the state was considering a wholesale adoption of a fifth technology: electronic voting machines. These five technologies represented the range of available technologies at the time, though there are variations on each.

A brief review of the five main technologies in use in 2000 reveals two basic truths about voting technology. First, any given election technology applies the computing technologies of the day to improve the speed of counting, the ease of use, and the security of the system.[2] Second, the way that particular technologies are implemented can fundamentally alter campaign strategies and political organizations.

At the beginning of the nineteenth century, voting was a public act. To state one's preference, one stood up at a town meeting to be counted. As the United States grew and as large cities emerged, town-meeting democracy became practically impossible, and hand-counted paper ballots emerged to make elections work. This innovation was also driven by technology—fast, cheap, mechanized printing—and by the 1880s, widespread use of paper ballots made possible the shift to a secret ballot. Once adopted, the secret ballot changed political organizations and campaigns. Vote buying and coercion—the bread and butter of machine politics— became exceedingly more difficult, and many local machines lost control of the electoral process.

But paper ballots also introduced a problem of accountability: who controlled the ballot itself? For most of the nineteenth century, formal election administration did not exist in most places, and political parties and campaigns printed and distributed ballots. As reforms sought to stamp out machine politics, printing and management of paper ballots became the responsibility of county and municipal clerks, and political parties and campaigns lost an important electoral instrument. To this day, county and municipal clerks are the backbone of election administration in the United States. The paper ballot, however much it changed elections and campaigns, began to fade with the beginning of the twentieth century.

The story of voting technology in the twentieth century is driven by speed and security. Lever machines were introduced at the end of the nineteenth century to secure the vote further and to speed up tabulations. These 500-pound steel machines spoke security and durability. Compared with paper ballots, they were not easily tampered with. They were self-contained voting booths that guaranteed one's privacy. Lever machines also exploited the most advanced computing available. These machines contained internal dials that advanced one click when a voter registered a set of choices and pulled a lever that recorded all of those choices. At the end of the day, the election officers would record the readings on the dials, and others could verify that the counts were correct. In 2000, approximately one in five voters used lever machines.

Punch cards automated the count still more. Punch card technology made computing easier and faster, and seeing a new market for their computing division, IBM purchased the license for punch card technology for voting. Punch cards squeezed out much of the market for paper ballots. IBM packaged the punch card technology to have many of the features of lever machines, including privacy booths and secure ballot boxes, without the 500 pounds of bulk.

Early on, though, cards suffered from problems with usability and ballot formatting, leading to recounts and election controversies. IBM quickly abandoned the market when tabulation problems brought bad publicity to the firm. Nonetheless, the technology spread throughout the 1970s and 1980s and, by 2000, approximately 40 percent of voters used punch cards.

In the 1980s, Unisys introduced scannable paper ballots, similar to standardized tests. Optically scanned paper ballots were designed to avoid many of the formatting and usability problems of punch cards. Voters could verify that they recorded their preferences, and votes could be counted at the precincts. Counting got even faster. Almost a third of voters used scannable paper ballots in 2000.

Electronic voting emerged in the 1990s, first as an adaptation of the lever machine (the Shouptronic) and then as a wholly new form of voting machine based on ATM touch screen technology, called direct recording electronic machines (DREs). By 2000, at least five firms stood ready to vend the new technologies, including Shoup, ES&S, Global, Sequoia, and Hart Intercivic. In 2000, less than 10 percent of ballots were cast with electronic voting machines, but they stood ready for adoption.

The 2000 election precipitated a massive overhaul of U.S. voting technology. Paper, lever, and punch card voting employed cutting-edge communications and computing technology of their day, but by 2000 they were legacy systems that had glaring problems. In the months following the 2000 election, social scientists were quick to measure the performance of voting equipment. Professor Henry Brady and a team of political scientists at Berkeley published findings showing that punch card problems in Florida accounted for a 6-percentage-point differential in the number of ballots counted for president.[3] Professor Charles Stewart and I followed suit with a report showing that over the course of the 1990s approximately 2 percent of votes cast for president were not counted by punch cards, and optically scanned paper ballots would cut that error rate in half.[4]

Our research further emphasized that voting equipment failures affected all campaigns equally, regardless of who runs the election. Voting machine failures tend to occur randomly and are uncorrelated with political and demographic indicators, with one important exception: voting machine error rates are systematically higher in rural areas than in urban and suburban areas. Why this is true remains a matter of speculation.

The simple results from social science inquiries informed public debate over election reform in 2001 and 2002. Drawing on these findings, the National Commission on Federal Election Reform (also known as the Ford-Carter Commission) and various state commissions recommended that governments buy out of legacy technologies and adopt optically scanned and electronic voting equipment.[5]

The Voting Technology Project and other researchers envisioned that innovations in communication technology would revolutionize voting in the future. New electronic voting machines were specialized computers that could accommodate many ballots, including audio ballots for low-literacy or blind voters. For the first time we could imagine that a voter could vote anywhere because the technology would allow an individual to call up the appropriate ballot on any computer at any polling location rather than going to a dedicated location where the ballot and technology were formatted to that specific location. Absentee voting had taken off, with 20 percent of votes cast absentee or early in 2000. Why not allow people to vote on the Internet? New technology opened the possibility not just of improving the speed and security of the count but of rethinking the entire voting process.

REFORMS OF THE 2000s

The decade following the 2000 election witnessed some of the most far-reaching reforms of election administration in U.S. history. Only the reapportionment and voting rights revolutions of the 1960s and the introduction of the secret ballot and the Australian ballot in the 1880s brought more sweeping changes in the way we vote.

The Help America Vote Act (HAVA), which codified many of the recommendations of the Ford-Carter Commission, took a two-pronged approach to technology change. First, HAVA authorized funds to buy out legacy systems. Congress appropriated funds to state and local election offices to replace punch cards and lever machines with optical scan and electronic voting. Nearly all counties and states upgraded their technology by 2006. Second, HAVA authorized NIST and the EAC to develop new voting technology standards. Voluntary voting systems standards had been adopted by most states, but they were developed for the older technologies, especially punch cards, and mainly concerned durability of equipment, not usability or security. By 2001 these standards were in sore need of revision. NIST and EAC brought together election administrators, voting machine vendors, computer scientists, and social scientists to develop new voluntary voting standards.

Upgrading technologies had an immediate impact on the accuracy and completeness of vote counts. The Voting Technology Project estimated that roughly 2.5 percent of ballots cast had no vote recorded for the top of the ticket over the course of the decade from 1990 to 2000, and that figure dropped to about 1 percent as a result of technology upgrades.[6] That improvement represented a substantial reduction in uncertainty in the count and the need for campaigns to worry about questionable vote counts.

The states took even more dramatic actions than the federal government. Until 2000, few state governments had much authority over election administration; that was left to the counties and municipalities. Nearly every state revamped its elections code between 2001 and 2002, resulting in greater concentration of authority in the state election office (usually the secretary of state). Some states, such as Georgia and Maryland, undertook field tests to gauge equipment performance, and several centralized their purchases of equipment.

HAVA also required states to develop statewide voter registration systems, which gave the state election offices even more influence over the management of election administration. Now the states could insist that voter registration lists meet high-quality levels, and they could assist counties that lacked the administrative capacity to do so. This innovation has made voter lists much more accessible and usable for campaigns.

Computerized voting creates tremendous opportunities. They are yet to be realized fully, but some significant experiments have been launched. For example, Colorado saw the potential synergy between statewide voter files and electronic voting machines. The secretary of state implemented "vote centers" for the state's 2008 and 2010 elections. Vote centers are multiprecinct voting locations, usually in shopping malls and other high-traffic areas. Colorado integrated the voter registration system with its electronic voting systems so that people could access any ballot in the state on any voting machine in the state.[7] Vote centers create new opportunities for get-out-the-vote activities, as people no longer need to vote in their neighborhood.

The next obvious step is Internet voting. The Department of Defense has already taken significant steps toward the development of Internet voting, at least for military ballots. In 2000, VoteHere.net sought to crack into the wider market of elections and gain adoption by some counties, and Accenture undertook an important study for the Department of Defense on the feasibility of implementing Internet voting for overseas military called the Federal Voter Assistance Program's Secure Electronic Registration and Voting Experiment.[8] Several states, such as Virginia, allow military voters to submit ballots online, and most allow military personnel to send ballots via fax. By 2002, then, the United States was on the verge of electronic voting, either in the form of stand-alone DREs or online.

The movement toward electronic voting came to a screeching halt in 2003 and 2004 when, during the debate over HAVA, a number of prominent computer scientists raised concerns about the security and transparency of DREs. In 2003, a group of computer scientists at Johns Hopkins circulated an analysis of the actual code inside one of the DREs, exposing a large number of flaws and vulnerabilities. Worse still, the Johns Hopkins team identified critical security problems with the procedures for the implementation of the equipment in the polling places—how the election offices handle and store the equipment, who has access to cards, how testing and validation procedures are performed, and the near-total dependence on firms to format software. The team argued that voting in the electronic age would become a "black box" for the election offices, where the local election officer no longer controls the process and cannot verify completely that the software and machines work.[9]

Black-box voting became a rallying point for opponents of electronic voting. The concern is not just the potential that a given ballot is hacked, destroyed, or fraudulent but one of scale. With paper ballots or stand-alone voting machines, it would take a massive, coordinated effort to perpetrate fraud on the scale needed to reverse all but a handful of elections. But with electronic voting machines it is possible for a small number of individuals, or possibly just one, to carry out a large-scale attack by altering the software inside the machines. In this new world, one needs to certify the people with access to the machinery as well as the machines themselves and to provide some independent way of auditing the vote, say by a verifiable paper record.

Voting technology firms responded by designing and developing electronic voting machines with verifiable paper audit trails. These machines are hybrids of paper ballots and DREs, and today there are at least five such machines produced in the United States. These designs take two forms—a DRE that prints a paper ballot that the voter then casts and a DRE that shows a paper recording of the voting session that the voter can see but not change. Few counties or states have adopted these costly hybrid machines. Several states and counties, mired in controversy over purchases of DREs, abandoned electronic voting in favor of scanned paper. Most significantly, California reversed its decision to adopt electronic voting equipment in the mid-2000s and cancelled contracts with vendors, at some cost to the state. Most California counties now use optically scanned paper ballots.

By the end of the 2000s, the majority of states and counties in the United States had chosen to use optically scanned paper ballots. For many, that was the natural transition from punch cards. For others, the controversy over the security of DREs caused states and counties to scrap plans to use electronic voting. For now, most of the country has adopted the optical scan ballot, a form of the old paper ballot. Both that technology and the

DRE feel antiquated, given advances in computing and communication technologies.

Once the technological challenges of securing electronic voting are resolved, I expect a revolution in voting technology, one that will change not just how people vote but where and when as well. The greater convenience offered by the coming adoption of communication technology will undo completely the notion of Election Day and the precinct and will force campaigns to adjust the GOTV, advertising, and other strategies. The technologists' challenge is how to solve the security problem, and the first one who does will capture the U.S. (and possibly global) market.

VOTING TECHNOLOGY CHALLENGES

The first and most immediate challenge for the coming decades is a familiar one—*obsolescence*. Paper ballots and lever machines were used for many decades without any changes, but the computer software in most DREs is already out of date. System failures with DREs could easily throw an election into doubt in the coming decade. Newer, better technology is needed. The experience of local election offices circa 2000, though, was that new technology was hard to acquire because funds were highly limited and the contracting process was protracted. Federal funds helped counties afford to upgrade to new technologies between 2002 and 2004, but those funds are no longer available.

Obsolescence could be solved if counties did not have to rely on highly specialized, expensive, and ultimately outdated hardware. We need systems that use the most current computing technology, can be easily upgraded, or rely on very inexpensive hardware that costs little to replace. One can easily imagine Internet technology addressing these challenges. Online voting systems today do not meet the fundamental security criteria for voting technology laid out by the computer science community. There has been considerable theoretical research over the past decade on the development of verifiable Internet voting, especially the work of Andy Neff and David Chaum. At least in theory, a verifiable, provable Internet voting system is now possible.[10] The problem with using this or any new technology is sustainability—how to get it to market in a timely manner and how to establish a healthy market for it.

A second substantial challenge for future technology arises from *absentee and early voting*. Absentee voting accounts for one-third of the ballots cast in the United States and half of all votes in the western states. Some of the increase in absentee voting is driven by the campaigns themselves. Most states have changed their laws over the past three decades making absentee voting more readily available, and campaigns have adapted to these laws by getting their partisans to vote early. We have, then, not one election administration system but two—the traditional polling place and the absentee system. These typically use different technologies and have very different procedures for guarding against abuses. It is widely thought that the absentee system is the most susceptible to failures, ranging from vote buying to undelivered mail to simple errors that would have been correctable in the polling place. Suitable methods of voting that guard against failures in the absentee system are sorely needed.

A third challenge is *Internet voting*. Online voting offers a tantalizing option that is currently used on a limited basis for some specialized populations, like military personnel. Internet voting could eliminate the need for dedicated voting machines entirely and remove the costs borne by counties. Were it not for the risks associated with large-scale hacking, Internet voting would be widespread today. The challenge is how to make Internet voting verifiable and the veracity of the count provable. Solving that problem would allow counties and states to get out of the business of acquiring equipment and convert voting into a software business. Counties could set up voting at dedicated locations, such as schools and libraries, and use existing computers (rather than specialized devices) for voting machines. Absentee voting could be conducted over a similar system, and military personnel would no longer have to rely on the postal system to handle ballots. Audio systems for blind voters would be easy to develop. As transformative as those advantages would be, it seems that we are still some years away from a workable, provable Internet voting system.

The fourth major technology challenge for voting over the coming decade is *sustainability*. The problem is that the voting technology has a poor business model. In most places, individual counties, not the states, purchase voting technology. Firms must devote considerable effort to sales rather than research and development. Once they have sold equipment to a county, the county wants to keep the machines operating for decades in order to amortize the costs. There is neither sufficient demand for new equipment nor sufficient investment in new technologies to create a robust market.

Not surprisingly, the bigger information technology firms get out of this sector quickly or do not enter at all. IBM vended punch cards for a short while but quickly got out when it realized that the bad publicity outweighed the revenues. Unisys developed one of the most widely used optical scanners but abandoned the market in less than 10 years. Diebold, which vends ATM technology, purchased Global Voting Systems in 2001, hoping to sell its touch screens in this market. By 2004 Diebold had become the villain in the black-box voting saga, and it sold its voting technology division in 2009. National Cash Register, the other big ATM firm, took a close look at this line of business in 2001 and decided not to get in.

The problem with sustainability, then, is that there is too little demand for technology and a marketplace that is fractured into too many small buyers (individual counties). With the withdrawal of Diebold, most of the voting technology business goes to just one company, ES&S. It is not a large company, but it is approaching the position of a monopolist, which, if Economics 101 instructs us correctly, will likely mean higher prices and less innovation.

REFORMING THE BUSINESS MODEL TO STIMULATE INNOVATION

How might we break out of the voting technology trap? The obstacles seem, at first glance, technical, but they are really rooted in government contracting. The U.S. election system devolves decision making to the counties. As noted above, this fragments the market and forces technology firms to invest heavily in their sales force (which goes county to county). In the large majority of counties, election administration is performed as a secondary activity in the county clerk's office; there is a lack of staff and resources to devote to voting technology. Market fragmentation, weak demand, and lack of competition stifle innovation.

Fifteen years ago, Brazil leap-frogged the United States in voting technology. Brazil had a hand-counted paper ballot system that was rife with corruption. Following the 1995 election, widely criticized for rampant vote fraud, the national government decided to change to an electronic voting system. Rather than rely on its federal system, which was modeled on the United States, Brazil set up a national system for contracting. The country's Supreme Court, Election Commission, and Department of Science and Technology developed a set of standards and criteria that new voting equipment must satisfy and requested proposals for the purchase of new technology for the entire nation. Bidders on this technology included Unisys, Hewlett-Packard, and IBM as well as many other information and voting technology firms—many of the very firms that had stayed out of the U.S. market. Unisys won the initial contract and developed equipment that has served as the platform for subsequent voting technologies used in the country.

At every national election, Brazil seeks a new national contract for voting equipment and purchases entirely new machinery. Although there are still flaws with this system, the case of Brazil demonstrates that centralized contracting can realize economies of scale that will attract a much wider range of technology firms, including many of the leading U.S. companies. This approach has allowed Brazil to incorporate much newer technology into its voting system and has allowed the country to address some of the most difficult problems in guaranteeing universal access to voting, including low literacy rates in the country and providing voting in the jungle.[11]

More centralized contracting for voting technology will likely have similar benefits in the United States. A large state like California or Texas could have enormous influence on the development of voting technology if it regularly upgraded its technology (say every four years) through a single request for proposals issued statewide that specified the features of the desired technology to be used in precinct and absentee voting. Regular technology purchases on a large scale would attract significant firms to submit bids and would entail frequent upgrading of equipment and software, giving firms the incentive to develop voting systems based on new computing and information technology.

The exact criteria would, of course, have to be set by the relevant political agency, such as the state legislature. Such efforts usually pile on unnecessary provisions, but the core requirements of voting technology are already well established and have evolved over the past two centuries. Voting technology must (1) be secure; (2) accurately record the vote; (3) be easy for voters to use; (4) be easy for election offices to maintain, manage, and operate; (5) operate reliably and durably; (6) protect the secrecy of the ballot; (7) produce an accurate count of votes that can be audited, verified, and proved correct; and (8) be accessible to all, even those with low literacy, limited vision, or who are absentee. We have not always attained these goals, but over our long history of elections the United States has moved steadily closer through the adaptation of advanced communication and computing technology.

Today, we are at an impasse. It is obvious what those technologies are, but it is not obvious how to use them in voting. Eventually the problems will be solved and a new era of electronic voting will be upon us. That will change where we vote and when, it will likely take voting further out of the public domain, and it will force politicians to change when and how they seek the support of voters. Hopefully, it will remove the uncertainties about vote tabulation and the ready descent into the courts that has followed very close elections over the past decade.

Conclusion

Nathaniel G. Pearlman

Those of us in the business—at least the partisans, of which I am proud to be one—are driven by the belief that political technology, creatively applied, can produce the margin of victory. We cope with all sorts of challenges in the faith that helping our side will ultimately elect better candidates and produce a better government.

But when I step back and think about how all this work fits into the big picture, how it affects the United States' democratic experiment, I must confess that I am not alarmed about the future. I do not believe that the continued development of political technologies will lead to a dystopia of political manipulation. I do not see sedentary masses controlled by politicians wielding mathematical models. Even an unparalleled facility with the mechanics of campaigning will not substitute for an effective candidate with a persuasive message or override the electorate's impression of the competence of the winners of the last election. It is a comfort that the basic rules of politics are in fact not being rewritten.

I am as frustrated as the next person with the shortcomings of U.S. government, but in the long run it is probably a good thing that a rough technological parity exists between the parties. It takes effort to discern it at times, but one reason that we have as good a government as we do (and there are far worse in this world) is that both parties are peopled by many well-meaning individuals who simply believe in different versions of the American creed.

In the late fall of 2006, I was asked to serve as the chief technology officer for Hillary Clinton—if she decided to run for the presidency. I was naturally energized by the idea that I could be a tiny part of history, if only by pulling together a good technical staff and the hardware, software, databases, and information technology for a concerted national effort. I had recently read Harold Holzer's book, *Lincoln at Cooper Union: The Speech That Made Lincoln President*, and was struck by the way that Lincoln had conducted his 1860 campaign. Lincoln took on the biggest issue facing the republic. He analyzed the founders' individual positions on slavery and argued in a carefully constructed speech that the newly formed Republican Party was the true heir to the founders' majority view; that is, against the extension of slavery and in favor of its ultimate extinction. According to Holzer, that speech by Lincoln, which was printed in newspapers across the country, was pivotal in helping him capture the Republican nomination. I impulsively sent Senator Clinton a copy of Holzer's book; it was my presumptuous but shy way of asking the senator to consider Lincoln's speech as a model for crafting her campaign.

I soon received a reply from the senator, thanking me for my efforts on her behalf and for the book. She wrote that she was "very familiar with the speech and appreciate[d] that you thought to send the book to me." I quickly Googled "Hillary Clinton Harold Holzer" and discovered, as I ought to have guessed, that Senator Clinton knew the book and the speech quite well. Indeed, she had attended the book's launch party with its author. One of the gifts that the Clintons took with them when they left the White House was a copy of that speech. Clearly, Hillary Clinton did not need to be introduced to the campaign of 1860 by me.

Even though I exposed my naïveté, I had one thing right: the best and most admirable campaigns cannot be constructed out of fundraising or advertising tools, essential though they be to modern campaigning. The essential element—the heart of a great campaign—resides where it ought to, with an animating idea and the character and competence of its standardbearer. The role played by political technologists is and should be a supporting one. All we do is attempt to harness innovations in the service of a grander cause.

Notes

INTRODUCTION

1. John G. Nicolay and John Hay, eds., *Complete Works of Abraham Lincoln: Comprising His Speeches, Letters, State Papers, and Miscellaneous Writings*, Vol. 1 (New York: Century, 1894), 38–39.

CHAPTER 1

1. Stephen Ansolabehere, Alan S. Gerber, and James M. Snyder Jr., "Does TV Advertising Explain the Rise of Campaign Spending?" MIT working paper, October 2001, http://economics.mit.edu/files/1211.

2. "Statistics of the Congressional Election of November 7, 1978," U.S. House of Representatives, April 1, 1979, http://clerk.house.gov/member_info/electionInfo/1978election.pdf.

3. Walter Isaacson and Evan Thomas, "Running with the PACs," *Time*, October 25, 1982.

4. Ansolebehere, "Does TV Advertising Explain the Rise of Campaign Spending?"

5. Bill Gorman, "Where Did the Primetime Broadcast TV Audience Go?" TV by the Numbers, ZapToIt.com (April 10, 2010), http://tvbythenumbers.zap2it.com/2010/04/12/where-did-the-primetime-broadcast-tv-audience-go/47976/.

6. Ansolebehere, "Does TV Advertising Explain the Rise of Campaign Spending?"

7. Andrew Rosenthal, "Politicians Count on Computers," *New York Times*, May 9, 1988.

8. Chuck Raasch, "A Gut Level Politician in a Techno Age," *USA Today*, July 9, 2010.

9. See also Lynn Reed, "Online Campaigning" in *The Manship Guide to Political Communication*, ed. David D. Perlmutter (Baton Rouge: Louisiana State University Press, 1999): 234–35.

10. "Request by Bill Bradley for President," Federal Elections Commission, March 18, 1999, http://saos.nictusa.com/saos/searchao?SUBMIT=ao&AO =750&START=1006866.pdf.

11. Richard Davis et al., "The Internet in U.S. Election Campaigns," in *Handbook of Internet and Politics*, eds. Andrew Chadwick and Philip N. Howard (New York: Routledge, 2009): 18.

12. Bill Gorman, "Where Did the Primetime Broadcast TV Audience Go?"

13. "Mail Volume: What Goes Up?" *Pushing the Envelope* (blog), December 12, 2008, http://blog.uspsoig.gov/?p=411.

14. "National Do Not Call Registry Opens," Federal Trade Commission (press release), June 27, 2003, http://www.ftc.gov/opa/2003/06/donotcall.shtm.

15. Tom Scheckt, "Campaigns Go High Tech to Get Out the Vote," Minnesota Public Radio, August 17, 2004, http://news.minnesota.publicradio.org/features/ 2004/08/17_scheckt_hitechcampaigns/.

16. "National ADS and Wired Cable Penetration Trends," Television Bureau of Advertising, Inc., http://www.tvb.org/planning_buying/184839/4729/72512.

17. Jasmin Melvin, "US Lagging in Broadband Speed, Adoption," Reuters.com, May 20, 2011, http://www.reuters.com/article/2011/05/21/us-usa-broadband -adoption-idUSTRE74J7D920110521.

18. Erick Schonfeld, "Netflix Now the Largest Single Source of Online Traffic in the US," Techcrunch.com, May 17, 2011, http://techcrunch.com/2011/05/17/ netflix-largest-internet-traffic/.

19. Robert Seidman, "DVR Penetration Grows to 39.7% of Households, 42.2% of Users," TV by the Numbers (March 23, 2011), http://tvbythenumbers.zap2it. com/2011/03/23/dvr-penetration-grows-to-39-7-of-households-42-2-of-viewers/ 86819/.

20. "DVR Viewing of Programs and Commercials Varies Based on Time Elapsed between Original Airing and Playback, Nielsen Says," Nielsen.com (press release), February 15, 2007.

21. Jorge Cino, "Email Use Declines 59% Among Teens . . . Can Messages Surge?" AllFacebook.com, February 8, 2011, http://www.allfacebook.com/email -use-declines-59-among-teens-can-messages-surge-2011-02.

22. Tim Peterson, "Email Volume Drops but Click, Open Rates Flat," Direct Marketing News, August 30, 2011, http://www.dmnews.com/email-volume-drops -but-click-open-rates-flat-study/article/210897/.

23. Marc Cohen, "Text-Message Marketing," *New York Times*, September 24, 2009.

24. "State of the Media: The Social Media Report," Nielsen.com, 2011, http:// blog.nielsen.com/nielsenwire/social/.

25. "US Wireless Penetration Hits 96%," *The Cell Phone Junkie* (blog), March 23, 2011, http://thecellphonejunkie.com/2011/03/23/us-wireless-penetration-hits-96/.

26. "Percentage of Cell-phone Only US Homes Doubles," CBSNews.com, April 23, 2011, http://www.cbsnews.com/stories/2011/04/23/earlyshow/saturday/ main20056730.shtml.

27. Horace Dediu, "Switching Rates for US Smartphone Users Suggest 50% Penetration by August 2012," Asymco.com, July 9, 2011, http://www.asymco.com/2011/07/09/switching-rates-for-us-smartphone-users-suggest-50-penetration-by-august-2012/.
28. "State of the Media," Nielsen.com.

CHAPTER 3

1. Jack W. Germond and Jules Witcover, *Wake Us When It's over: Presidential Politics of 1984* (New York: Macmillan Pub Co, 1985).
2. "What Americans Do Online," Nielsen.com, http://blog.nielsen.com/nielsenwire/online_mobile/what-americans-do-online-social-media-and-games-dominate-activity/.
3. Alexis Rice, "The Power of the Internet," CampaignsOnline.org, Johns Hopkins, http://www.campaignsonline.org/reports/1104.html.

CHAPTER 4

1. Sam Youngman, "White House Unloads Anger over Criticism from 'Professional Left,'" *The Hill*, August 10, 2010.
2. Interview between Kaili Joy Gray and Dan Pfeiffer, Netroots Nation, June 17, 2011, http://www.livestream.com/freespeechtv/video?clipId=pla_bb941dac-f73b-44cd-a3ab-ac6ba476082e.
3. Ibid.
4. Ibid.
5. Michael Calderone, "Republicans Flock to *The Huffington Post*," *Politico*, May 22, 2009.
6. Mayhill Fowler, "Obama: No Surprise That Hard-Pressed Pennsylvanians Turn Bitter," *Huffington Post*, April 11, 2008.
7. Ibid.
8. Cision and Don Bates, "2009 Social Media & Online Usage Study," George Washington University, December 2009.
9. "Use of Social Media among Business Journalists," Brunswick Group, Spring 2011.
10. "Major Senate Race Shakeup," *Not Larry Sabato*, August 13, 2006.
11. Tim Craig and Michael D. Shear, "Allen Quip Provokes Outrage, Apology," *Washington Post*, August 15, 2006.
12. Nancy Scola, "Dems' Money Infrastructure Gets a Wisconsin Workout," *TechPresident*, March 10, 2011.
13. http://www.votenaturally.org.
14. Toby Harnden, "The Most Influential US Conservatives," *Daily Telegraph*, October 30, 2007.
15. Erick Erickson, "Not One Dime to the NRSC," *RedState*, May 13, 2009.
16. Hoffman was the Conservative Party nominee for the seat.

17. It bears noting that the NRCC's e-campaign director, John Randall, has done much to maintain positive relationships with bloggers including those at *RedState* since taking the helm at the beginning of the 2010 cycle; the NRSC also engaged with bloggers throughout that same cycle including via its consultant, Hynes Communications, cementing solid relationships, including with writers at *RedState*.

18. John Heilemann and Mark Halperin, *Game Change* (New York: Harper Collins, 2010), 128.

19. Stephen Dinan, "Blogger Outreach Boosts McCain," *Washington Times*, March 31, 2008.

20. Ibid.

21. Ibid.

22. Calderone "Republicans Flock to *The Huffington Post.*"

23. White House press conference, February 9, 2009.

24. Sam Stein "White House Beefs Up Online Rapid Response," *Huffington Post*, May 23, 2011.

25. Tribbett is a Virginia Democratic operative and the author of *Not Larry Sabato*; Dayton is a writer at *RedState* and other sites who has advised several national-level Republican figures and candidates; Holtsberry handled online communications for Senator Rob Portman's 2010 campaign.

CHAPTER 6

1. Carly Carioli, "Walking Edge: The iPhone App That Killed Coakley," *Boston Phoenix*, January 21, 2010.

2. CTIA—The Wireless Association, "Wireless Quick Facts," http://www.ctia.org/media/industry_info/index.cfm/AID/10323.

3. Ericsson, "From Apps to Everyday Situations," http://www.ericsson.com/res/docs/2011/silicon_valley_brochure_letter.pdf.

4. Burson-Marsteller, "Evidence-Based Communications: The State of Mobile Communications," http://www.slideshare.net/BMGlobalNews/the-state-of-mobile-communications-5068995.

5. comScore, "comScore Releases First Comparative Report on Mobile Usage in Japan, United States, and Europe," October 7, 2010, http://www.comscore.com/Press_Events/Press_Releases/2010/10/comScore_Release_First_Comparative_Report_on_Mobile_Usage_in_Japan_United_States_and_Europe.

6. Aaron Smith and Lee Rainie, "Politics Goes Mobile," Pew Internet and American Life Project, December 23, 2010, http://pewInternet.org/Reports/2010/Mobile-Politics.aspx.

7. David A. Lieb, "Candidates Get Creative to Build Text-Message Lists," *Washington Post*, October 3, 2010.

8. Sylvie Barak, "Political Campaigns Turn to Text Messaging Harassment," *RCR Unplugged*, November 11, 2010, http://unplugged.rcrwireless.com/index.php/20101111/content/5096/political-campaigns-turn-to-text-message-harassment.

9. Nancy Scola, "ActBlue Profitably Tweaks Mobile Giving," *TechPresident* (blog), December 20, 2010, http://techpresident.com/blog-entry/actblue-profitably-tweaks-mobile-giving.

10. comScore, "Number of U.S. Mobile Display Advertisers More than Doubles in Past Two Years," June 7, 2011, http://www.comscore.com/Press_Events/Press_Releases/2011/6/Number_of_U.S._Mobile_Display_Advertisers_More_than_Doubles_in_Past_Two_Years.

11. Sara Yin, "Tech Industry Facing Shortage of Mobile App Developers," *PC Magazine*, October 22, 2010, http://www.pcmag.com/article2/0,2817,2371308,00.asp.

12. Brian Ries, "Killer Election Apps," *Daily Beast*, October 21, 2010, http://www.thedailybeast.com/blogs-and-stories/2010-10-21/midterm-elections-killer-smartphone-apps.

13. David Berkowitz et al., *Mobile Marketing Playbook*, 360i. September 14, 2010, http://www.google.com/url?q=http%3A%2F%2Fwww.scribd.com%2Fdoc%2F37405970%2F360i-s-Mobile-Marketing-Playbook&sa=D&sntz=1&usg=AFQjCNGtPB-jD02ZYPWYGLXVwED34ywqOw.

14. Burson-Marsteller, "Evidence-Based Communications: The State of Mobile Communications."

15. Nielson, "Global Faces and Networked Places," March 2009, http://www.google.com/url?q=http%3A%2F%2Fwww.scribd.com%2Fdoc%2F13117994%2FNielsen-Global-Faces-and-Networked-Places&sa=D&sntz=1&usg=AFQjCNHmMCoJ5QPzcmiZqmYpaImT-ywkOg.

CHAPTER 7

1. Taken from New Models National Brand Survey, February 22–23, 2010.

2. Aaron Smith, *The Internet and Campaign 2010*, Pew Research Center, March 17, 2011, http://www.pewInternet.org/Reports/2011/The-Internet-and-Campaign-2010.aspx.

3. Kristen Purcell, R. Entner, and N. Henderson, *The Rise of Apps Culture*, Pew Internet & American Life Project, September 15, 2010, http://pewInternet.org/Reports/2010/The-Rise-of-Apps-Culture.aspx.

4. Carl Bialik, "Press 1 for McCain, 2 for Obama," *Wall Street Journal*, August 1, 2008, A8.

5. Reg Baker et al., "AAPOR Report on Online Panels," American Association for Public Opinion Research, March 2010, http://www.aapor.org/AM/Template.cfm?Section=AAPOR_Committee_and_Task_Force_Reports&Template=/CM/ContentDisplay.cfm&ContentID=2223.

6. 2010 AAPOR Cell Phone Task Force, Paul Lavrakas, et al., *New Considerations for Survey Researchers When Planning and Conducting RDD Telephone Surveys in the U.S. with Respondents Reached via Cell Phone Numbers*, paper presented at the annual meeting of the American Association for Public Opinion Research, Chicago, May 13–16, 2010.

7. Leah Christian et al., *Assessing the Cell Phone Challenge to Survey Research in 2010*, Pew Research Center, May 20, 2010, http://pewresearch.org/assets/pdf/1601-cell-phone.pdf.

8. Richard Curtin, Stanley Presser, and Eleanor Singer, "Changes in Telephone Survey Nonresponse over the Past Quarter Century," *Public Opinion Quarterly* 69, no. 1, 87–98.

9. "New York Times Polling Standards," http://www.nytimes.com/ref/us/politics/10_polling_standards.html.

10. Baker, "AAPOR Report on Online Panels."

11. Lavrakas, *New Considerations for Survey Researchers*, 19.

12. Christian, *Assessing the Cell Phone Challenge to Survey Research*.

13. Telephone Consumer Protection Act, 47 U.S.C. 227, http://www2.fcc.gov/cgb/policy/TCPA-Rules.pdf.

14. Lavrakas, *New Considerations for Survey Researchers*.

15. Courtney Kennedy and Steven E. Everett. "The Use of Cognitive Shortcuts in Landline and Telephone Surveys," *Public Opinion Quarterly* 75, no. 2 (Summer 2011): 346.

16. Pulse Opinion Research, http://www.pulseopinionresearch.com/.

17. Nate Silver, "Rasmussen Polls Were Biased and Inaccurate; Quinnipiac, SurveyUSA Performed Strongly," http://fivethirtyeight.blogs.nytimes.com/2010/11/04/rasmussen-polls-were-biased-and-inaccurate-quinnipiac-surveyusa-performed-strongly/.

18. Ibid.

19. Brian Schaffner, "Polling: Innovations in Survey Research," in *New Directions in Campaigns and Elections*, ed. Stephen K. Medvic (New York: Routledge, 2011): 51.

20. Doug Rivers, "Sample Matching: Representative Sampling from Internet Panels," http://www.rochester.edu/College/faculty/mperess/srm2010/Polimetrix_Methodology.pdf.

21. Baker, "AAPOR Report on Online Panels."

22. Matthew DeBell, Jon A. Krosnick, and Arthur Lupia, *Methodology Report and User's Guide for the 2008–2009 ANES Panel Study*, American National Election Studies, August 2010, revised December 13, 2010, http://electionstudies.org/studypages/2008_2009panel/anes2008_2009panel_MethodologyRpt.pdf.

23. Doug Rivers, "Sample Matching."

24. "Prediction Markets," http://www.intrade.com/v4/misc/howItWorks/predictionMarkets.jsp.

25. David Rothschild, "Forecasting Elections," *Public Opinion Quarterly* 73, no. 5, 913.

26. Keith N. Hampton et al., "Social Networking Sites and Our Lives," Pew Research Center Internet & American Life Project, June 16, 2011, http://electionstudies.org/studypages/2008_2009panel/anes2008_2009panel_MethodologyRpt.pdf.

27. Jolie O'Dell, "How the GOP Debate Exploded on Twitter," June 14, 2011, http://mashable.com/2011/06/14/republican-debate-twitter/.

28. Mark Memmott, "Jobs, the Future, and Salmon: Key Words from the State of the Union: The Two-Way," *National Public Radio*, January 26, 2011, http://www.npr.org/blogs/thetwo-way/2011/01/26/133234249/jobs-the-future-and-salmon-key-words-from-state-of-the-union.

CHAPTER 8

1. Dennis W. Johnson, *Congress Online: Bridging the Gap between Citizens and Their Representatives* (Routledge, 2004), 2.

2. Eric O'Keefe and Aaron Steelman, "The End of Representation: How Congress Stifles Electoral Competition," *Cato Policy Analysis* 279 (1997).

3. Brad Fitch and Kathy Goldschmidt, *Communicating with Congress: How Capitol Hill Is Coping with the Surge in Citizen Advocacy* (Congressional Management Foundation, 2005), 4.

4. Johnson, *Congress Online*, 2.

5. Chris Casey, *The Hill on the Net: Congress Enters the Information Age* (Morgan Kaufmann, 1996).

6. Graeme Browning, *Electronic Democracy: Using the Internet to Transform American Politics* (Information Today, 2001), 7–8.

7. Jeffrey W. Seifert and R. Eric Petersen, "House of Representatives Information Technology Management Issues: An Overview of the Effects on Institutional Operations, the Legislative Process, and Future Planning," Congressional Research Service, April 2, 2003.

8. Johnson, *Congress Online*, 5.

9. "Generations 2010," Pew Internet & American Life Project, 2010.

10. Ibid.

11. Matthew Eric Glassman et al., "Social Networking and Constituent Communications: Member Use of Twitter during a Two-Month Period in the 111th Congress," Congressional Research Service, 2010, 2.

CHAPTER 12

1. "Dole-Kemp Site Flawed," *CNET News*, October 8, 1996, http://news.cnet.com/Dole-Kemp-site-flawed/2100-1023_3-235969.html.

2. Advisory Opinion, Federal Election Commission, June 10, 1999, http://saos.nictusa.com/aodocs/1999-09.pdf.

3. "Fund-raising Champ Bush Being Outdone Online," *Post and Courier*, February 5, 2000.

4. Laura Meckler, "Bush Plan Supporters Not All 'On Message' at GOP Web Site," Associated Press, April 8, 2005.

CHAPTER 13

1. Chris Cillizza, "Romney's Data Cruncher," *Washington Post*, July 5, 2007.

2. M. G. Siegler, "Eric Schmidt: Every 2 Days We Create As Much Information As We Did Up To 2003," Techcrunch.com, http://techcrunch.com/2010/08/04/schmidt-data/ (accessed July 25, 2011).

3. "Moore's Law and Intel Innovation," Intel.com, http://www.intel.com/about/companyinfo/museum/exhibits/moore.htm (accessed July 25, 2011).

4. Christopher C. Shilakes and Julie Tylman, "Enterprise Information Portals," Merrill Lynch, http://en.wikipedia.org/wiki/Unstructured_data#endnote_ML, November 16, 1998.

5. "Twitter Used to Predict Box Office Revenues," Technology Review, The Physics arXiv Blog, http://www.technologyreview.com/blog/arxiv/25000/ (accessed July 25, 2011).

6. "Twitter Can Predict the Stock Market," Lisa Grossman, Wired.com, http://www.wired.com/wiredscience/2010/10/twitter-crystal-ball/ (accessed July 25, 2011).

7. Brendan O'Connor, Ramnath Balasubramanyany, Bryan R. Routledge, Noah A. Smithy, "From Tweets to Polls: Linking Text Sentiment to Public Opinion Time Series," Proceedings of the International AAAI Conference on Weblogs and Social Media, Washington, DC, May 2010, http://www.cs.cmu.edu/~nasmith/papers/oconnor+balasubramanyan+routledge+smith.icwsm10.pdf.

8. Anscombe's Quartet, Wikipedia, http://en.wikipedia.org/wiki/Anscombe's_quartet (accessed July 25, 2011).

CHAPTER 14

1. I pick on Williams-Sonoma in this example because the company was the subject of a lawsuit, *Pineda v. Williams-Sonoma*, in which a customer sued— and won— because of the privacy implications involved when Williams-Sonoma asks for customers' zip codes.

2. Since, in most social circles, the socially acceptable decision is to vote, much of the fibbing on this question is by people who say they will vote but don't. However, a significant proportion also indicate to pollsters that they won't vote even though they actually will, either because they don't want to take a survey or because they mispredict their own actions.

3. The Bradley Effect is a well-known cause of voters misrepresenting their true beliefs. The term comes from the 1982 California governor's race, in which public opinion polls overstated the support for the African American candidate, Los Angeles Mayor Tom Bradley, among white Californians. Whites were also more likely to state that they were "undecided" when they were actually planning to vote for the Caucasian Republican candidate, George Deukmejian.

4. Media markets are the geographic regions in which broadcast television advertisements run. For example, if you're in the Columbus, Ohio, media market, you get your news and local commercials from Columbus.

5. Catalist, a private company, follows voters for Democrats, and Voter Vault, controlled by the RNC, follows voters for Republicans.

6. Much of what I know about Dick Wirthlin was passed on to me by my polling mentor, Mark Mellman, who recounts Wirthlin's contributions to our field in his column, "Wirthlin: The Passing of a Giant," *The Hill* (newspaper), March 22, 2011.

7. David Broder, "Engineering Reagan's Big Victory," *Schenectady Gazette*, November 6, 1980.

8. The total electoral votes of the four close states that Gore won was 29, which is more than Florida's 25. Thus, abandoning all those states for Florida was not an option; the Gore campaign had to win some combination of the five, and that combination had to include Florida.

9. Nascent Republican and Democratic microtargeting programs appeared to be very effective at boosting turnout in Ohio in 2004. Between 2000 and 2004, the turnout rate (voters divided by eligible population) jumped 10 percentage points for the Buckeye State, compared with a 5 percentage point increase in the rest of the country.

10. I would be remiss if I didn't mention Hal Malchow's early microtargeting efforts, which preceded the main thrust of the movement. By early 2003, he had

already published a book on political microtargeting, *The New Political Targeting* (Campaigns & Electrons). Ken Strasma, the founder of Strategic Telemetry, was also influential in early microtargeting endeavors and continues to be a leader in the field.

11. Alan S. Gerber and Donald P. Green, "The Effects of Canvassing, Telephone Calls, and Direct Mail on Voter Turnout: A Field Experiment," *American Political Science Review* 94, no. 3 (September 2000): 653–63.

12. Allison Dale and Aaron Strauss, "Don't Forget to Vote: Text Message Reminders as a Mobilization Tool," *American Journal of Political Science* 53, no. 4 (October 2009): 787–804.

13. Academics call this statistical procedure "indentifying heterogeneous treatment effects," but I think that label is a bit too unwieldy for practitioners.

14. I thank Kosuke Imai, Avi Feller, and several people at the Analyst Institute for their help in working with me on solving the persuasion microtargeting problem.

15. A notable exception is the 2006 Rick Perry gubernatorial primary campaign in Texas, which (with the help of political scientists) randomized its advertising buys and learned a great deal for subsequent campaigns.

CHAPTER 17

1. Roy G. Saltman, "Accuracy, Integrity, and Security in Computerized Vote-Tallying," National Bureau of Standards Special Publication 500-158, August 1988, http://www.itl.nist.gov/lab/specpubs/500-158.htm.

2. For a more thorough discussion of the technologies available in 2000 see, "Voting: What Is, What Could Be," Caltech/MIT Voting Technology Project, California Institute of Technology and Massachusetts Institute of Technology, July 1, 2001, http://vote.caltech.edu/drupal/node/10.

3. Jonathan Wand et al., "The Butterfly Did It: The Aberrant Vote for Buchanan in Palm Beach County, Florida," *American Political Science Review* 95 (2001): 793–810.

4. Stephen Ansolabehere and Charles H. Stewart III, "Residual Votes Attributable to Technology," *Journal of Politics* 67 (2003): 365–389.

5. National Commission on Federal Election Reform, *To Assure Pride and Confidence in the Electoral Process* (Washington, DC: Brookings Press, 2002).

6. Charles H. Stewart III, "Residual Vote in the 2004 Election," *Election Law Journal* 5 (2006): 158–169.

7. Robert M. Stein and Greg Vonnahme, "The Effects of Vote Centers on Voters' Experiences," paper presented at the Midwest Political Science Association Meeting, April 2009.

8. For a description, see "Secure Electronic Registration and Voting Experiment," http://www.fvap.gov/reference/reports.html.

9. Tadayoshi Kohno, Adam Stubblefield, Aviel Rubin, and Dan Wallach, "Analysis of an Electronic Voting System," IEEE Symposium on Security and Privacy 2004. IEEE Computer Society Press, May 2004.

10. D. Chaum, P. Ryan, and S. Schneider, "A Practical Voter-Verifiable Election Scheme," in *Proceedings of the 10th European Symposium on Research in Computer Security* (ESORICS, 2005): 118–139.

11. See "Security in the Electronic Voting System" on the Superior Electoral Court of Brazil's Web site, http://www.tse.jus.br/internet/ingles/voto_eletronico/voto_eletronico.htm.

About the Editor
and Contributors

ABOUT THE EDITOR

NATHANIEL G. PEARLMAN has worked in the field of political technology for more than two decades. In 1997, he founded NGP Software,
Inc. (now NGP VAN, Inc.) a 130+ person firm that assists Democrats and
their allies in fundraising, compliance, organizing tools, and new media.
Pearlman earned a bachelor's degree in computer science from Yale College.
He also studied American politics and political statistics in the doctoral
program at the Massachusetts Institute of Technology. Pearlman is
also president of Timeplots, LCC, a creative analytic design and niche
information enterprise.

ABOUT THE CONTRIBUTORS

STEPHEN ANSOLABEHERE is professor of government at Harvard
University. He was professor of political science at MIT, where he led the
Caltech/MIT Voting Technology Project. He is author of *Going Negative:
How Political Advertising Shrinks and Polarizes the American Electorate*, *The
Media Game*, and *The End of Inequality: Baker v. Carr and the Transformation
of American Politics*.

ROBERT BLAEMIRE, director of business development at Catalist, LLC,
holds a BA and MA from George Washington University. After serving on
the staff of U.S. Senator Birch Bayh (D-IN) for 13 years, he went on to
become the president of a PAC organized to fight the New Right, the Committee for American Principals. After that, he worked for eight years as

vice president of Below, Tobe & Associates, a political computer firm. In 1991 he formed his owned company, Blaemire Communications, finally merging with Catalist in 2007.

ANDREW BLEEKER and NATHANIEL LUBIN are veterans of the Obama 2008 Internet marketing operations. After running all online marketing for the Democratic Party in 2008, Bleeker founded Bully Pulpit Interactive and has since become a leading counselor on digital marketing to progressive campaigns, nonprofits, and corporate social responsibility efforts. Lubin was one of the first to join Bleeker at Bully Pulpit and is currently now back on the Obama campaign as the on-the-ground lead for digital marketing in 2012.

MINDY FINN, cofounder and partner at digital agency Engage, has consulted for some of the United States' most well-known politicians and brands including former Minnesota governor and 2012 presidential candidate Tim Pawlenty, Virginia governor Bob McDonnell, speaker of the U.S. House of Representatives John Boehner and U.S. House Budget Committee chairman Paul Ryan. Finn served as the director of digital strategy for former Massachusetts governor Mitt Romney's presidential campaign and was the deputy director of the Republican National Committee's first new media department after working on similar efforts for the Bush-Cheney 2004 campaign. She earned a master's degree in political management from the George Washington University and graduated magna cum laude with her bachelor's degree in journalism from Boston University.

JULIE GERMANY is the vice president of digital strategy at DCI Group, an international grassroots public affairs firm headquartered in Washington, DC. She previously served as the director of the Institute for Politics, Democracy & the Internet. She has authored chapters in *The Routledge Handbook of Political Management*; *Campaigning for President 2008: Strategy and Tactics*, *New Voices and New Techniques*; *Voting in America*; and *Rebooting America*.

JOSH HENDLER has worked in political technology since 2004, beginning with Wesley Clark's presidential campaign. He recently served as the chief technology officer at Jumo—a social platform for connecting individuals and organizations working to change the world. He managed Jumo's technology and product offerings. Prior to joining Jumo, he was the director of technology for the Democratic National Committee and Organizing for America, overseeing the national party's technology efforts, software development, infrastructure, and data warehouse. He has held many roles in political and nonprofit technology, including Labour's 2005 election in Britain, Rock the Vote, and John Kerry's 2004 presidential campaign. He has also worked at ThoughtWorks as a strategic consultant and was an early technology hire for MLB Advanced Media.

ALEXANDER LUNDRY is vice president of research at TargetPoint Consulting, where he works as a political pollster, microtargeter, data miner, and data visualizer. His client list includes political work on behalf of the Republican National Committee, Senator John McCain, Governor Mitt Romney, Governor Chris Christie, Congressman Dave Camp, Resurgent Republic, and American Crossroads. Alex earned his undergraduate degree in political science at Swarthmore College, and his masters of public policy at Georgetown University, where he focused on public opinion research.

LIZ MAIR is the founder and president of Mair Strategies LLC, a political consulting firm based in Arlington, Virginia. Best known for her work as the Republican National Committee's online communications director during the 2008 presidential cycle, she also served as former Hewlett-Packard CEO Carly Fiorina's online communications strategist during her 2010 U.S. Senate run. A recovering lawyer, she attended law school in England, having previously obtained her MA in international relations from the University of St. Andrews in Scotland and having studied at Sciences Po in Paris, France.

NICCO MELE is a leading expert in the integration of social media and Web 2.0 with politics, business, and communications. As the webmaster for Governor Howard Dean's 2004 presidential race, Nicco and the campaign team pioneered the use of technology and social media that revolutionized political fundraising and American politics. Later that year, Nicco founded **EchoDitto**, a leading Internet strategy consulting company. Through EchoDitto, Nicco continues to consult with Fortune 500 companies and nonprofit groups. Now an adjunct faculty at Harvard's Kennedy School, Nicco teaches graduate-level classes on the Internet and politics. In 2009, Nicco was named the Spring 2009 Visiting Edward R. Murrow Distinguished Lecturer at the Harvard Shorenstein Center for the Study of Press, Politics and Public Policy.

WILL ROBINSON is a founder and partner at the New Media Firm, a progressive advertising agency that specializes in the integration of traditional and new media and has worked on over 63 U.S. House, Senate, and gubernatorial races. He also served as media director and senior advisor to Senator Bill Bradley's presidential campaign and as the campaign director of the Democratic National Committee. Robinson has also produced media for 51 referendum and initiative campaigns in 14 states and the District of Columbia. A good Democrat, Robinson went to the same college as Bill

Clinton (Georgetown University) and the same high school as Joe Biden (Archmere Academy).

PATRICK RUFFINI is currently president at Engage, a political media firm he founded in 2007. Formerly, Ruffini served as e-campaign director at the Republican National Committee and served as webmaster for Bush-Cheney 2004. Ruffini is a 2000 graduate of the University of Pennsylvania and currently resides in the Washington, DC, suburbs with his wife and three children.

EDWARD SAATCHI cofounded NationalField and serves as the CEO. He received a double–first class degree from the University of Oxford in England and a master's degree in philosophy and theology from the Sorbonne in Paris, France.

KRISTEN L. SOLTIS is the director of policy research at the Winston Group, a Washington, DC-based Republican polling and strategy firm. She frequently provides political analysis for outlets such as MSNBC, CNN International, *Politico*, the *Huffington Post*, and Bloggingheads.tv. She received her master's degree in government from Johns Hopkins University and was awarded best thesis honors for her research on young voters in the Republican Party.

AARON STRAUSS is a senior analyst and director of decision analytics at the Mellman Group. He has invented new strategies for integrating data into campaigns since 2000. Dr. Strauss received his PhD in politics from Princeton University in 2009 with a dissertation on political microtargeting.

MARK L. SULLIVAN founded Voter Activation Network in 2001, building the voter file and field management tools now distributed to campaigns through the United States by the Democratic National Committee. Following a 2011 merger with NGP Software, he serves as founder and board member of NGP VAN, Inc., the largest provider of campaign technology to Democrats and progressives. Sullivan grew up on a farm in southeastern Michigan, graduated from the University of Michigan, earned a master's degree in public policy from Harvard University, and today lives in Cambridge, Massachusetts.

MICHAEL TURK has worked at the intersection of technology and politics since 1994. He served as e-campaign director for Bush-Cheney 2004 and the Republican National Committee. He is a partner in CRAFT | Media/Digital, a uniquely integrated communications firm that creates innovative communications strategies across all media. Turk lives in McLean, Virginia, with his wife and two children.

KEN WARD is CEO of Fireside21, a company that creates easy-to-use Web-based tools that help legislators keep in close contact with their constituents. Fireside21 currently works with over 100 members of Congress. Ward was a contributor to *Constituent Relationship Management: The New Little Black Book of Politics*, published by the George Washington University's Institute of Politics, Democracy & the Internet. Ward previously served as a policy and communications aide to former U.S. representative Richard Pombo and earned his BS in computer science from Georgetown University.

Index